Advance Praise

"A comprehensive introduction to psychedelics in psychotherapy and the exploration of human consciousness with rich case presentations and intriguing perspectives from philosophy, comparative religions, physics, literature, neuroscience and personal experience. Wow! Enjoy!"

—William A. Richards, Author of *Sacred Knowledge: Psychedelics & Religious Experiences*

"Gregor Hasler's Higher Self effortlessly moves between cutting edge psychopharmacology and functional brain imaging, Freud and Jung, and ancient Hindu Vedas and contemporary mindfulness research, all in the service of shedding light on how the skillful application of psychedelic-assisted psychotherapy can heal. What makes this book so useful are the many clinical cases that exemplify the real-life application of these multiple disciplines, perspectives, and tools in successful treatment."

—Rick Strassman MD, Adjunct Associate Professor of Psychiatry, University of New Mexico School of Medicine, author of *DMT: The Spirit Molecule and My Altered States*.

HIGHER SELF

Psychedelics in Psychotherapy

HIGHER SELF

Psychedelics in Psychotherapy

Gregor Hasler

Translated from the German by Noah Harley

SENTIENT PUBLICATIONS

First Sentient Publications edition 2025

A paperback original

Book design by Laura Johanna Waltje
Cover Design by Laura Johanna Waltje

Library of Congress Control Number: 2024953123
Publisher's Cataloging-in-Publication Data
Names: Hasler, Gregor, author.
Title: Higher self : psychedelics in psychotherapy / Gregor Hasler.
Description: Includes bibliographical references. | Boulder, CO: Sentient Publications, 2025.
Identifiers: LCCN: 2024953123 | ISBN: 978-1-59181-352-1 (paperback) | 978-1-59181-353-8 (ebook)
Subjects: LCSH Hallucinogenic drugs--Therapeutic use. | Psychotherapy. | Mental illness--Treatment. | BISAC PSYCHOLOGY / Psychotherapy / Spiritually Integrated | PSYCHOLOGY / Mental Health | BODY, MIND & SPIRIT / Entheogens & Visionary Substances
Classification: LCC RM324.8 .H37 2025 | DDC 615.7/883--dc23

SENTIENT PUBLICATIONS
A Limited Liability Company
PO Box 1851
Boulder, CO 80306
www.sentientpublications.com

Contents

Extreme remedies are very appropriate for extreme diseases.

—Hippocrates

Foreword

I was gratified to hear from Gregor asking whether I would write a foreword for his new book, *Higher Self: Psychedelics in Psychotherapy*. My reasons in part were obvious: It's a privilege to have the chance to write a foreword for a book and wish it safe passage onward to the widest possible audience. Yet I was also pleased on account of the decade-plus history that now connects the author of the present work and myself. In 2007, I obtained permission to begin a clinical study on LSD. In the broad wake of public interest that followed, two Swiss news shows did programs on the study. The second aired on 18 July 2011; the controversy surrounding the topic led the channel to seek out expert voices critical of LSD in medicine. The role was ultimately filled by Dr. Gregor Hasler, who expressed his opposition to using LSD in psychotherapy on the broadcast. Nearly ten years later, in the course of a personal conversation about a separate topic, I asked how he had come to change his opinion in the meantime. Gregor responded with a grin that there were things in life that you simply changed your mind about. He had also read a large amount of fascinating and illuminating material since that brought about a shift in his thinking.

His answer cheered me, because it is precisely this sort of fact-based evolution in opinion that I view as my primary task whenever I've been able to speak publicly on the subject of LSD in psychotherapy. Rick Doblin—founder of the MAPS (Multidisciplinary Association for Psychedelic Studies) foundation in the US, a colleague of many years, and an exponent of psychedelics in medicine—once told me that it was critical to speak about our work, since it was a form of public education.

In shifting from a stance of critical opposition to critical acceptance regarding the use of consciousness-altering substances, Gregor has now written a book of his own that falls within the best tradition of public education. When he first told me about the book, he introduced it as a work of popular science. Having now read it, I would like to impress upon him what an understatement this is. It is a book for lay people and experts alike—extraordinarily well-researched, technically sound, and personally honest. It unfailingly sets discoveries and work related to consciousness-altering substances in a broad comparative context, drawing on religious studies, philosophy, biomedical research, resilience research, and much more. Dr. Hasler also brings his own experiences as a psychotherapist to bear, including numerous and convincing case studies that tell of astounding and positive results. Finally, he shows courage in openly describing personal experiences that have given him a profound look into his own soul.

By working across disciplines and tying his own personal experiences as a human being and therapist to discoveries in neurobiological research—climbing down from the proverbial ivory tower—Gregor has written a book that isn't just intellectually stimulating, but full of lessons and insight. In doing so, he never shies away from working out and offering his own concepts and explanatory models—the helioscope effect, for example. I learned a great deal from this book, even though I've been engaged with psychedelics for some time now.

I wish Gregor all the best, and great success with this book. May it find its way into the hands of a broad and keen readership, critics included, whose careful reading makes them a critically accepting and well-informed audience that realizes what exactly is being talked about when the subject turns to psychedelic "drugs." Hopefully, this book will help abolish the unfortunate, lopsided use of the term "drug." Often used colloquially to indicate "a harmful and illegal, intoxicating substance," the term draws an arbitrary line at alcohol and nicotine. It would be better to talk about "psychotropic substances," to really know their risks, but also their potential. The present book represents an important stepping stone on the long path toward that goal.

Peter Gasser

Introduction

In early 2020 I was contacted by an optometrist from western Switzerland. His wife was suffering from severe depression, he told me, and had expressed a desire to end her life. The distinguished psychiatrist she was seeing had tried every form of treatment conceivable, including different combinations of antidepressives at high doses, lithium, and electroconvulsive therapy. Nothing had helped. Now, however, her husband had read in the *New England Journal of Medicine*—the most important medical journal of the day—that very low doses of esketamine, a component of ketamine, had a rapid and strong antidepressive effect, even in cases of severe depression that did not respond to standard antidepressants.

I had some previous experience with ketamine treatment, initially with ketamine infusions and later with esketamine as a nasal spray, so I invited in the optometrist and his wife, Aline. When we met, Aline expressed how happy she was that her husband had arranged the appointment. She may have given up all hope of improving herself, but she was still open to trying out any sort of treatment at all that might help. She let her husband tell her story.

Aline grew up the youngest in a seven-person family. Her parents ran a restaurant and had little time to spare on the children. From an early age, Aline had to look after one of her brothers who had been left severely disabled from a serious head injury after a bike accident. Around the time Aline reached puberty, three of her sisters died in rapid succession from cancer. She later trained as a professional health worker, specializing in caring for cancer patients. She then met her husband and they had two children. Though Aline loved her work, she was forced to give up her position at the hospital when her daughter developed a severe case of epilepsy. The decision came as a heavy blow. Then, when Aline was fifty-two, her daughter died after falling down a flight of stairs. Aline stopped eating and lost all interest in her surroundings. Any volunteer spirit vanished completely. Her husband no longer recognized her. Prolonged bouts of anxiety and insomnia induced her to take more and more tranquilizers, leading to an on-and-off addiction.

Her husband handed me a folder thick with failed treatments. "I'm eternally grateful for my husband and son's help," Aline said, looking at me. "They're the ones I'm still living for. For me personally, I'd be better off dead."

The diagnostic assessments showed Aline to be eligible for esketamine treatment. She had a depression score of forty-two before her first session, indicating severe depression. She sat on the hospital bed holding her husband's hand as I administered the esketamine spray. Then she lay down. Within half an hour her face was beaming—it was the first time I had seen that Aline could be happy. After two hours' supervision, I asked her how she was. "Great," she replied. "I went on a trip that did me a lot of good. A tunnel opened up and I entered another world. It was a world where everything was very easy, full of warm, satisfying colors. I felt my body again, for the first time in years. I could feel myself again. My anxieties were still there, I could see them, but from a safe distance."

Before our second session Aline's husband came up to me in excitement: "It worked. It's like a miracle. My wife has blossomed like a flower. Thank you, thank you so much. I hope the effects last. But even if it doesn't work today, the treatment has already been more than worth it." He continued, "These last few days I've been able to see all of my wife's former liveliness, her care and attention toward me and our son—it's been a tremendous gift, even if it's passing."

As we continued with the esketamine treatments, first twice, then once a week, Aline went on other trips. "I was walking through a field of flowers, like I used to do as a kid on my grandmother's farm," she reported once. "You know what," she said another time, "I met my brother again, who passed away. He was sitting in a wheelchair and I was able to help him again. The love I have for my brother—that's who I am. That's why this depression is so catastrophic for me; it robs me of love."

The effects of the esketamine held up; Aline's depression score now ranged between three and nine points. Months later, as I write this, it is at six. This sort of treatment result is termed "remission," meaning symptoms have grown so slight that depression in the clinical sense no longer exists. Aline is again able to take part in life, to cook for her husband and son, meet up with girlfriends, or look after her grandchild. She no longer relies on tranquilizers.

Around the same time Aline was encountering such positive results in her treatment, I had another experience that led me to write this book. As a psychiatrist and scientist, it brings me a great sense of honor and satisfaction to belong to the American College of Neuropsychopharmacology (ACNP). Admission requires a significant track record of research and publication, and evidence that one's professional work is cited regularly. For me, 2016 was the year the organization voted me in as a full member. Since then, I've attended the annual conferences and served as a mentor for young researchers. I also receive regular emails from the organization, some sad, as the ones announcing "Death of a Colleague" in the subject title. So it was in February 2020, while on ski vacation in the Swiss mountains, that I opened up one such announcement in the course of my daily email routine. To my horror, I discovered the deceased was an acquaintance, Ronald Duman, whose work had brought perspective to my own scientific and therapeutic endeavors. Although I only knew Ron from lectures and brief interactions at international congresses, I grew quite emotional on reading the news; tears came to my eyes.

Ron had died at just sixty-six, amidst an extraordinarily productive period in his career. In a series of studies, he had been able to show depression to be an illness of neuroplasticity. Neuroplasticity refers to the brain's ability to adapt to changing environmental conditions, and recover from stressful or traumatic experiences. Mental flexibility, openness, and a capacity for learning and forgetting are all common facets of neuroplasticity. The fact that the blind are able to see with their hands, or that stroke victims learn to walk again are striking examples of our neurons' ability to transform. In cases of severe depression, neuroplasticity as a whole is reduced in order to shield us from overstimulation. Our brains developed at a time when catastrophes—be they droughts, floods, or plagues of locusts—regularly provoked experiences of horror that made more sense to simply weather by switching to power-save mode, as it were, rather than expending all the energy necessary to assimilate them cognitively. [1] In today's world however,

1 At many points throughout the book, I liken aspects of the human psyche to a computer, much like Sigmund Freud's earlier comparisons of the mind to a steam engine, a camera, or a microscope. Every era draws on its own pool of images and metaphors, which are beholden to the contemporary state of technology. Their impact in shaping our understanding of the psyche makes them worth careful consideration.

where mental stasis rarely makes sense and improved neuroplasticity often leads to success, this type of cerebral shutdown has emerged as a major health issue begetting tremendous personal and economic costs.

In subsequent studies, Ron demonstrated it was possible to liberate the brain from mental freeze using ketamine and other psychedelic substances. Building on Ron's research, other groups were able to show LSD and psilocybin to be especially effective at bolstering neuroplasticity, followed by DMT (the active psychedelic substance in ayahuasca), ketamine, esketamine, and MDMA (better known as ecstasy). The findings laid the scientific groundwork for researching the value of psychedelics in treating illnesses that essentially required increased neuroplasticity. Aside from depression, those include obsessive-compulsive and anxiety disorders, stress and trauma disorders, bipolar disorders, autism, eating disorders, attention-deficit disorders, addictive illnesses, learning and developmental disorders, dementia, neurological illnesses like paralysis, and cognitive impairment associated with strokes or Parkinson's disease.

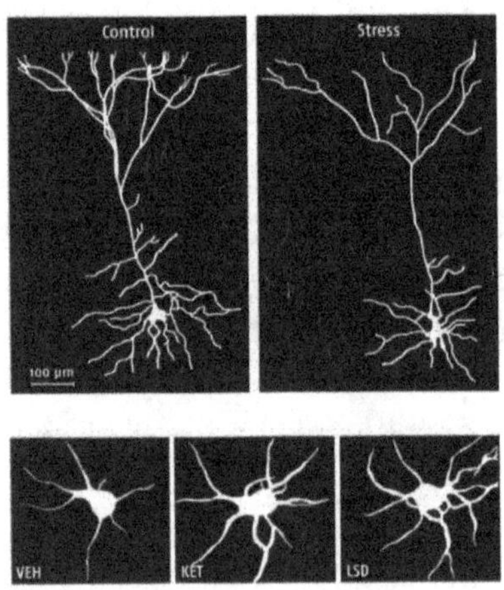

Psychedelics promote both functional and structural neuroplasticity, visible here in the increase of dendrites and spines (not shown here). VEH = no psychedelics, untreated nerve cells; KET = ketamine; LSD = lysergic acid diethylamide.[2]

"What's up?" my son asked, after noticing that I had been sitting motionless in front of my computer for a while.

2 Calvin Ly, Alexandra C. Greb, Maxemiliano V. Vargas, Whitney C. Duim, Ana Christina G. Grodski, Pamela J. Lein et al., "Transient Stimulation with Psychoplastogens Is Sufficient to Initiate Neuronal Growth," *ACS Pharmacology & Translational Science* 4, no. 2 (September 11, 2020): 452–60.

"Nothing," I replied, "I'm just thinking about a new kind of treatment that works like fertilizer on your brain." I showed him an image from one of Ron's studies demonstrating how nerve cells atrophy under stress. In response to stress, dendrites—the short, branched extensions of nerve cells responsible for receiving impulses from other cells—grow smaller and thinner, branching out less but also producing fewer of the dendritic spines that form synapses with other nerve cells. This in turn restricts the flow of information along neural pathways, leading to mental shutdown. Psychedelics by contrast cause dendritic spines and synapses to branch out and return to their normal, healthy state (see "control" in the figure).

"That's cool," my son said staring at the image, "a little like mom's orchids when they dry out and she makes them bloom again with some fertilizer." His words made me think of Aline, whose husband had described her as blooming like a flower under the influence of esketamine.

"You're right," I replied. "They are astonishing results."

"I think you should write your next book about that," my son added, before turning back to his comic book.

In early 2020 I was also contacted by the mother of Susan, a patient on whom I had performed a psychiatric assessment a couple of years before. Doing so had been difficult because Susan hadn't been able to express herself clearly. Asked whether she had lost pleasure and interest in things that once brought her happiness, she replied, "Yes, it's possible, but I'm not entirely sure. Yesterday and today, joy or no joy, it's hard for me to judge." In talking about her relationships, she had said, "Love is very important to me, but it's also total chaos, a game and a lot of illusions, so it also isn't important at all. I have no idea what to say."

The term "pseudodementia" had passed through my mind at the time, a severe impairment in thought or the ability to judge that can arise during a depression. Susan also seemed to be suffering from a distorted sense of time, an inability to recall temporal sequences accurately. In Susan's case, it left her unable to tell her own life story, or how a given relationship had developed. Speaking with Susan and her mother, then reviewing her file, confirmed what the colleague who had referred them assumed: Susan was struggling with severe depression.

Since then, Susan had undergone treatment with various antidepressants and psychotropic drugs, as well as lithium—none had improved her condition. Many of the psychotherapy sessions had been broken off not by Susan but her therapists, who classified her as incurable. A lack of response to conventional treatments in a patient is called "treatment resistance." Susan's mother told me her daughter "was at the end. She registered with Exit. I'm calling you to find out what options are left. We're ready for anything."[3] Step-by-step, I talked them through all the treatment options that were available for cases where treatment resistance and a heightened risk of suicide were involved—electroconvulsive therapy, deep brain stimulation (which requires neurosurgical intervention), ketamine, and other psychedelics—providing relevant information and scientific articles about each.

Susan called a week later: "I've decided on LSD. My parents support my decision." In speaking with her, I got the impression that she had been well advised by her family doctor and her parents, both of whom were professional academics. And even though her thinking was impaired, I considered her capable of making certain judgments. So I applied to the Swiss Federal Office of Public Health for a course of treatment with LSD, which was accepted two weeks later. Once the pharmacy had delivered the LSD, I invited Susan in for two preparatory sessions.

In our meetings Susan and I talked about the common side effects of LSD like nausea, fear or other strong emotions, sensations of coldness, headaches, and muscle cramps, which thankfully are nearly always acute and pass in time. We also discussed logistical and practical matters like getting to and from the session, clothing, eating and drinking, emergency medication, what to do about physical restlessness, music during the treatment, and the follow-up conversations planned for afterward to help integrate the LSD experience psychologically. I encouraged Susan to come up with something to concentrate on, questions she hoped to clarify for example, or desires connected with the session, but she didn't feel capable of working with a focal point. This left me skeptical, and wondering whether I wasn't overestimating LSD's efficacy in therapy, or even my own use. I didn't have all that much experience of my own, and maybe it wasn't such a good idea to treat a patient who had been turned away as untreatable by multiple colleagues whose work I held in high esteem. Would LSD make her thinking even less clear, still more vague?

The first hour of the LSD session seemed to confirm my skepticism: Susan was visibly nervous, bothered by hiccups, and drifted between bouts

3 In Switzerland euthanasia is legal, and registering with the organization Exit means someone is preparing for assisted suicide.

of giggling and sad, serious states, where she said things like: "Yoga is a burden but also a support, but I can't do any yoga, but that doesn't matter anyway." Then she fell silent, closed her eyes, and lay down. I played slow, calming music, "183 Times" by Greg Haines, as her body noticeably relaxed. After an hour, she sat up. "Something became clear to me," she said.

An insight after such a short time—it's probably just a new version of her confusion, I thought to myself.

Yet my fears were unfounded. Aided by the LSD, Susan succeeded in formulating an extended, clear train of thought, and told a story: "Not long after I started studying, I met Pierre. Through him I got to know myself, my passions and my strengths. I also got to know the world. He showed me tucked-away fish restaurants in Venice and jazz cellars in New York. It was a wonderful time. We blossomed. Instead of writing essays about Voltaire or Rousseau, we began to write a novel together in French, our novel.

"Pierre was an enthusiastic mountain climber. His friends assured me that he didn't take any risks, and knew the mountains well. I was never afraid, since I knew he would always come back. But one day he didn't come back. His cell phone was dead. I was in a panic. Finally, late that night, somebody called. It was the police. I had crying fits the whole night. The next day I had to identify the body of a mountain climber who had fallen. They were body parts in a sack. One hand and a part of the face were oddly familiar to me. It was Pierre.

"My reaction to his death was strange. I didn't cry anymore, I wasn't even sad. I froze, and my body became my armor. It protected me for a while, but over time I began to develop muscle cramps and awful stomach pain. What was especially difficult was that I couldn't think properly anymore. I couldn't gather my thoughts, I had lost the through line. I felt like unimaginative, untalented Katya in Chekov's *A Dreary Story*. I had to give up studying. As a kid my parents had lovingly referred to me as 'bookworm.' I haven't read a single book since Pierre's death."

LSD's ability to generate such clarity in Susan awakened me out of a false conviction that I had clung to for years. I was already convinced of ketamine's efficacy from numerous studies, but I was still quite skeptical at the time about using classic psychedelics in a therapeutic setting. My skepticism was rooted in an episode I had as a medical student on a strong dose of LSD, during which I had experienced dramatic changes in space and time and other nonsensical distortions in my perception. In any text I read, for instance, the letter "e" stood on its head. The effects might have been fascinating, but they seemed unlikely to be of much use in therapy. Yet now I was learning through Susan that LSD's impact can vary drastically according to the person and the situation. I was witnessing, for myself and in real time, that LSD had the potential to improve—or even normalize—thinking in people suffering from pessimistic self-evaluations and rumination.

Immediately the *Rig Veda* came to mind, the first and oldest part of the Indian Vedas, and the book I had read as I was preparing for my own LSD trip. Over hundreds of pages, the work hails the effects of the psychedelic substance soma, most often praising it for its "clarification" or "clarifying" qualities. Over countless repetitions, which in my own reading came across as both exaggerated and dubious, the text asserts that soma clarifies one's thinking and allows a clear view of things, that it bestows the vision of an eagle, is a pathfinder, and finds ways out. Susan's clarity of thought, which offered her a way out of her depression, now suddenly cast these hymns in an entirely new light. It seemed I had been wrong to abandon my previous plan of expanding neuroscience's view on psychotropic substances by turning to the millennia-old psychedelic experiences contained in the *Rig Veda*. I had made an error in reasoning, drawing general conclusions from individual experience. It was an error that stood in urgent need of correcting. The project I had tucked away among my files had to be revived, even turned into my main pursuit. My son was absolutely right: I had to write this book.

Academic opinion holds that psychotropic substances function primarily by altering our brain chemistry. What both my patients and the *Rig Veda* indicate, however, is that psychedelics like LSD, psilocybin, MDMA, ketamine, and esketamine operate at the level of direct experience. This makes them unique. Aline discovered new paths toward love and affection, Susan a way back to recalling and healing her trauma. Direct experience is one of the most powerful tools psychotherapy has at its disposal, making it entirely plausible to consider psychedelic therapy, or treatment with psychedelics. Consider the following scenarios: (1) watching a couple in love on a screen; (2) reading a book about the psychology of love; and (3) actually being loved. There's no doubt that the last option offers the most direct, basic, and effective way for understanding and learning about love. It is a lesson psychotherapists discovered long before psychedelic therapy in any modern form began to develop: Sigmund Freud and Carl Jung were continually emphasizing that it wasn't abstract knowledge that was decisive in the therapeutic setting, but insight gained from experience.

In behavioral therapy, exposure is considered the most important element at play—a patient directly experiencing a phobia she has been avoiding, for example. The meditation techniques used in modern mindfulness-based psychotherapy similarly help patients experience themselves and their environments in the here and now as directly as possible. And since direct experience and consciousness are one and the same, these kinds of experiences always mean an expansion of consciousness.

Direct experience is essential in psychotherapy because the contemporary world is constantly getting better at avoiding it, which is to say our experiences are growing less and less intense in nature. That, or even more problematic from a psychological standpoint, we now often have "unlived experiences" that never actually occur and are never fully processed—watching a video of a plane crash on YouTube, for instance. As every facet of life falls increasingly subject to technology, digitalization, and scientific modes of thought, we know more and more about a world that we experience less and less of. We have to keep in mind here just how much more information, differentiation, and intuitive insights direct experience contains compared to indirect experience, and how much more strongly it stimulates neuroplasticity. Who would you sooner trust to pilot your airplane—a man who has read a hundred books about flying but never actually flown himself, or a woman who has flown a hundred times over the Atlantic but has never laid a finger on an aviation manual? We avoid learning through direct experience because it is stressful and demanding. The growing gaps in our experiential knowledge have led to a rise in psychological disorders where we systematically avoid interacting with other people and their environment. Psychedelic therapy is one method for reestablishing contact to the world and ourselves.

This sort of rapprochement can be especially difficult in cases of severe trauma, at times dangerous. Aline and Susan both had good reasons for avoiding demanding experiences over the years. Yet as a strategy, avoidance carries the risk of a person remaining trapped in his or her traumatic experiences, stuck in a psychological cul-de-sac. Patients suffering from these sorts of post-traumatic issues thus pose a real quandary for psychotherapy and psychiatry. The latest research shows that even so much as naming or giving linguistic form to an undefined negative feeling can strengthen it over the long term, and without any therapeutic benefit.[4] Meditation, meanwhile, leads to retraumatization in up to 10 percent of patients with mild mental disorders, with negative long-term consequences.[5] This means nothing less than that in many instances, our current psychotherapeutic models are inappropriate for treating patients who are avoiding negative feelings and memories.

It is this very reason that led one of the world's leading trauma experts, US psychologist Rachel Yehuda, to open the Center for Psychedelic Psychotherapy in New York in 2021, and publicly announce that the method of trauma psychotherapy she had helped to develop would be replaced by psychedelic therapy. In part this is because psychedelics possess a built-in protective mechanism, something I call the "helioscope effect," and discuss in greater detail in chapter 1. The helioscope effect allows us to look directly into our pain or emotions without being burned by their "heat." The discriminating ways in which psychedelics are thus able to expand consciousness, paired with their ability to promote neuroplasticity, gives them an important role as catalysts in the psychotherapeutic process.

This book describes those catalyzing effects over the course of eight chapters; each chapter focuses on one essential aspect of psychological resilience and health, pairing it with at least one psychedelic effect that amplifies it.

Chapter 1 delves into perception, exploring the fundamental ways in which direct perception expands consciousness. Here, a sense of embodiment and vividness are the key elements in our experience that psychedelics strengthen.

Chapter 2 addresses time, a vital facet of our consciousness and a frequent source of psychological suffering. Fearing the future or remaining trapped in a traumatic past easily rank among the most common psychiatric problems that exist. Psychedelics alter our sense of time by allowing us to experience it in different modes, whether as narrative time, archetypal time,

4 Erik C. Nook, Ajay B. Satpute, and Kevin N. Ochsner, "Emotion Naming Impedes Both Cognitive Reappraisal and Mindful Acceptance Strategies of Emotion Regulation," *Affective Science* 2, no. 2 (April 20, 2021): 187–98.

5 Willoughby B. Britton, Jared R. Lindahl, David J. Cooper, Nicholas K. Canby, and Roman Palitsky, "Defining and Measuring Meditation-Related Adverse Effects in Mindfulness-Based Programs," *Clinical Psychological Science* 9, no. 6 (May 18, 2021): 1185–1204.

or even suspended time. Expanding our notion of time helps us put into perspective whatever suffering it causes us.

Chapter 3 is about gratification, which is capable of throwing both our experience of time and our perceptions seriously out of balance. Craving and addiction do not just rob us of our breath, but our awareness. Through positivity and peak experiences, psychedelics can strengthen the joy we find in everyday things and help us discern what truly matters.

Chapter 4 leads from reward to meaning. Despite everything in their lives going well, more and more people suffer from a feeling of meaninglessness. Psychedelics invite profound experiences of meaning that reveal manifest truths and foster forward-looking visions. In a severe crisis, this shift in perspective can be lifesaving.

Chapter 5 explores the intense lived experience of positive social feelings like love, gratitude, and reconciliation, and the psychotherapeutic benefit of these sorts of experiences when it comes to improving actual relationships and showing us a path out of loneliness.

Chapters 6 and 7 deal with the self and identity. Our everyday, egotistical self functions like a strong magnet that filters, blunts, and warps our perceptions, leading us to avoidance of direct experience, mental vacancy, social isolation, and negative thought patterns. By dissolving the self, psychedelics allow us to experience ourselves and the world anew. "Ego death" while on psychedelics helps us interrogate and revise our concepts of self and identity.

Finally, chapter 8 draws attention to the psychedelics that occur naturally in our brains and help us withstand extreme periods where everything changes—childbirth, for example, or near-death experiences. Achieving a sort of existential resilience through openness is a central topic in wisdom teachings and religions both Eastern and Western. It is also an important skill for remaining secure, courageous, and happy in a modern, uncertain, and rapidly evolving world.

A couple notes on terminology. The adjective *right*—as it appears in each chapter title—is borrowed from the Buddha's "Middle Way" or the "Noble Eightfold Path" for reaching enlightenment. All eight elements in the path begin with "right," under headings like "Right View," "Right Resolve," "Right Mindfulness." While the actual argument of my book doesn't tie in directly to these elements, I do employ the term *right* as it is used in a

Buddhist context, in terms of holistic and realistic understanding—as opposed to a moralistic or legal sense.

The term *higher self* that shows up in the title of the book refers to the holistic aspect of a person, which embodies their true, authentic selves as distinguished by its spiritual wisdom and intuitive capacity. The higher self is comparable to a tree whose roots extend down and up simultaneously. The lower roots are associated with our individual life stories, personal needs, and values while the upward-reaching roots connect us with a greater whole that goes beyond the individual self.

Despite psychedelics' undeniably positive effects, access for treatment remains quite restricted at present. In Germany, Switzerland, and a handful of other countries, psychedelics are currently being used for treatment in ongoing studies. Switzerland has also made certain legal exemptions for the use of MDMA, LSD, and psilocybin in a therapeutic setting. To obtain permission, the therapist must be fully trained and experienced, while the patient must reside in Switzerland and be unresponsive to other sanctioned treatments (various antidepressants or different forms of psychotherapy in the case of depression). The Swiss Physicians Society for Psycholytic Therapy offers a training course for doctors on using psychedelics in psychotherapy. Germany offers training courses in psychedelic studies to hospital staff.

For several countries—England, Canada, and the US—it appears likely that certain psychedelics will be approved for psychotherapy in the next ten years; MDMA stands the best chances for treating PTSD, psilocybin for depression. Regardless of the legal standing of these medicines around the world, as you'll see in the following pages their efficacy is undeniable.

Chapter 1

Right Perception: The Path to Direct Experience

I learned firsthand about the tremendous importance of perception for our well-being as a child, when over the course of several months my grandmother began to experience sudden, crushing bouts of facial pain. Diagnosed by a neurologist with trigeminal neuralgia, my grandmother turned down the recommended medication for preventing or stilling the pain. She opted instead for a radical surgical solution that destroyed a part of her trigeminal nerve. It was true that she didn't experience any pain after the intervention, but her perception was unmistakably altered. The food in her mouth was no longer perceived as such, but as bothersome clumps. Red wine suddenly tasted so salty that she had to spit it out. The apple tart she loved so well tasted like paper. Her hearing also worsened, while a loving touch on the face now felt as though she were being worked over with sandpaper. In short, her sense perception had changed entirely, and with it the things that she held to be real or true. She became a stranger to herself, and she couldn't understand the world around her. Her mental and physical health subsequently took a dramatic turn for the worse. My grandmother, the artist overflowing with ideas and plans, who sat with us grandkids tinkering with church windows because they refracted the light so beautifully, grew sluggish and apathetic, until she finally lost all interest in life and was left waiting for death. A couple of months later, she passed away from a lung infection.

The final years of my grandmother's life suggest what many studies confirm: Perception plays an important role in our psychological health. Losing the ability to see, for instance, often leads to severe psychological disorders; hearing loss can bring on depression, paranoid delusion, and dementia. Prolonged exposure to noise pollution or tinnitus, the perception of phantom noises and tones, can provoke severe stress disorders. Certain changes in perception are especially frequent among certain illnesses. In the case of PTSD, complex changes in perception may deaden our senses, make us overly sensitive to light, and cause sensory intolerances of all kinds. Severe depression can trigger olfactory hallucinations, leading patients to complain of spoiled, rotten, or burning smells. Within the modern industrial world, a lack of sensory experience is by far the most common psychological affliction, expressing itself among the general population in a range of troubles, from overly abstract and vague thoughts to brooding and feelings of alienation.

Right perception is central to our well-being. It is through seeing, hearing, feeling, and bodily perception that young children first establish basic trust in themselves and their surroundings. It comes as small surprise, then, that psychiatry has developed a range of treatments aimed at altering perception.[6] Exposing patients to bright light has become a standard method of treating depression. Hearing aids and ear training hold the potential to slow dementia. Positively stimulating the ear, with music for example, lessens anxiety and strengthens positive social feelings. Still, these kinds of treatment are just the tip of the iceberg when it comes to methods for altering perception, which stretch back thousands of years to the origins of human culture and philosophy. Those that hold most sway currently spring from Indian and Buddhist psychology. *Vipaśyanā* or *vipassanā* serves as a central concept in this context that means "attentive seeing," "clear seeing," "direct seeing," or "insightful seeing," where seeing stands for perception as such. The mountain of research papers on how mindfulness impacts depression, anxiety, pain, addiction, and the aftereffects of trauma, as well as its great popularity within psychotherapy and relaxation techniques, point to how direct, attentive, clear, and insightful perception of ourselves and the world can strengthen our sense of well-being and psychological resilience.[7]

---

6 Reşit Canbeyli, "Sensorimotor Modulation of Mood and Depression: An Integrative Review," *Behavioural Brain Research* 207, no. 2 (March 1, 2010): 249–64.

7 Joseph Wielgosz, Simon B. Goldberg, Tammi R. A. Kral, John D. Dunne, and Richard J. Davidson, "Mindfulness Meditation and Psychopathology," *Annual Review of Clinical Psychology* 15, no. 1 (May 7, 2019): 285–316.

Early Psychedelic Experiences in India

The importance of right perception in Eastern psychology has its roots in the *Rig Veda*, the oldest section of the Indian Vedas. Over hundreds of hymns, the authors describe changes in perception brought on by soma, a psychedelic likely obtained from the fly agaric mushroom. Among its various properties, soma is said to

- clarify and purify perception
- confer a broad vision that sees all sides
- be the possessor of one thousand eyes
- grant the wisdom of the seer and visionary
- grant insights that instill courage
- allow for treasure to be found and seen[8]

The *Rig Veda* also contains the first written reference to an ascetic: He wears his hair long, the future sign of ascetics and yogis in India, and is named Kesin. Under the influence of soma, Kesin perceived a connection between winds of the cosmos and his own breath. The experience provided a tremendous source of inspiration in the development of Indian thought, culminating in the phrase "Atman is Brahman," a formula given in the Upanishads that I will return to later. *Atman* derives from the Sanskrit for "essence or breath," and refers to the breathing body and the self, where *Brahman* signifies the cosmos, or ultimate reality. In this context, it is important to know that at the time adherents to the tradition of the *Rig Veda* were not ascetics themselves, and the changes in perception they praised were primarily practical, not spiritual in nature: securing cows and land, choosing the right partner, staying courageous in the face of conflict, recognizing interpersonal conflict more adeptly, and taking the right path through life. At the time, the cosmic scope of Kesin's perception left him a curious outsider among his contemporaries.

From today's perspective, one might say that soma's effects on our sensory perception led Indian psychology to the same findings that underpin research topics in modern neuroscience, consciousness studies, and psychotherapy: the way our brain operates as a filter or valve. Tasked with

8 Wendy Doniger, *The Rig Veda* (Penguin Classics, 2005); Karl Geldner and Peter Michel, *Rig Veda: Das Heilige Wissen Indiens* (Marix, 2008); Stephanie Jamison and Joel Brereton, *The Rigveda: The Earliest Religious Poetry of India* (Oxford University Press, 2017).

shielding our waking minds from anything that isn't of practical interest, human consciousness is comparable to an eagle able to recognize a mouse or other small animal of prey from a great height, even as it lacks acute hearing. This type of consciousness tends toward overfocus and seeing and thinking on rational and instrumental grounds, or in terms of use value. It quickly grows bored and exhausted if it stands no chance to benefit. Its weakness is openness. It also struggles to gain awareness of itself; it suffers from tunnel vision and is externally oriented to an excessive degree.

The brain's role as a filter makes it clear that we will have a better or worse connection to our environment and ourselves depending on how we perceive them. That connection arises through a process of consciously and unconsciously filtering and assembling partial pieces of information into meaningful overall impressions. Perception is an active process in which our attention and movement through space determine the content of what we perceive. Modern neuroscience has shown the tremendous influence preconceived expectations and value judgements exert over that content throughout the process, and how it is continuously weighed against our notions of the world. This back-and-forth plays a critical role in our lives; in German for example, the verb for perceive is *wahrnehmen*, which is literally "take to be true." What we perceive directly, then, establishes what we take to be true and real.

Modern technology has given us an increasingly abstract and technical view of the world; the Internet provides a wealth of information about the makeup of the world, while wearables and health apps seemingly communicate more important information about ourselves than our own bodily awareness. More and more, we are able to forego immediate perception, which is often stressful and emotionally charged, in favor of a life led by concepts. The problem is that in doing so we surrender direct connection, and with it the fullness of life and the complexity of the world.

The tension between the greater demands of direct perception and a more abstract, computerized, energy-efficient mode of interaction is even on display in robotics. In the field of artificial intelligence research, Moravec's paradox refers to a discovery that contrary to older assumptions, higher-level logical thinking actually requires very little computation, whereas lower-level sensorimotor and perception skills take tremendous computational resources.[9] It makes sense for the same reason that a robot would beat the best chess player in the world but have difficulty in climbing down the stairs or opening a door. Chess players are also much easier to replace with computers than barbers or nurses, whose work relies on complex, direct perception. Hans Moravec, the Austrian-Canadian intelligence researcher partially responsible for formulating the paradox, explains it along evolutionary lines: Our physical, intuitive, sensory intelligence developed over the course of a billion years, learning to perceive a changing and complex world in a way that granted us an intimate connection to ourselves and our surroundings. Abstract thought is a relatively recent phenomenon by contrast, less than a hundred thousand years old, and hasn't yet come to terms with our much older physical intelligence. This means that when we align ourselves too closely with what is ultimately a new trick, we end up robbing ourselves of the fullness of life.

The REBUS Theory

One leading theory about the effects of psychedelics argues that they weaken abstract thinking, opening us up to our physical, intuitive, and sensory intelligence in the process. Developed by British researchers Robin Carhart-Harris and Karl Friston, the theory is called relaxed beliefs under psychedelics, or REBUS for short, an acronym that plays on the term *rebus*, Latin for "in the middle of things."[10] In this chapter I concentrate on personal preconceptions; later chapters seek to address the fundamental structures of perception itself such as time, gratification, and the sense of self.

Our sense of touch is a good way to illustrate the REBUS effect. Imagine a blind woman feeling her way through a pathless forest. She does not perceive her surroundings all at once but bit by bit, using the information she gathers to best plot out her movements and whatever tactile sensations she will need along the way. If she has an image of a forest in mind, she won't need to touch much—she will know, for instance, that trees do not normally grow closely together, and does in fact make it through the forest

9 Hans Moravec, *Mind Children: The Future of Robot and Human Intelligence* (Harvard University Press, 1988), 28.

10 Robin Carhart-Harris and Karl J. Friston, "REBUS and the Anarchic Brain: Toward a Unified Model of the Brain Action of Psychedelics," *Pharmacological Reviews* 71, no. 3 (June 20, 2019): 316–44.

without bumping into a tree. If the same woman were now to take psychedelics, the mental map of the forest vanishes. Consequently, she will have to inch her way through the woods, touching every centimeter of earth and every tree as she does. While this is an exceedingly impractical way of crossing through a forest in principle, it offers the woman an incredibly rich experience of her environment. She will discover many new things that are irrelevant as a means to an end (i.e., for the purposes of navigation), but are rewarding as an end in themselves: the damp cushion of moss or the harmonious pattern of birchbark.

People who wrestle with psychological disorders have bad or even foolhardy plans and overestimate their accuracy. They will usually generalize negative experiences, saying for example that the forest is always wet and cold, while overlooking the fact that new trees, plants, and paths are constantly emerging. This is merely intended to illustrate that nearly all psychological disorders go hand-in-hand with a fixation on expectations. This means people suffering from these disorders rely on a model that bases their course of action on abstract thoughts and notions, while the physical, practical aspects of life go neglected. Once I am convinced that the people around me don't deserve any trust I stop engaging in social interactions and my social life withers, closing me off to experiences that might show me otherwise. If I sit down all by myself in my little room to set goals for the coming years, things will most likely turn out totally differently than planned. The result can either be an illusory, compartmentalized life or, at the other end of the spectrum, an uninspired, uncreative accommodation to one's surroundings, to the point of subjugation.

It isn't just psychotherapists and intelligence researchers; among politicians and business managers as well, the importance of direct perception is a current topic. In his book *Reinventing Organizations*, Belgian business coach Frédéric Laloux makes a case for direct perception's growing role in the business world, proposing a concept of "sensing" to replace leadership that emphasizes planning, strategizing, or change management. Observing that companies grow by evolving, through a continual process of "sensing" and adapting to their internal and external climates, he detects a shift in modern organizational forms from "predicting and controlling" to "perceiving and responding."[11]

---

11 Frédéric Laloux, *Reinventing Organizations: A Guide to Creating Organizations Inspired by the Next Stage of Human Consciousness* (Nelson Parker, 2014), 23.

Author Aldous Huxley stressed the primary role perception plays in religion and art, basing the title for his famous book on psychedelics, *The Doors of Perception*, on lines from the English poet William Blake: "If the doors of perception were cleansed every thing would appear to man as it is: Infinite. For man has closed himself up, till he sees all things thro' narrow chinks of his cavern."[12] Huxley himself foresaw great opportunities in researching and using psychedelics:

> We must learn how to handle words effectively; but at the same time we must preserve and, if necessary, intensify our ability to look at the world directly and not through that half opaque medium of concepts, which distorts every given fact into the all too familiar likeness of some generic label or explanatory abstraction.... Systematic reasoning is something we could not, as a species or as individuals, possibly do without. But neither, if we are to remain sane, can we possibly do without direct perception, the more unsystematic the better, of the inner and outer worlds into which we have been born. This given reality is an infinite which passes all understanding and yet admits of being directly and in some sort totally apprehended.[13]

Other psychedelic pioneers like Terence McKenna even see psychedelics as necessary for addressing environmental issues, given that direct perception of and creating intimacy with our ecological surroundings begets activism, conservation, and solution-seeking.[14]

Thanks to psychedelic research over recent decades, we now know how these substances alter perception in the brain. The thalamus operates as a primary switchboard for nerves located near the center of the brain. The thalamus also serves an important filtering function known as "thalamic gating" or "sensory gating," as nearly all sensory signals pass through it to the cerebral cortex, which is responsible for higher cognition. Psychedelics like ketamine, LSD, or psilocybin loosen this filter, with broad implications

12 William Blake, *The Marriage of Heaven and Hell and a Song of Liberty* (Andesite Press, 2015), 24.

13 Aldous Huxley, *The Doors of Perception and Heaven and Hell* (Harper, 2009).

14 Terence McKenna, *Food of the Gods: The Search for the Original Tree of Knowledge: A Radical History of Plants, Drugs, and Human Evolution* (Bantam Books, 1993).

for how the brain operates.[15] Under psychedelics, greater resources are allocated toward processing information physically or through the senses at the expense of higher-level processes like abstract thought. Yet psychedelics also work directly on the cerebral cortex, reducing the influence of prejudice and preconceived expectations. Overall, the changes mean hierarchical structures and organizational units exert less influence throughout the brain, explaining why this state is sometimes described (exaggeratedly) as the "anarchic brain."

How does that feel? Usually quite good. Abstract thought dissipates while sounds, images, smells, and tactile sensations come through more intensely. The result is an inner calm that again reinforces perception. This relaxed state of inner peace might best be described in English by the adjective *rapt*, meaning either "completely fascinated by what one is seeing or hearing" or "filled with an intense or pleasurable emotion" (as in *enraptured*). Originally, the term meant being transported by religious feeling.

We begin to feel more, hear more, see more, experience more. Words often fail for some of these new sensations, although changes in visual perception are relatively easy to describe. Things become more vivid, more real, contain greater shades of red, orange, and yellow. This arrives as a surprise, since colors indicate that we are dealing with reality, not fantasy—our dreams are usually colorless, for example. All in all, the image of a deeper, richer, less processed, more fundamental reality comes into view. The impression of a deeper, or more natural reality is admittedly difficult to explain; Aldous Huxley describes the experience as "seeing what Adam had seen on the morning of his creation—the miracle, moment by moment, of naked existence." For Huxley, this sort of fundamental or naked existence arises from a lack of judgement and the direct experience of what is.

Our perceptions not only feel more profound, but more whole. The *Rig Veda* describes soma as conferring a broad eye that can see all sides, an impression that experiences of synesthesia (literally "perceiving together") can help create as different sensory impressions cross wires with one another in the anarchic brain. Sounds suddenly have colors; smells make music.[16] One

15 Sam Vesuna, Isaac V. Kauvar, Ethan Richman, Felicity Gore, Tomiko Oskotsky, Clara Sava-Segal et al., "Deep Posteromedial Cortical Rhythm in Dissociation," *Nature* 586, no. 7827 (September 16, 2020): 87–94.

16 Devin Blair Terhune, David P. Luke, Mendel Kaelen, Mark Bolstridge, Amanda Feilding, David Nutt et al., "A placebo-controlled investigation of synaesthesia-like experiences under LSD," *Neuropsychologia* 88 (July 1, 2016): 28–34.

patient saw a conversation I was having with a coworker as a set of colors that transformed into a shimmering light, for example.

The most reliable consequence of these changes is that any and all sense of boredom vanishes. Before taking psychedelics, patients will sometimes grow bored and strike up a conversation with me, play with their smartphone, or read. Yet as soon as the psychedelics take hold, any form of diversion or entertainment becomes unnecessary, and they quietly lie down. Looking at a picture or a vase can suddenly provide hours of fulfillment. Aldous Huxley spent hours on end inspecting his pants after taking mescaline, for example: "Those folds in the trousers—what a labyrinth of endlessly significant complexity! And the texture of the gray flannel—how rich, how deeply, mysteriously sumptuous!" French author and poet Charles Baudelaire gave an account of his psychedelic fascination with the scent of a flower; it held him captive for an entire day, all without Baudelaire feeling tempted to describe or elevate it in a poem. After hours spent marveling at a rose on LSD, one patient of mine, an Anglicist, said that she had truly grasped the writer Gertrude Stein's line "A rose is a rose is a rose" for the first time.

The psychedelic state, Chilean psychiatrist and psychedelics pioneer Claudio Naranjo writes, "is linked with a special mode of perception in which the world of persons and objects is neither distorted nor left behind (along with the body itself and one's sense of identity), nor is it hidden behind a screen of half-materialized fantasies; it becomes more of itself, we might say. Everything becomes clearer, sharper, not only appearing to be more 'present' than usual, but with a density of formal relationships that creates the impression that each thing is a miracle of perfection even in its imperfections."[17]

In therapy, feelings that trigger a more direct, less filtered perception of self are particularly important; the keen interest patients will at times develop in visual or acoustic changes to their environment, meanwhile, can distract from the therapeutic process. This explains music's role in treatment—a way of encouraging patients' emotional and introspective capacities. Music has therapeutic value in its own right; as neurologist Oliver Sacks writes, "Perception of music activates more brain regions than any other activity. It activates an extensive network including the acoustic and

17 Claudio Naranjo, *My Psychedelic Explorations: The Healing Power and Transformational Potential of Psychoactive Substances* (Park Street Press, 2020).

the visual cortex, the motor cortex, the basal ganglia, the cerebellum, the amygdala, the hippocampus. That's why music therapy is effective in so many health conditions."[18] The effects Sacks describes are all the more intense under psychedelics, which have already activated the neural networks music typically triggers. It is mostly quiet and slow music that is appropriate in the therapeutic context, such as the psilodep playlists (short for "psilocybin for depression") assembled on Spotify by psychedelic music expert Mendel Kaelen. Yet unlike the perpetual drone of a supermarket soundtrack, it is important for the music to be used in a fully intentional way, for otherwise the effect will fizzle out or even disrupt the treatment. I myself only play music for about a third of the time, selecting each piece to match the patient's current state, much like a DJ. Music at the beginning of the treatment should be very slow and peaceful; at the high point of the trip it can be somewhat faster and include singing, and toward the end return to its original calm.

Having described the general changes in perception that occur under psychedelics, I'd like now to delve into three specific effects of psychedelics that are particularly important for psychotherapy. The first two—mindfulness and a sense of embodiment—have long been discussed in therapy research at large and are merely amplified by psychedelics. The third however—what I call the helioscope effect—is unique to psychedelics and of tremendous value to psychotherapy. To my mind, it is enough to justify the use of psychedelics in treating patients.

Mindfulness

When talked about as a relaxation technique, mindfulness refers to a specific kind of attention that is intentional, trained on the present moment, and nonjudgmental. Within this clear, wakeful state, people can experience their surrounding environments, bodies, and psyches directly, i.e., without growing distracted by abstract thoughts, preconceived notions, or memories.

Historically, mindfulness has mostly been found in yoga teachings and Buddhist meditation practice, both of which trace their own roots back to the psychedelic experiences described in the *Rig Veda*. It hardly comes a

18 Oliver Sacks, *Musicophilia: Tales of Music and the Brain* (Knopf Press, 2007).

surprise then that meditative states exhibit many similarities with psychedelic states. In Western culture on the other hand, practicing mindfulness has gained broader recognition as a technique used in psychotherapeutic methods. Mindfulness is also a term used within the context of care ethics to designate a specific practice of attention.

Below I've summarized the differences between meditative and psychedelic mindfulness:

> *Intentionality*: Mindfulness is an intentional action with a clear beginning and end, as opposed to spontaneous perception or moments of self-recognition. In meditation, as in psychedelic therapy, there is a clear and deliberate process of planning and execution.
>
> *Clarity*: Clarity is a central aspect of soma's effects in the *Rig Veda*. The Buddha also placed great value on monks' inner clarity and was constantly reminding them that hypnosis and trance are not meditative states but hindrances. More than anything, mindful clarity pertains to perception and simple, fundamental, and vivid insights—not the clarity of abstract thought. You might find it a little difficult to give a presentation on fractions in math while under the influence of psychedelics.
>
> *Non-action*: Meditative and mindful psychedelic states are distinguished by a sense of physical calm and instructions not to yield to the impulse to move. In hunter-gatherer societies that use psychoactive plants for hunting, they call them "plant-of-power-to-sit-still" or "gifts of stillness."[19] Improving one's impulse control is a long-term goal in mindfulness training.
>
> *Effort*: Like meditation, the psychedelic state should be compared to work. Psychedelics aren't used in a therapeutic context just for the fun of it, which also explains why neither meditation nor psychedelics pose much risk of addiction. You might more easily compare it to a mountain hike that is strenuous, but also highly satisfying.

19 McKenna, *Food of the Gods*.

Non-judgement: Both meditative and psychedelic awareness are permeated by an attitude of attentive neutrality and withholding judgement. Aldous Huxley describes the state as a form of liberation in *The Doors of Perception* by comparing his own condition to that of two sober companions: "But both belonged to the world from which, for the moment, mescaline had delivered me—the world of selves, of time, of moral judgments and utilitarian considerations, the world (and it was this aspect of human life which I wished, above all else, to forget) of self-assertion, of cocksureness, of overvalued words and idolatrously worshiped notions."[20] A feeling of liberation isn't uncommon for patients undergoing psychedelic treatment; as one patient wrestling with negative thought patterns reported, "Now I've experienced how beautiful and marvelous the world is when I can do without my negative thoughts."

Fellowship: Freedom from judgement and concepts doesn't mean the freedom to exist outside any and all human relations, and does not generally have an asocial effect. Quite the contrary—it usually is accompanied by feelings of connection, empathy, and love. It is no coincidence that many spiritual and religious traditions share the assumption of a mindful attitude spontaneously leading to empathy for oneself and others, and a deep appreciation for the intimate connection that exists between everything. This is owed in part to the fact that filtering our perceptions through abstract concepts and judgements often puts us at a remove from the world around us. In many cases, shutting this filtering function off leads to profound insights about giving and receiving love.

Timelessness: Mindfulness exercises set the goal of concentrating on the present moment. With psychedelics, this happens of its own accord, with support from the therapeutic setting. During periods of mindfulness, attention to the present moment can increase to such an extent that one temporarily loses a sense of time (more on this in the following chapter).

20 Huxley, *The Doors of Perception*.

Eternity: The natural sciences and medicine focus in large part on tangible, finite things; philosophy, art, and religion, for their part, will also delve into the intangible and eternal. The potential for mindfulness to impart feelings and ideas about eternity gives it—along with contemplation and psychedelics—an important place in the broader humanities, not just in psychotherapy. "Behind the cloud of thoughts there appears a small corner of blue sky," wrote Harvard professor-turned spiritual teacher Ram Dass about the feeling of eternity on psychedelics. I will discuss the aspect of eternity as it relates to psychotherapy in greater depth in the final chapter about right openness.

As in medicine and health care, mindfulness is widely used in psychotherapy as a method for calming patients. Agitated patients are instructed to focus less on anxiety-inducing thoughts, to sit down, and to focus on bodily or breathing sensations. Adjusting in this way allows patients to calm down, trust the attending personnel, and stay open to suggestion, even if unpleasant perceptions arise (backaches, for example, or intestinal issues), since it is really their worries and not the sensations themselves that are the primary cause of anxiety. Without exception, patients have relaxed in every instance of psychedelic treatment that I have led to date, even in cases where they perceived their pain more distinctly and precisely or were grappling with deeply traumatic experiences. In one pilot study I participated in, we were able to show that a reduction in negative judgement and abstract thought coincided with a significant increase in activity of the vagus nerve, even when patients were experiencing intense pain. The vagus nerve is a part of the calming, parasympathetic nervous system that connects the brain to the lungs, heart, and intestines.[21]

Loni, a former figure skater plagued by extreme stomach and bone aches, had a very strong experience of mindfulness while on psychedelics. I treated Loni with LSD because her pain left her unable to meditate. At the start of the session, she reported that her burning stomach pain had increased. She also felt pain in her feet and knees, everywhere, in fact, where she had been operated on due to injuries. I was still an inexperienced therapist at the time when it came to psychedelics, and her words left me frightened at the thought that her pain was increasing.

---

21 Gregor Hasler, *Die Darm-Hirn-Connection: Revolutionäres Wissen für unsere psychische und körperliche Gesundheit* (Klett-Cotta Verlag, 2020).

That was when Loni said, "Please don't worry. I see these pains from a long ways off. I'm observing them as though they didn't belong to me at all." Later, she described "seeing my burning gut in front of me, extremely clearly. I can see the barriers to my intestines opening and closing. When they close, the pressure on my bowels increases, and so does the psychological weight. When they open, the pressure lessens and the depression goes away." She perceived her entire body as a large wound; not just her intestines, but every last bone. "It isn't bad at all though, I'm seeing it from far away." She remembered her father coming home drunk, and her mother holding her when Loni started crying from fear. She said, "This not knowing what was happening, the fear of uncertainty, maybe that is at the root of my angst and my pain." Yet in spite of the intense pain and traumatic childhood memories resurfacing, Loni was completely relaxed. She said, "This is the most relaxed I've been since I was a kid. It's crazy—the pain is there, and I'm relaxed."

The following graph shows psychological and physical relaxation preceded by a dramatic rise in vagus nerve activity. Loni only sat for one LSD session; after she purchased a device to stimulate the vagus nerve through electrical impulses on the ear. With her psychedelic experience still in the back of her mind and the stimulator, she's since been able to do mindfulness exercises on her own.

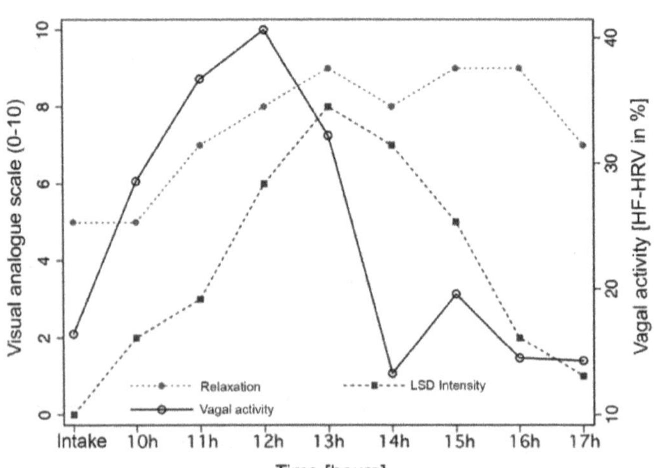

Fig. 1–1: A chart illustrating the course of subjective relaxation, perceived intensity of LSD, and vagus activity measured physiologically during an LSD session.

Abstract Thinking as a Source of Anxiety

It is especially difficult to foster mindfulness in patients who exhibit disorders in attention or speech, as is all too often the case. With generalized anxiety disorder for example, constant focus on relatively abstract negative thoughts is the primary cause of chronic worry and indefinite fears. People will find it difficult to visualize concrete situations or memories (more on this under the "Vision" subtitle in chapter 4), thinking instead in abstract, imprecise terms that have little to do with direct perception.[22] Someone might ask, for instance, "Who knows whether a trip to Brazil would really do me good? Is my daughter in safe hands on her stay in England? What will happen if my pension fund goes belly-up?" On closer look, one quickly notices that a term like "pension fund" doesn't refer to a particular building or person. By the same token, the "safe hands" of the daughter's host family remain empty, without definite form. As for Brazil, the person is scarcely able to say anything more concrete about what kind of trip they would like to take. It is the same with memories: "It was bad!" one patient replied when I asked about her childhood, without being able to elaborate any further.

Psychological research has shown abstract worries and vague memories to be one way of avoiding direct perception.[23] Negative, abstract thought leads to chronic activation of the stress system; clear, concrete images with a basis in direct perception, by contrast, activate the stress system in a way that promotes active coping: "Today I will read the annual report for my pension fund. Tomorrow I'll call my daughter's British host family. The day after that I'll speak with my former coworker João, who knows his way around Brazil." Cognitive behavioral therapy is one way of helping to support the strategy of filling concepts with concrete and intuitive views and direct experience.

It isn't uncommon for an underlying speech disorder to be the cause of chronic worries and troubling thought patterns, in which case more

22 Colette R. Hirsch, Sarra Hayes, Andrew Matthews, Gemma Perman, and Tom Borkovec, "The Extent and Nature of Imagery During Worry and Positive Thinking in Generalized Anxiety Disorder," *Journal of Abnormal Psychology* 121, no. 1 (February 1, 2012): 238–43.

23 Evelyn Behar, Sarah Kate McGowan, Katie A. McLaughlin, T. D. Borkovec, Michelle Goldwin, and Olivia Bjorkquist, "Concreteness of Positive, Negative, and Neutral Repetitive Thinking About the Future," *Behavior Therapy* 43, no. 2 (June 1, 2012): 300–312.

straightforward methods of behavioral therapy unfortunately won't work. For people suffering from these sorts of disorders, speech has fundamentally retreated from reality; words have lost their direct connection to sensory, emotive, and physical experience, and with it the ability to evoke clear images. This doesn't just lead to undefined fears, but severely limits a person's experiential and narrative capacities. Aldous Huxley pointed this problem out repeatedly in calling for a dedicated effort by schools to employ language that is sensory, vivid, and direct. Huxley himself suffered from severe visual impairments and limitations on his imagination since childhood—a grave deficit for an author and art historian. Through psychedelics he was thankfully able to develop an exceptionally vivid style of language, and eventually become one of the great writers of the twentieth century. In Huxley's case, it reveals his enthusiasm for psychedelics was less politically or religiously motivated then it was based in practical and existential reasons.

More recent linguistic research has shown the importance of synesthesia (where one type of sensory stimulation evokes the sensation of another, as often occurs under psychedelics) in the development of language.[24] There is even increasing evidence that language as such may have first originated in synesthetic experiences. The theory behind the ideas goes as follows: Otherwise meaningless sounds stimulate the imagination. New words emerge out of associations between word-like sounds and images that point either to external or internal realities, which are then tested through social exchange as a means of communication for understanding oneself and the surrounding world. If the theory holds, it's not impossible that just as Huxley intuited, psychedelics help us to experience the origin of language, the ultimate ground of words and meanings, and learn speech anew. Given the protection that concrete, descriptive language offers against anxiety and fear, and the importance of verbalizing conflicts and emotions as a tool in therapy, it can be helpful to return to the foundations of language to free up therapeutic processes that may have gotten stuck.

---

24 Yasmin Schmid, Florian Enzler, Peter Gasser, Eric Grouzmann, Katrin H. Preller, Franz X. Vollenweider et al., "Acute Effects of Lysergic Acid Diethylamide in Healthy Subjects," *Biological Psychiatry* 78, no. 8 (October 1, 2015): 544–53; Nicholas Root, Romke Rouw, Michiko Asano, Chai-Youn Kim, Helena Melero, Kazuhiko Yokosawa et al., "Why Is the Synesthete's 'A' Red? Using a Five-language Dataset to Disentangle the Effects of Shape, Sound, Semantics, and Ordinality on Inducer–concurrent Relationships in Grapheme-color Synesthesia," *Cortex* 99 (February 1, 2018): 375–89.

I emphasize this linguistic aspect so strongly because by far the most common reason patients consult with me about psychedelic treatment is that they have gotten stuck with other forms of psychotherapy. They've often sought help from a host of different psychotherapists in the past, only to slide back into an endless loop in their conversations. There's no end of things to talk about or fascinating ways of analyzing them; it is a connection to the suffering and the actual problem to the world of direct perception that is missing.

Mindfulness and Moving Past Suffering

A leading question in psychotherapy research is how mindfulness contributes over the long term to successful therapy. The same applies for psychedelic research, and once again it is the Indian tradition that provides us with important signposts. The Buddhist model of mindfulness sets out three elements in its comprehensive set of teachings on how to overcome human suffering:[25]

- Sense impressions and mental events (thoughts, for example) are impermanent. They arise and cease to exist.
- Habitual reactions, in the sense of attachment or aversion to sense impressions and mental events, and a lack of awareness about those reactions, lead to suffering.
- Sense impressions and mental events do not contain or form an enduring, separate entity that could be called a self.

Simple mindfulness exercises are enough for us to ascertain the first element; there is no need for psychedelics. Studies have shown, for instance, that depressive symptoms will change much more over time than is generally supposed.[26]

The second element has become a hot topic in psychotherapy research. As we saw in Loni's case, psychedelics can help patients consciously

25 Andrea Grabovac, Mark A. Lau, and Brandilyn R. Willett, "Mechanisms of Mindfulness: A Buddhist Psychological Model," *Mindfulness* 2, no. 3 (April 6, 2011): 154–66.

26 Gregor Hasler, U. Schnyder, R. Klaghofer, and J. Angst, "Treatment of Depressive Disorders with and Without Medication—A Naturalistic Study," *Pharmacopsychiatry* 35, no. 6 (November 1, 2002): 235–38.

"accept" even severe physical pain without attachment or aversion. "Acceptance" in the psychotherapeutic sense does not mean simply giving in, whether to a conflict at one's job, a marriage in crisis, or an illness. The term refers instead to accepting the negative emotion tied to a given case as the only path toward self-exploration, i.e., right perception of the situation, and taking the appropriate steps. Nonacceptance, repression, and avoidance weigh as heavily as they do because we usually repress and avoid the very things that are most important to us, since their importance makes us vulnerable. Other people are often especially important to individuals who isolate themselves from social anxiety, for example; so important, in fact, that they are a source of fear.

While "acceptance" may be a relatively new and somewhat fashionable term, it describes a factor that figures in most methods of psychotherapy. Early in his career Sigmund Freud developed a perception-based theory of psychological suffering. He assumed that a strong, unpleasant perception—being bitten on the left hand by a large poisonous spider, say—is made weak psychologically by separating out the source of excitation (i.e., the emotional element). The emotion is then transferred either into a physical symptom like tension in the left hand, or attaches itself to another previously harmless idea, which then becomes an obsession: mentally avoiding all words that begin with an "s" as in "spider," in our example. Freud describes a broad range of possibilities the psyche has at its disposal for rendering direct perception impossible, and the extreme contortions it will undertake to maintain its defenses over the long term. Freud termed this sort of avoidance "blocked affect."[27] The feeling that would be necessary for direct, full perception is blocked, and thus lingers on in the subconscious over the long term. Therapy in this context aims to revive the feeling by recalling the traumatic event then "discharging it," i.e., living the "unlived experience" after the fact.

Discovering and reawakening blocked feelings for Freud occurs through methods that bear a great similarity to the contemporary notion of mindfulness. Discharging the feeling, also called "catharsis," should cause the psychological disturbance to vanish, much like lancing a festering abscess—it hurts a great deal at first, but after being cleaned brings relief and healing over the long term. The Czech psychiatrist and psychedelic pioneer Stanislav Grof, whose study *LSD Psychotherapy* remains instructive and well

---

27 Sigmund Freud, *Werke Aus Den Jahren 1892–1899* (S. Fischer Verlag, 2010).

worth the read today, leans heavily on the theory of blocked affect both in explaining how and why unpleasant feelings arise and resolve during psychedelic therapy sessions, and for conceiving of the therapy process overall.[28]

Exposure therapy (or confrontation therapy), one of the best researched methods of classical behavioral therapy, also centers around accepting unpleasant feelings. The underlying principle is for the patient to be confronted by the fear-inducing object (the spider) or situation (the dark forest where the spider bite occurred). Here, too, the goal is to practice direct perception of something unpleasant. Exposure therapy is only possible in cases where the object is clearly defined, as with a fear of spiders or heights. Parallel to Buddhist psychology, the goal is to overcome one's reactions to sensory input, whether that reaction is attachment or aversion. In the case of simple phobias, psychedelics are appropriate only for patients who find themselves overwhelmed by exposure. As it is, recent research has shown that this is not infrequently the case, and that the risks of exposure therapy are much greater than originally assumed, potentially resulting in traumatization or retraumatization (more on this important aspect in the helioscope section later in this chapter).

Mindfulness and Holistic Perception

Psychedelics' effects on mindfulness also bring many patients to report more holistic, integrated experiences of perception. One depressive patient, a former dancer, told me: "With psilocybin I relearned how to listen to music not just with my ears, but with my whole body, as a whole person." If we take "person" in the sense of the Latin term *personare*, literally "to sound through" (*per* means "through" and *sonare* means "sound"), we begin to approach what my patient meant—a person is a being whose spirit and body are in vibration and resound like an instrument. The word *persona* originally meant the mask through which an actor spoke, announcing himself as an individual. Another patient told me that LSD had allowed him to detect half tones in music, as though his hearing had suddenly improved. Parallel to his discovery of musical nuances, he also found new nuance in

28 Stanislav Grof, *LSD Psychotherapy: The Healing Potential of Psychedelic Medicine* (Multidisciplinary Association for Psychedelic Studies, 2008).

his emotional life. Before stress had simply been stress; now he recognized how varied it truly was, and the subtle differences in his reactions—that, and how feelings of love were able to ease his response.

Rediscovering beauty can also have therapeutic value in my experience, bringing a sense of joy and enthusiasm to life and connecting us to a greater whole. The following example hopefully illustrates one way in which abstract thinking directly limits our ability to perceive beauty. I once treated a professor of physical chemistry for depression with LSD; for years on end she had felt listless and worn-down. As one of the first patients I was treating in this way, at one point I asked out of pure scientific curiosity how she understood the phrase "not all that glitters is gold" under the influence of the LSD. At first she didn't even attempt an answer, replying that she wasn't "ready at the moment to think it over in higher-level concepts. The colors are too important, too rich, too beautiful to think about color as non-color, as a value or a play on words. Right now I am seeing things as they really are. They're so beautiful, so brilliant if you remove abstract meaning. Language isn't enough to describe what I'm experiencing. Nothing occurs to me that would be of any use. I feel embarrassed by how much beauty I'm seeing, because I'm able to see beauty." Like many others, the therapy brought her attention to the high price of abstract thought subsuming more and more realms in life, an insight that often brings long-term positive consequences for patients.

Before continuing, I want to stress that psychedelic mindfulness effects do not simply arise on their own, but come about first through the interplay of setting and substance. The organizers of the storied LSD parties on the East and West Coasts of the US in the 1960s and '70s, for instance, weren't interested in cultivating mindfulness among partygoers—playing music at full blast, setting up strobe light shows, instigating social and sexual games, and introducing a powerful cocktail of other substances like alcohol, cocaine, and heroine into the mix. Tom Wolfe's *The Electric Kool-Aid Acid Test* describes the scene in detail; his sketches leave one feeling that party organizers and guests were ultimately just as afraid of psychedelics opening their minds and hearts as the politicians who later banned the substances. The therapeutic setting is the opposite of a party. I repeatedly encourage my patients not to let themselves be distracted by the external world but stick to their experience, as in meditation. A sleep mask like the kind used on airplanes can support mindfulness, as can peaceful music. The minute music starts to distract, I turn it off.

Embodiment

In his best-selling book *How to Change Your Mind: What the New Science of Psychedelics Teaches Us About Consciousness, Dying, Addiction, Depression, and Transcendence*, Michael Pollan describes his own experiences with psychedelics. The title refers to both a change of opinion as well as a broader shift in consciousness. Before taking psychedelics, Pollan's first trip guide advised him to experiment with holotropic breathing, a method developed by Stanislav Grof after psychedelics were banned for therapy in the US. Holotropic breathing produces a mild psychedelic state by means of hyperventilation, or very rapid breathing. About his experience Pollan wrote that "it felt fantastic to so fully inhabit my body, as if for the first time."[29]

The concept of "embodiment" helps situate Pollan's experience in a scientific context, a thesis in contemporary research that supposes consciousness to require a physical body, as opposed to the simplified model of consciousness in computers described earlier. Perception is not just the rote reconstruction of sensory inputs in the form of an internal model of the world; it is a physical and sensory event that calls on the entirety of a living, acting being. The point is not that inner psychological events like wishes or thoughts are externalized, but rather that they are embodied to begin with. The concept is a scientific version of non-duality where inner and outer—subject and object—collapse: The hand that touches is also the hand that is touched.

To dynamically interact with our environment as an embodied self requires a body schema. A body schema denotes the fact that our body is not just any body, but our own unique, subjective opportunity to perceive and act as an integrated whole. The term also describes the overarching perception of our body in its structure and composition, movements, and limits. The phantom arm that people are sometimes able to feel after an amputation is a striking instance of a body schema. It is a sign that even after mutilation, we do not want to surrender the practical field that the arm presided over. The amputation means the person will not have any new experiences with their arm; nothing concrete, no direct perceptions will arise in this part of

---

29 Michael Pollan, *How to Change Your Mind: What the New Science of Psychedelics Teaches Us About Consciousness, Dying, Addiction, Depression, and Transcendence* (Penguin, 2019).

their body schema. That particular aspect of reality remains frozen, with the sensation of a phantom arm that can last years.

Phantom limbs are obviously one extreme example of disruptions that can occur to a body schema. Yet more subtle disturbances occur for us all when we don't use our entire body or avoid certain physical sensations, which leads our body schema to age, wither, or freeze. Traumatic experiences that leave one's physical integrity in doubt will also often leave traces behind in a body schema. It isn't surprising that people no longer feel at home in their own body and seek help in such cases.

These are not new problems. The *Rig Veda*'s proclamation: "Soma, o self-purifying one, you drive to great fame with your brilliant rays. Vaunting yourself, you keep smashing away all the dark shades in the house of the pious man," sounds a lot like a run-down body schema being rejuvenated or updated, as with Pollan's psychedelic experience of "fully inhabit[ing] my body." Yoga instruction also works closely with body schemas, building off the *Rig Veda* by placing special emphasis on the connection between breath and consciousness. This echoes Pollan's experience of simple hyperventilation leading to a pleasant sensation of inhabiting his body. Early yoga used symbiotic or embryonic breathing—a method of respiration that draws on the entire body, head to toe—as a means for unifying consciousness. In yoga, unifying oneself means becoming aware of the totality of one's body, perceived as a unity. For all their cosmic reach, the chakras—discussed in detail in chapter 3—are first and foremost conceived as a form of embodied consciousness; in many Indian writings, the body provides the bridge to the cosmos. The Buddha praised those who used their bodies to try to contact the undying nirvana by means of direct perception. In later yoga teachings, as in alchemy, the set goal is to transform living material, to "decondition" it, making it freer and more flexible, and place it in a new era—to perform an update, in other words.[30]

The sense of embodiment that arises under psychedelics is a result of the lifting of filters that otherwise shield our consciousness from internal stimuli. The changing perceptions of the psychedelic state also cause our consciousness to rely more heavily on information drawn from the central nervous system in creating a stable and meaningful world. This lowers the alpha oscillations within our neural networks, in turn privileging concrete

30 Mircea Eliade, *Yoga: Immortality and Freedom* (Princeton University Press, 1958).

over abstract thought.[31] People are well documented as expressing things in a more physical, personal, and emotional way while under the influence of psychedelics; their autobiographical memory also improves and grows livelier. All of these changes can lead to greater efficacy in psychedelic-assisted therapy. Several studies show extroverted people responding especially well to psychedelics, likely because they access the less-accessed terrain of introspective experience. In psychedelic therapy, this sense of embodiment is encouraged further by instructing patients to focus on their body, or having them do a body-scan meditation before the session. Peter Oehen, a Swiss psychiatrist who introduced me to psychedelic psychotherapy and accompanied me on my own experiences with psychedelics, further recommended occasionally reminding patients to concentrate on the regions of their chest and heart.

Feeling disembodied is a common symptom of depression. As one patient described, "It isn't tiredness in the body that leads to listlessness. It feels as though my spirit has left the body. A feeling of a complete lack of security in myself...my legs and arms hang off me like dead flesh. A feeble, spineless, even lifeless body lying there in bed. Feeling alienated from my body and the crushing waves of guilt have me constantly thinking up new ways to kill myself." In this patient's case, a weekly treatment with esketamine nasal spray helped her find the way back. "It feels like I'm back in my body," she said afterward, "and with it the depression has also largely gone away."

Another depressive patient who felt cut off from his body described his new state of being six months after a single session with LSD: "The treatment had a lasting effect on me. Like a blow with an axe on the frozen sea within me. A door opened inside me and a narrow sliver stayed open. I can feel my body again, which means my feelings, too." One of Claudio Naranjo's patients described her experience with embodiment during an ibogaine session as feeling "through the perineum, a warm energy began to emanate that went up my vagina, passed through my womb, and my entire body up to the crown and it began to envelop my whole body. I felt a lot of heat, but it was very pleasant. It was an energy that moved in waves, that had a very fast, but very soft vibration."[32]

---

31 Adam L. Halberstadt, Franz X. Vollenweider, and David E. Nichols, *Behavioral Neurobiology of Psychedelic Drugs* (Springer, 2018).

32 Naranjo, *My Psychedelic Explorations*.

In Western modernity, body dissatisfaction, or body image disorder, is one of the most common forms of disruption to body schemas. These disorders are an important source for feelings of low self-esteem, social isolation, depressive moods, obesity, and eating disorders like anorexia, which can be fatal. Telltale signs include:

> *Body dysmorphia*: regarding certain body parts as either too large or small, or disfigured.
>
> *An overly idealized body image*: considering an entirely flat stomach, or a large gap between the upper thighs when standing to be normal.
>
> *Judgement disorders*: belittling one's own body or body parts according to incoherent criteria.
>
> *Behavioral disorders*: compulsively checking whether one's body is "all right," whether looking in the mirror or by constantly weighing oneself.

The complex and truly oppressive difficulties that can arise in inhabiting our own bodies is not just a problem for women. Jan was twenty-three when he was referred to me for an unspecified eating disorder. At sixteen Jan had suffered an inflammation of the epididymis that left him deeply insecure, scared that he had cancer and that his testicles would have to be removed to stop the disease from spreading. His insecurity persisted even after the inflammation was cured without complications. Within a matter of months he had turned his life upside down; instead of reading or meeting with friends as usual, he started going to the fitness studio, jogging, and drastically altering his diet. He ate only low-fat products and would often skip meals. A well-defined six-pack, narrow waist, and broad shoulders became an absolute necessity. Before, he had loved Franz Kafka's short story about Gregor Samsa's metamorphosis into an insect; now he wanted nothing to do with reading. His new idol was Andy Hug, a Swiss martial artist who had won European and world championships in kickboxing and Thai fighting. "Andy was successful, invincible, a millionaire," he observed, awestruck.

Over the years Jan's perfectionism had only grown where his diet and appearance were concerned. He found work for a spell as a junior trainer at a karate school, though he soon became too weak and unfocused to continue, with the lack of calories in his diet leaving him exhausted. "Jan has completely changed," his father said. "Before he devoured books and was quite funny. We were always laughing. Now he's very grim, never laughs, rarely talks, and is withdrawn. He spends the whole day focused on his body, constantly looking at himself in the mirror and weighing himself multiple times a day."

His mother was also worried: "His life consists exclusively of sleeping and strength training." In truth, Jan's strength training was rapidly becoming a form of compulsive control. Missing so much as a single training session left him in a panic. As he grew steadily weaker and found it harder and harder to do his strength training, he ended up in a vicious cycle—the greater his panic and despair, the less he ate, increasing his despair and exhaustion all the more. His muscle mass decreased, and Jan thought more and more about taking his own life. Various psychotropic drugs hadn't improved his condition, and he had left inpatient treatment at a center for eating disorders after just one week.

Jan and his parents were immediately enthusiastic when I floated the possibility of an LSD session. I mentioned it as an option based on my experience of LSD bringing new life to patients in therapy who had reached an impasse. This comes in part from LSD's ability to loosen inflexible or hardened neural pathways, making room for new perceptions, experiences, and behaviors to emerge. This effect impacts the insular lobe, which operates differently within the brain on LSD, giving patients a different experience of their body.

For the first three hours after taking the LSD, Jan remained withdrawn. His answers were brief, and he didn't want to be distracted from his internal experience. Then he suddenly sat up on the bed, looked around, and let his eyes come to rest on the Buddha that I keep in my office, sitting fully relaxed on a small, unassuming throne. "Is that a toilet the Buddha's sitting on?" Jan asked in amazement. I didn't understand what he meant at first, until we both broke out in laughter. It was the first time I had seen Jan cheerful and in high spirits. The ice had been broken.

Jan normally viewed his muscles as armor offering him protection and feared its collapse. Yet now, under LSD, that armor had changed in his mind's eye into a soft, hilly surface. "That's what I looked like before," he said, astonished. "I was so brave then, marching through the world with a body like that!" He went on to experience other body images: now he was corpulent and broad, now bony and thin. At one point he experienced himself with a large stomach, observing, "Normally I get all in a panic at the thought of a stomach like that, but I think it's totally fine now, even nice." Later, he said, "You know, I always thought I was two people: Jan One, who reads Kafka; and Jan Two, the martial artist. But I can see it clearly now: Kafka's Gregor and Andy Hug are the same! Jan One is Jan Two!"

Jan wasn't fully cured after the session, but he felt motivated to continue his healing in therapy. "I'm in a dead end! I have to free myself of my armor!" he declared. As an inpatient at a psychotherapy clinic, Jan was finally able to abandon his pathological eating behavior, and for the most part give up checking his body compulsively. He lost interest in teaching karate, and instead began organizing events for a youth club. "With you I learned that fun is important," he said to me at the end of one session.

Unlike the healthy Michael Pollan, for whom a feeling of physical perfection set in after a single breathwork session, Jan wasn't able to accomplish this even in the context of complex therapy. Psychotherapists can't work magic with psychedelics. Still, in many instances psychedelics can catalyze a fresh start and greater impact in psychotherapy.

Directing one's gaze inward and embodying the spiritual are not the exclusive domain of Eastern philosophy or psychedelics. Shamanistic practices in Oceania hold that to be initiated as a shaman, the dead must appear to the initiate in order to turn his gaze inward; only by looking inward will they be able to eat from the castor bean and reach the source of life.[33] Albert Hoffman, the Swiss chemist who discovered LSD, set the embodiment effects of LSD within the context of Christianity, writing in a letter that "the most worthwhile spiritual benefit from LSD experiments was the experience of the inextricable intertwining of the physical and spiritual. 'Christ in matter' (Teilhard de Chardin)."[34] For feminist theologian Elisabeth Moltmann-Wendel, the opening and transformation of the body is the principal theme in Christianity, which asserted the physicality of spirituality so vehemently that it vouched for a concept of God incarnate. This provoked violent resistance within society that led to the body being tortured on the cross. The Christian story of flight from the body into the soul led to religion's

33 Mircea Eliade, *Shamanism: Archaic Techniques of Ecstasy* (Princeton University Press, 2020).

34 Albert Hofmann, *LSD: My Problem Child: Reflections on Sacred Drugs, Mysticism and Science* (Oxford University Press, 2013).

modern-day denial of the body. "When we embed ourselves in our bodies," Moltmann-Wendel writes, "we are able to broaden its constraints, to leave the container of our bodies, or make it permeable...and suddenly we notice all the new spaces that have opened, which coffins we are leaving behind and what returns: Fantasy, desire, energy, pain and sadness as well...we're able to trust in ourselves and the living matter."[35] She proposes thinking with the body as a way of reconciling ourselves with nature, and bridging the gap between subject and object. This echoes the goals of psychedelic psychotherapy.

The Helioscope Effect

As I've discussed, direct perception and coming to accept negative experiences or physical pain are generally recognized as effective means of healing within the psychotherapeutic process. In such processes, a temporary increase in symptoms has been considered tolerable, though systematic research was long outstanding as to whether the increase is only ever temporary, and ultimately beneficial. Recent research has taken a closer look at the side effects of direct perception, and now show concerning results.[36] According to one study, 40 percent of patients with mild psychological disorders who used meditation as a means of reducing stress experienced symptoms in therapy that had a negative impact on their lives. Around a quarter of these symptoms persisted; the most common involved retraumatization, where the patient became newly aware of a traumatic experience but wasn't able to address it properly with meditation. This is a risk with which talk psychotherapists are also familiar, since they always contain a confrontational aspect of direct perception, looking toward instead of looking away.

One Harvard University study for example reported that simply naming a negative experience did not on average lead to sorting through or accepting it. On the contrary—it "crystallized" psychologically, growing

---

35 Elisabeth Moltmann-Wendel, *Wenn Gott und Körper sich begegnen: Feministische Perspektiven zur Leiblichkeit* (Gutersloher Verlagshaus, 1989).

36 Britton et al., "Defining and Measuring Meditation-Related Adverse Effects in Mindfulness-Based Programs," 1185–1204.

more resistant to change.[37] This is supported by research on psychological debriefings, an emergency intervention technique used after natural catastrophes or accidents to prevent against trauma-related disorders. In debriefings, victims, aid workers, or witnesses receive psychotherapeutic support immediately following a potential source of trauma to work through their experiences. Yet studies now show that this sort of psychological help brings no benefit, and may even be harmful.[38] In short, any form of therapy that encourages direct perception must include protective mechanisms that prevent retraumatization and negative experiences from becoming entrenched.

Unlike psychotherapy studies, which still lack a strong regulatory framework, psychedelic studies are legally categorized as medical research, making them subject to strict regulations. Among other things, this means that side effects must be systematically examined. Thanks to these regulations, we know that when professionally conducted, psychotherapy supported by psychedelics almost never leads to retraumatization, even in patients dealing with severe and complex trauma-related disorders.[39] To my mind, this is one of the most astounding and important findings in psychotherapy research in recent decades and makes a strong case for the use of psychedelics.

In addition to expanding our perceptions, psychedelics also provide a protective mechanism that does not simply remove our perceptive filter but replaces it with another.[40] The psychedelic filter, however, seems more porous and less rigorous in separating out anything that does not serve an immediate practical purpose or short-term self-interest. Psychedelics thus seem to function more like a helioscope, an astronomical instrument for observing the sun where most of the sunlight is either refracted through a lens, or attenuated by a polarization filter, much like a pair of sunglasses. This makes it safe to look at the sun, but it also sharpens colors and contours and prevents reflections from disturbing the view. Applied to psychedelics,

37 Nook et al., "Emotion Naming Impedes Both Cognitive Reappraisal and Mindful Acceptance Strategies of Emotion Regulation," 187–98.

38 Gregor Hasler, *Resilienz: Der Wir-Faktor: Gemeinsam Stress Und Ängste Überwinden* (Schattauer Verlag, 2017).

39 Jennifer Mitchell, Michael Bogenschutz, Alia Lilienstein, Charlotte Harrison, Sarah Kleiman, Kelly Parker-Guilbert et al., "MDMA-assisted Therapy for Severe PTSD: A Randomized, Double-blind, Placebo-controlled Phase 3 Study," *Nature Medicine* 27, no. 6 (May 10, 2021): 1025–33.

40 Gregor Hasler, "Toward the 'Helioscope' Hypothesis of Psychedelic Therapy," *European Neuropsychopharmacology* 57 (April 1, 2022): 118–19.

it means they offer us a chance to see something through a different set of filters that we could hardly peek at under normal circumstances. In contrast, finding the doors of perception wide open without any filter would lead to severe sensory overload, as with fatal familial insomnia, an extremely rare brain disease that gravely disrupts the filter in the thalamus. Victims are beset so forcefully with direct experiences, visions, and internal images that they are unable to sleep. The disease is always fatal; some patients die fully conscious, flooded by images, others fall into a coma due to sensory overload.

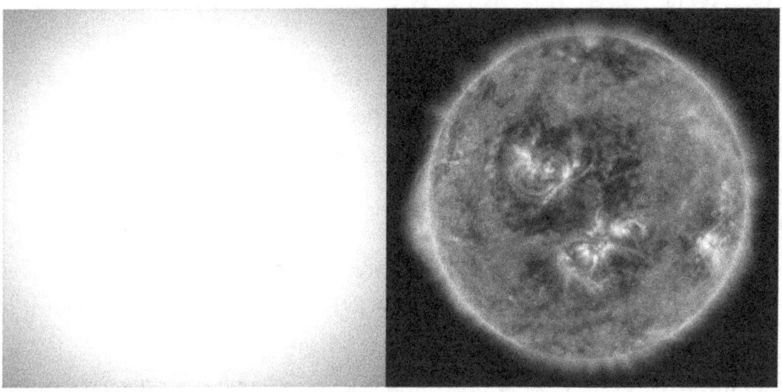

Fig. 1–2: A view of the sun with and without a helioscope. The polarization filter allows for the structure of the sun to be seen clearly and examined, in spite of the incredible heat and light that it emits.

The focal points or "hot spots" of an illness, injury, or healing process have long been associated with intense sensations of heat. At the physical level, heat arises simply from inflammation and the body's healing processes increasing blood flow, which raises body temperature. In village life, it was the shaman who was able to work with and withstand this heat. Passages in the *Rig Veda* that describe soma as granting an ability to look at the sun can also be applied to the healing process. In a therapeutic context, I am thinking primarily of severe traumatic experiences.

One woman who was referred to me grew up in France, the child of Moroccan parents. From an early point in her life, she knew that she was lesbian. When her parents noticed that she preferred toy trucks to puppets, they decided to marry her off against her will when she was still in puberty. For years she was violently raped by her husband, something she kept quiet about for fear of losing her entire social network. When she finally found the courage to break off her marriage, she was cut off by her family and endured years of threats until she finally found asylum in Switzerland under an adopted name. Her story came to me through official documents and doctors' reports, and she told me in no uncertain terms that she was incapable of speaking about her past. "It would burn me like the sun," she said. It was thanks to the helioscope effect of MDMA that it did in fact prove possible for her to work through her traumatic personal history.

The helioscope effect may be where the greatest differences lie between various psychedelics. MDMA likely offers the best protection against retraumatization, making it the method of choice for post-traumatic stress disorders. Retraumatization means that the patient relives a previous traumatic experience in a distressing way, something that doesn't improve the disorder and may even worsen it. A disadvantage of MDMA is that things can appear in an overly rosy light. One patient even talked about the "sweet frosting," that it gave her life. Nor does MDMA bring about changes in the self or identity, important effects of some psychedelics that I'll discuss in later chapters. All these qualities make MDMA a good starting point and option for patients with severe, "burning," traumatic experiences.

LSD likely offers the most profound and direct view of past experiences, though it may be harsh or unflinching at times, provoking forceful and unforeseeable reactions including paranoid anxiety. Psilocybin probably strikes a middle ground between the two, offering more safety than LSD and less "frosting" than MDMA. Ayahuasca seems to leave people especially open to instinctive parts of their unconscious, often conjuring visions of power animals like panthers, tigers, or snakes. Ibogaine opens the floodgates of physical sensation.

In individual cases it may make sense to combine these different filters; MDMA and LSD have proven especially effective in combination when treating trauma. Yet, these understandings are of a provisional nature; a pressing need exists for more comparative studies on the shielding effects of psychedelics. Dosage does not seem to be a deciding factor where the therapeutic effects of psychedelics are concerned, however. To keep side effects at a minimum, it makes sense to start with a somewhat lower dose of 75 milligrams MDMA, which can then be increased to 125 milligrams MDMA if there is insufficient response.

A Manual for MDMA-Assisted Psychotherapy in the Treatment of Posttraumatic Stress Disorder provides a good summary of the helioscope effect:

> One of the qualities of MDMA is that it makes it easier to face memories and not be overwhelmed and actually work through them and the painful emotions in a way that is healing rather than retraumatizing. In everyday life, flashbacks and memories can come up spontaneously and overwhelm you. We are trying to change this by inviting whatever comes up to come up in a safe setting, with the medicine helping you approach it without being overwhelmed. The idea is to approach your memories with less fear and less defensiveness.... This combination of drug effects should support the participant in overcoming the emotional numbing of PTSD and allow her/him to be more fully open to experiencing the full range of emotions (grief, fear, rage, as well as joy, happiness, love, comfort) without the subjective feeling of being overwhelmed.[41]

One of my patients described the helioscope effect as they experienced it under psilocybin as being "like I had a point of access to the deepest regions of my brain, under the strong, peaceful protection of psilocybin."

Psychedelics feature a second important protective mechanism in addition to their "polarization filter." Unlike exposition in behavioral therapy, modern psychedelic therapy does not purposely select or prescribe stimuli, memory cues, or objects to provoke a pathological reaction. The focus of a session instead emerges from the interaction between the psychedelic and the patient's unconscious, ensuring that the patient is not confronted by something they are unprepared to handle in the first place. It may be this aspect of the helioscope effect that the *Rig Veda* is referencing when it describes soma as seeking suns. Psychedelic "sun seeking" will often take the form of an "unwinding" that can stretch out over multiple sessions. Just like the good old telephone cord that gets tangled up in itself, unwinding plays out according to its own logic, time, and structure, not unlike the way genetic material unfurls in the cell nucleus, guided by growth signals like the brain-derived neurotropic factor, or epigenetic markers. Psychedelics

41 Michael C. Mithoefer, *A Manual for MDMA-Assisted Psychotherapy in the Treatment of Posttraumatic Stress Disorder* (The Multidisciplinary Association for Psychedelic Studies, 2017).

loosen the tangled cord, searching out "hot spots" in the process. At times it may be necessary for the therapist to help untangle more complicated knots.

I am continually brought up short by the pinpoint precision with which psychedelics target the hot topics in my patients' psyches, leading them true as an arrow to the areas of conflict or growth whose resolution offers the greatest therapeutic potential. The same holds even in patients who tend to systematically avoid important topics in normal conversation, or who lack intuition as to which topics might be fruitful in therapy. Conversely, I have observed that particularly severe instances of trauma whose reappearance might prove overwhelming do not cross the lens of the psychedelic helioscope. If they do, it is only several sessions into the overall course of the therapy, once the patient feels surer of themselves and their resilience has improved.

One such case involved a patient who had experienced severe sexual abuse as a child, later became depressive, and developed panic attacks. Panic attacks are nearly always prompted by an ambiguous bodily symptom (heart palpitations, for example) that trigger unconscious fears of death (a heart attack, for instance). The thoughts lead to physical anxiety, strengthening the palpitations and seeming to confirm the fearful thoughts. One term for the self-reinforcing process, which ultimately ends in a panic attack, is the "vicious cycle of anxiety." In therapy, one tries to make the patient aware of this cycle, illustrating it by discussing specific attacks so that he or she can interrupt future cycles. This method unfortunately wasn't effective with my patient, who was too unstable in her self-perception, and wasn't able to recognize the course her reactions were running. "The panic comes on all at once, out of nowhere. There isn't a set path," she told me. I considered at first whether I might not have to address the patient's early trauma before treating the panic attacks but it wasn't an option either, as the mere notion of discussing her childhood led her to break out in tears.

In the end, I referred her to one colleague whom I considered exceptionally competent and sensitive, but they didn't get anywhere in talk therapy either. The colleague suggested I conduct a session with psychedelics, to which the patient agreed. I was extremely curious before the treatment as to which "sun" the MDMA would choose—the patient's childhood, her panic, or something entirely different? MDMA selected the panic. Feeling, hearing, and seeing her heartbeat through the helioscope of the psychedelic, the patient said: "It's my heart that makes me afraid, this beating that might stop at any moment. But it doesn't. It keeps on beating." She later arrived at another insight: "I have to listen more to my heart, have more trust in my heart." Her psychedelic experience left her able to peer through the vicious cycle of fear, and subsequently helped her respond in behavioral therapy.

The helioscope effect is also what allows cancer patients to confront their approaching death directly, much like protective eyewear allows one to look at the sun. Some patients see it as a sort of dress rehearsal for death, shedding some of their fear in the process. Others go beyond death to discover vast spaces or expansive levels of consciousness, transforming into water or the roots of mighty trees (I return to this in chapter 8 about right openness). In general, patients emerge from their experience stronger than before, thus confirming the hymns in the *Rig Veda* attesting to soma's sensitivity and strength, and its capacity for giving people courage.

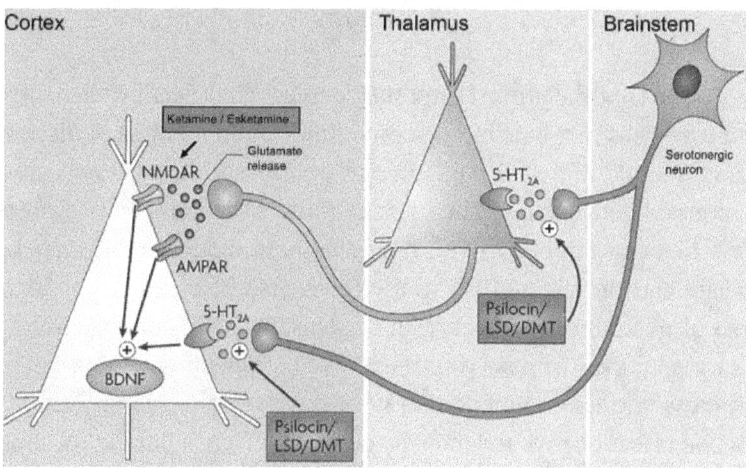

Fig. 1–3: The helioscope effect of psychedelics and increased neuroplasticity result from the complex way they effect the reciprocal pathways of communication between the thalamus, which bundles pathways of information from the sensory organs, the brainstem, and the outer cerebral cortex. Serotonin and glutamate play the most important role as messenger substances in the psychedelic effect. 5-HT2A is the serotonin receptor, the site at which psychedelics take effect; BDNF stands for brain-derived neurotrophic factor (a nerve growth signal); NMDA-R and AMPAR are two types of glutamate receptors that are responsible for learning, among other things.

Getting acquainted with the helioscope and understanding its different facets is an important part of training as a therapist who works with psychedelics. Repeat personal experience as well as supervised therapy are both necessary to gain the sort of trust that will allow therapists to credibly communicate the protective effects of psychedelics to patients while instilling confidence in patients' ability to engage with their deepest wounds and existential challenges in a healing way. Even if patients continue to find their psychedelic experiences confusing or distressing in the weeks after treatment, follow-up studies have shown that integration will happen in time, and no lasting retraumatization occurs.[42]

Of course, trust does not mean blind trust. Not all patients are fit for psychedelic therapy, and time will tell to which cases psychedelics offer little or no benefit. Nor can a harmful impact ever be ruled out entirely, as with any form of psychotherapy.

Summary

Perception is of the utmost importance to psychological well-being. Undefined fears, abstract worries, disembodiment, and feelings of disconnectedness or boredom are all signs of the perceptual disorders so common throughout modern society. The sense of mindfulness and embodiment that psychedelics can establish within patients help them inhabit their bodies once again and participate fully in life. They also help patients break out of patterns of avoidance, and confront unpleasant feelings and sensations, a necessary precursor to resolving them. Yet therapeutic methods involving mindfulness and embodiment also pose the risk of retraumatization. The helioscope effect of psychedelics, by contrast, offers a unique form of protection. Like a strong pair of sunglasses, the intense rays of traumatic experience can be explored and worked through without patients being blinded or burned in the process.

42 Liridona Gashi, Sveinung Sandberg, and Willy Pedersen, "Making 'Bad Trips' Good: How Users of Psychedelics Narratively Transform Challenging Trips Into Valuable Experiences," *International Journal of Drug Policy* 87 (January 1, 2021): 102997.

Chapter 2
Right Time: The Path to the Source

Nothing unsettles us more greatly than time. Nearly every complaint or difficulty my patients express is related to time. The most common symptom of this fixation on time is fear in all its forms: fear of failure, isolation, loss, the future, growing old, illness, and finally the fear of death, which lurks behind so many of our everyday worries. Yet it isn't just the future we fear; the past is also a source of anxiety. Freud discovered that many of his patients were suffering from traumatic memories and were exhausting themselves in the struggle to deal with unprocessed past experiences. Problems related to identity and feelings of meaninglessness are likewise chronological, often prompted by questions about how to hold steady in the flow of time. More mild psychological issues frequently revolve around problems with time management or setting priorities (e.g., sleep vs. socializing, or work-life balance). Boredom—burnout in the form of a bore-out—is also time related.

Throughout my career as a psychotherapist, I have observed time and again how people with psychiatric issues suffer from a scarcity of time (even if they don't have to work themselves) and live less in the present moment than healthy people. Many also find it difficult to tell their life stories in a lively, coherent way. Disturbances in a temporal or circadian rhythms nearly always crop up in cases of more severe psychological disorders.

The Buddha considered time to be the central issue of human existence: birth is pain, separation is pain, illness is pain, decay is pain, death is pain. Clinging of any sort brings pain, since we will inevitably lose the thing we hope to hold on to. Yet the Buddha wasn't a pessimist but an optimist, with a vision for easing and even overcoming suffering related to time through psychological and spiritual methods. His idea also provides the topic for this chapter.

In addition to my work as a psychotherapist, I also coach people— politicians, economic leaders, business executives—who often are more resilient and accomplished, psychologically and physically speaking, than I am myself. They come seeking room for reflection outside of their busy professional lives. In counseling them, I am continuously struck by the impression they give of having a great deal of time. Even though I'll learn about everything they are doing or have done in the newspapers, on television, or in annual reports, it is never difficult to reach them and make time for an appointment. In conversation as well, they appear as though they had all the time in the world, and the hours I spend with them feel quite rich and full. They share the same fears about time that we all do, of course (possible changes in their work environment for example, or the feeling that their best days are behind them), but in the moment, at the point of contact, they have time. One might describe this as the "Roger Federer phenomenon"—especially at the height of his career, Federer gave the impression of having more than enough time to trace an incoming tennis ball and hit it back. In his essay "Roger Federer as Religious Experience," US author David Foster Wallace takes up the following thought experiment:

> Imagine that you're a person with preternaturally good reflexes and coordination and speed, and that you're playing high-level tennis. Your experience, in play, will not be that you possess phenomenal reflexes and speed; rather, it will seem to you that the tennis ball is quite large and slow-moving, and that you always have plenty of time to hit it. That is, you won't experience anything like the (empirically real) quickness and skill that the live audience, watching tennis balls move so fast they hiss and blur, will attribute to you.[43]

Foster Wallace describes what the Buddha and many Western philosophers have long observed: Time isn't a physical property, but a psychological phenomenon. In ancient Greece, the philosopher Plotinus asserted that time is the life of the soul, while Church Father Saint Augustine was convinced that time existed only within the human spirit, even though the view blatantly contradicted official church doctrine. Existentialist philosopher Martin Heidegger wrote that time exists only so long as people do. Today,

43 David Foster Wallace, "Roger Federer as Religious Experience," *The New York Times*, Aug. 20, 2006.

we would say that the brain creates time. This holds tremendous implications for psychiatry, since it means that we can change time, and thus any suffering related to it, by applying methods from the neurosciences.

In a fascinating parallel, modern physics has arrived at the same results, albeit by very different methods. Time plays no role whatsoever in the fundamental laws of physics.[44] Neither past nor future appears in Heisenberg's theory of quantum mechanics or Schrödinger's elementary particles. In the space-time continuum Albert Einstein researched, time does not travel in an irreversible direction; instead, it is conceivable that one could return to an initial event by means of traveling through space-time. For physicists, the directional, constant ebbing of time that we experience (and from which we suffer) is a specialized, local phenomenon, but does not represent a fundamental quantity or force in the physical cosmos. The neurosciences meanwhile have shown the brain to function as a time machine that spends an inordinate amount of energy registering and storing states within the timeless interplay of forces in an effort to predict their changes. Doing so gives rise to the directional, relentless form of time that more than any other phenomenon constitutes and creates our consciousness, shaping our feelings and fears, and indeed our entire existence.

Psychedelics possess an astonishing capacity to significantly alter our perception of time. The first self-experiment Albert Hofmann performed with the psilocybin he had discovered in mushrooms from Mexico gave him the experience of time standing still. In his subsequent report he wrote that "it seemed to me that 100 years would not be sufficient to describe the fullness of experience of a single minute."[45] The *Rig Veda* also describes soma's time-granting effects in detail, as "the lengthener of day, of dawn, of heaven. Soma brings us to the place where they stretch out life-spans."[46] To the authors of the *Rig Veda*, it seemed clear that lengthening the day, as Albert Hofmann had experienced, also lengthened one's entire life. For them soma led to a life that allowed one to die happy, as Abraham, "in a good old age, an old man and full of years."[47] They even had a clear idea about the mechanism by which soma prolongs time; at one point, the text explains that soma expands time by operating faster than thoughts. This

---

44 Carlo Rovelli, *The Order of Time* (Penguin, 2018).

45 Hofmann, *LSD: My Problem Child*,

46 Jamison and Brereton, *The Rigveda: The earliest religious poetry of India*.

47 Genesis 25:8.

corroborates findings in neuroscience that psychedelics allow the brain to operate more quickly, producing the impression of the external world slowing down. An airplane can move so slowly under the influence of LSD that one is left wondering why it doesn't crash. The effect is likely akin to the experience of elite athletes and top-ranking managers, or the way time expands in near-death experiences. In his interviews with mountain climbers who had survived life-threatening falls in the nineteenth century, Swiss geologist Albert Heim found that every last one had experienced a form of "mental speed" often connected to a retrospective look back over their lives. One way in which the brain measures time is by counting the changes in short-term synaptic strength, or the flow of information between nerve cells. "Mental speed," then, is a direct expression of psychedelics (in this case produced by the body) raising the rate at which neurons process information, and with it, neuroplasticity.

Outside the realm of psychedelics, focusing on the present moment is an effective method for time management, in the same way that dwelling in the past or the future is often a time sink. Attention to the present moment also makes us more social, since it allows for us to truly encounter each other in the here and now. When we are wrapped up in thoughts about the past or the future, we close ourselves off to social interaction.

For Portuguese poet Fernando Pessoa, the term *present* itself was too closely associated with time. He emphasized instead the quality of experience in a single timeless moment: "Live, you say, in the present; / Live only in the present. / But I don't want the present, I want reality; / I want things that exist, not time that measures them."[48] Psychedelics may not be able to fulfill Pessoa's wish to experience an absolute timelessness in which things are immutable and real. But I can say for certain that they do more than increase our mindfulness (see chapter 1). The way they change our sense of time opens realities beyond simply being in the present moment.

British philosopher and author Alan Watts described the temporal effects of LSD in a book entitled *The Joyous Cosmology*. The first aspect is the way time slows, and a concentration on the present moment emerges:

> One's normally compulsive concern for the future decreases, and one becomes aware of the enormous importance and interest of what is happening at the moment.... The speed of thought and association is

48 Fernando Pessoa, *Poems of Alberto Caeiro* (The Foolish Poet Press, 2018).

> increased so astonishingly that it is hard for words to keep pace with the flood of ideas that come to mind.... There is therefore time to perceive every detail of the movement with infinitely greater richness of articulation.... But here the depth of light and structure in a bursting bud go on forever. There is time to see them, time for the whole intricacy of veins and capillaries to develop in consciousness, time to see down and down into the shape of greenness, which is not green at all, but a whole spectrum generalizing itself as green—purple, gold, the sunlit turquoise of the ocean, the intense luminescence of the emerald. I cannot decide where shape ends and color begins. The bud has opened and the fresh leaves fan out and curve back with a gesture which is unmistakably communicative but does not say anything except, "Thus!"...The meaning is transparent in the same way that the color and texture are transparent, with light which does not seem to fall upon surfaces from above but to be right inside the structure and color. Which is of course where it is, for light is an inseparable trinity of sun, object, and eye, and the chemistry of the leaf is its color, its light.... A journey into this new mode of consciousness gives one a marvelously enhanced appreciation of patterning in nature, a fascination deeper than ever with the structure of ferns, the formation of crystals, the markings upon sea shells, the incredible jewelry of such unicellular creatures of the ocean as the radiolaria, the fairy architecture of seeds and pods, the engineering of bones and skeletons, the aerodynamics of feathers, and the astonishing profusion of eye-forms upon the wings of butterflies and birds. Time is so slow as to be a kind of eternity, and the flavor of eternity transfers itself to the hills—burnished mountains which I seem to remember from an immeasurably distant past, at once so unfamiliar as to be exotic and yet as familiar as my own hand.[49]

The sumptuous reality that unfolds within the temporal realm of psychedelics is akin to time as it is experienced by other life forms. Plant time moves much more slowly than our own, for instance. Under psychedelics, the expressions, gestures, and contortions of the plant kingdom become visible to us, as through a time lapse; if a similar technique existed for hearing,

49 Alan W. Watts, *The Joyous Cosmology: Adventures in the Chemistry of Consciousness* (New World Library, 2013).

one would most likely hear cries and whispers as well. Psychedelic time lapses and slow-motion effects allow us to encounter different parts of the world from which we would otherwise remain cut off, yielding the impression that everything participates in consciousness, and consciousness exists within everything. In other words, our alienation from the world is the price we pay for the temporal order we impose on it. Psychedelics can allow us to overcome this alienation over the short term.

Psychedelics stimulate a highly specific serotonin receptor called 5-HT2A, with 5-HT standing for 5-hydroxytryptamine, the chemical structure of serotonin. Serotonin is a derivative of the protein tryptophan that appears in many foods such as cheese, legumes, cereals, nuts, and eggs. A "receptor" refers to the protein to which naturally occurring materials in the body like serotonin or a drug like LSD bind, eliciting a reaction in the nerve cells. 5-HT2A receptors are distributed throughout the brain and intestine. An especially high concentration is located in the pineal gland, which lies in the middle of the brain directly between the two large hemispheres, at the juncture between the cerebrum and the brain stem. The gland plays an important role in how the body regulates time, and is known first and foremost by way of French philosopher René Descartes, who contended that it was the principal seat of the soul within the time-bound body. Long derided as nonsensical, Descartes's idea has now found new life through modern psychedelic research. It was the discovery of LSD that initially prompted the identification of the mood hormone serotonin, which is produced in large quantities by the pineal gland. The pineal gland also contains high concentrations of naturally occurring messenger chemicals with psychedelic properties such as DMT (dimethyltryptamine), which also appears in the ayahuasca brew. DMT is produced and distributed within the body under situations of extreme stress such as birth, near-death experiences, during death, or anytime when transcending or abandoning time becomes important (more on this in the chapter 8).[50]

To return to the more straightforward temporal effects of psychedelics: What is their therapeutic value? They can relativize time for us; we realize that our brain itself is what creates time, and therefore we don't need to fear or panic over it. For me personally, the effects call to mind the wonderful novels of Carlos Castaneda and his brilliant character Don Juan, a Mexican

---

50 Rick Strassman, *DMT: The Spirit Molecule: A Doctor's Revolutionary Research into the Biology of Near-Death and Mystical Experiences* (Park Street Press, 2001).

shaman who introduces his US apprentice to a wide range of realities and teaches him to see properly. The teaching often occurs by a brook or a waterfall, where the teacher directs the gaze of his student toward the air bubbles in the water: "Look, Carlos, there are fast and slow bubbles, all flowing in the same river."[51]

Below I describe two ways in which psychedelics act on our sense of time—their narrative effect and their archetypal effect—as they relate to scientifically acknowledged effects of psychotherapy.

Narrative

In the introduction I described the case of Susan, who had been left speechless in the face of her suffering and was first able to tell her story under LSD. This too is related to the filter function of the human brain—a capacity that does not just affect perception but memory as well.

Freud saw disorders in how we filter time as a cause of neurosis. The disturbance leads to a situation where a person is unable to recall traumatic memories of the past consciously, i.e., as an integrated memory that combines actions, feelings, thoughts, and physical states. The splintered traces of the memory still express themselves however, albeit in compulsively acting out childhood wishes. This explains why remaining sensitive to different kinds of time lies at the heart of psychoanalysis as a method of therapy. Freud listened to his clients on two channels at once, tuning in to their conscious experiences, thoughts, and feelings in the present moment, but also to repressed childhood memories. More than anything, Freud's "evenly-suspended attention" meant a receptivity to different timescales. The goal for patients in analysis is for them to better integrate different timelines—to reconstruct their life story, in other words—and spot the connections between their childhood experience and life as adults. Doing so allows for better reconciliation between childhood and the adult selves, enabling contact with one's inner child, for example.

Our brain has difficulty identifying connections over longer periods of time; temporal patterns and cause-effect relationships are largely short-term

51 Carlos Castaneda, *Journey to Ixtlan: The Lessons of Don Juan* (Washington Square Press, 1991).

affairs. It is easy to determine whether an insect spray is effective at killing flies or not. The extended period of time that often lies between cause and effect in psychotherapy or psychedelic therapy, meanwhile, makes it much more difficult to evaluate their overall value. If we speed up or slow down the tempo of music enough, in either case there will be a point beyond which we no longer experience it as such. Under the influence of LSD, long-term pattern recognition improves at the cost of short-term, letting us enjoy very slow music, for example, but growing nervous at faster-paced music. We also develop a better sense for long-term connections between important events. While on LSD, Jan, the patient with a body image disorder who I introduced in the last chapter, recognized that his old identity, "Jan One," was much more closely tied to his new identity, "Jan Two," than he ever would have thought in a normal state of consciousness. Another patient who had broken off relations with her parents repeatedly brought up during talk therapy how her mother had pressured her to dress up as a child. Under LSD however, she recognized this as part of a larger dynamics in which the patient herself had pressured her parents to make a better impression on her friends.

As with direct perception, biased opinion and abstract thought are large hurdles for directly recalling and narrating one's story. Blanket judgements like "I was always at a disadvantage" or "My parents were simply overburdened with me" often reflect a lack of direct recall. A good narrative does not judge but rather allows the story to unfold in all its nuance and ambiguity. These turn out to be the essential characteristics of psychedelic trips: They are journeys of looking, feeling, and perceiving with a guide who is either loathe to explain or interpret, or refrains entirely from doing so. In this regard, a psychedelic trip resembles the ecstatic journey of the shaman, which is a way of looking and sensing, not of thinking or assigning meaning.

The story of one's life stretches far back beyond childhood in Eastern teachings. The Buddha was able to recall every detail from every one of his previous lives, ascribing great importance to memory. The Brahmans also thought very highly of the ability to remember previous incarnations, a view expressed in one passage in the *Rig Veda* spoken from soma's perspective: "Even though still in the womb, I knew all their births through and through—those of the gods— but a hundred metal fortifications guarded me. Then the falcon!—and swiftly I flew away."[52] One of the aims of shamanic ecstasy, which can be amplified by psychedelics, has been to establish contact with ancestors. Stanislav Grof worked off the premise that psychedelics brought memories like pregnancy or birth to our waking conscious, allowing us to work through traumatic experiences that had occurred in utero or while being born. The notion is interesting in light of recent psychiatric research that shows pregnancy to be a critical period in the later development of psychological disorders—psychological stress, trauma, alcohol, environmental toxins, or malnourishment can all lead to epigenetic changes that leave a lasting impact on gene regulation.[53]

Modern memory research shows that a single moment lasts about three seconds for our brains. Everything that is experienced within these three seconds is gathered together as "now," also called the "experiencing self." Longer stretches of time are experienced as sequences of different moments. One day consists of around twenty thousand moments; a lifetime of a good half billion. Nearly all of these are inaccessible to our conscious minds. Could you say exactly what your experience was like twenty-four hours ago? Most likely you no longer know or never did. Maybe you were reading an email or looking out of the window. The remembering self is the part of our consciousness that collects the rare moments that the experiencing self doesn't tuck away or simply discard.

Psychologist and Nobel laureate Daniel Kahneman has explored the ways in which experience is selected or filtered in a brilliant series of memory studies. Kahneman recognized that we store memories according to a principle that he called the "peak-end rule." The rule states that an experience is evaluated and recalled based on its peak (the high point, or most intense moment) and its end. That means that our memory of events is not balanced, holistic, or representative, but distorted. It also means that the length of experiences is quite unimportant, an aspect Kahneman called "duration neglect." A single second of intense anxiety can leave behind more traces of memory than years of moderate happiness—a grave distortion of reality. One patient easily recalled in vivid fashion the unpleasant encounters she'd had with her mother, who suffered from addiction, even though she had been raised by her grandmother, who she almost never spoke of. It

52 Doniger, *The Rig Veda*.

53 Gavino Faa, Mirko Manchia, Roberta Pintus, Clara Gerosa, Maria Antonietta Marcialis, and Vassilios Fanos, "Fetal Programming of Neuropsychiatric Disorders," *Birth Defects Research* 108, no. 3 (September 1, 2016): 207–23.

was first with the assistance of MDMA that she experienced a wash of gratitude for her grandmother and was able to recall all the good moments they had shared. Granted, it remains an open question just how many moments are actually stored away and become accessible again through psychedelics. Still, the wealth of life images that can appear during near-death experiences speaks for the peak-end rule applying only to conscious memory, with a great deal more information stored in the unconscious mind.

Psychedelics have a complex effect on memory. The higher the dosage, the more strongly they disrupt short-term memory, making it easy to misplace one's glasses during a psilocybin session, for instance. In return psychedelics improve our autobiographical memory, which aides significantly with their narrative effect. They make autobiographical content more vivid and stimulate the retrieval and recollection of personal memories that have been avoided or forgotten by the conscious mind.[54]

Nearly every form of psychotherapy makes use of life narratives, or "narrative therapy." Simply having a patient tell their story can help them better understand their life, give it meaning and value, or view it from a different angle by exploring alternate versions of those pesky, looping stories. In narrative couples' therapy, each partner learns and comes to understand the other's story, and together they come up with one in common.

In narrative therapy, individual life events are woven together; the point of departure is not first and foremost the factual basis but the narrating subject as they exist in the here and now. Psychedelics can contribute to this form of therapy by the immediate experiences and vivid images they awaken in patients' autobiographical memory. One patient I treated with LSD had fallen into depression after a difficult childhood. She subsequently wrote about her experience that "with LSD it was as if I were to go back into my past and try it out with different feelings and interpretations, almost as if I were reliving it. In the moment I think that allowed me to come to peace with certain things in my head, which is already a big deal."

One dramatic example of the healing force of narrative comes in *A Christmas Carol* by Charles Dickens. On a cold, dark Christmas Eve, selfish old Ebenezer Scrooge has his autobiographical memory awakened by the Ghost of Christmas Past. It allows Scrooge to relive his lonely childhood and pressing need for love and connection. The Ghost of Christmas

---

54 Colm Healy, "The Acute Effects of Classic Psychedelics on Memory in Humans," *Psychopharmacology* 238, no. 3 (January 9, 2021): 639–53.

Yet to Come then takes him on a psychedelic trip into the future, where he witnesses the death of an unloved man—local businessmen only attend the burial because there is free lunch. The two journeys through time lead Scrooge to better understand his present predicament, and subsequently to an ecstatic experience of Christmas that transforms him into a gentler, more sympathetic person.

A sense of uninterrupted, narrative flow is an important aspect of stories. The same holds for the stories of our lives. Albert Hofmann, for instance, suffered from a problem that is common to many patients: Unlike time as perceived on psychedelics, ordinary life "is never 'total,' but instead divided, cut in pieces, and split up into the tiny fragments of seconds, minutes, hours, days, weeks, and years: there one is a slave of Moloch time, which devour[s] one piecemeal."[55] Yet psychedelics not only lend our experience of time greater coherence, they allow us to experience time as such. This is surprising since we don't have a sensory organ dedicated to time, let alone a proper vocabulary for it. We are forced instead to draw on spatial metaphors such as a "long" day or a "short" week. Our ears, which can measure sound waves as a way of roughly estimating time's passage, are the best option we have. Still, our bodies possess many clocks; every cell has multiple. Lacking coordination between them can lead to severe disorders like clinical depression or cluster headaches. Music is one of the best ways we have for experiencing time and recalibrating the different clocks to each other, and effect that psychedelics only bolster. There is no known disorder of the brain that impairs our perception of music, showing it to be a very basic capacity in the brain and the entire body. One patient I treated for depression described a lack of flow in her life, her thoughts, and body. Treatment with esketamine paired with music allowed her to reenter that flow and spin the next yarns in the story of her life.

From time to time, psychedelics will also ease the pain of experiencing time as ceaselessly ebbing away. One of Claudio Naranjo's patients reported a similar experience during an ibogaine session: "My inner world started flying and feeling, my head was spinning, and I was turning into many things that were leaping into the void, into emptiness, and I was falling and falling with such pleasure and trust."[56] This bears a surprising similarity to poet Rainer Maria Rilke's lines about transience: "We all are

55 Hofmann, *LSD: My Problem Child.*

56 Naranjo, *My Psychedelic Explorations.*

falling. This hand there falls. / And look at the others: it is in all of them. / And yet there is one, who holds all this falling / with infinite gentleness in his hands."[57] Showing tenderness toward time can slide into forgetting all about it, a flow state, or the consciousness of the child at play.

Having a story to tell isn't just of therapeutic value, it's an existential need. It gives us a location in time. Some patients who have had to spend a long time in hospitals seem to have very little narrative space left, with the referring doctor herself remarking "there's not so much to say about him." When working with hospital patients who have spent many years in hospitals or nursing homes, I find myself shocked and saddened at times that there could evidently be so little to talk about. Yet it isn't uncommon under the influence of psychedelics for a wealth of vivid narrative material to surface even within these patients, baffling the therapists who have worked with them year in and year out. I call this effect the "Proust phenomenon," as the blossoming of autobiographical memory reminds me of the novel *In Search of Lost Time*, in which Proust grants his characters' experiences an immense temporal space that extends over thousands of pages. About his own work, Proust wrote:

> If enough time was left to me to complete my work, my first concern would be to describe the people in it, even at the risk of making them seem colossal and unnatural creatures, as occupying a place far larger than the very limited one reserved for them in space, a place in fact almost infinitely extended, since they are in simultaneous contact, like giants immersed in the years, with such distant periods of their lives, between which so many days have taken up their place—in Time.[58]

---

57 Cliff Crego, *Rilke in the Wallowas: New English Translations & Photographs* (Printed by author).

58 Marcel Proust, *Finding Time Again: In Search of Lost Time*, Volume 7 (Penguin, 2023).

Archetypes

Psychotherapy typically plays out along the linear timeline of an individual life. Such is the case with psychoanalysis and behavioral therapy for example, though various attempts have been made to expand that temporal context over the course of psychotherapy's development; daseinsanalysis and existential psychotherapy extend outward to include the future, for example. Yet the most influential remains Swiss psychiatrist Carl Jung's model of archetypes, which traces the origin of psychological material, patterns, and conflicts back to a collective, transpersonal unconscious. The concept found favor especially with psychotherapists using psychedelics to initiate or strengthen therapeutic processes, turning the term "transpersonal," an English translation of Jung's *überpersönlich*, into somewhat of a buzzword within psychedelic therapy. Stanislav Grof, the key figure in the field, was the founding president of the International Transpersonal Association, which set the goal of supporting research into psychological phenomena that are more than purely personal experiences.

The following example illustrates the sort of power that transpersonal and archetypal experiences can hold. I treated a patient named Edi for PTSD; during one psilocybin session he saw himself standing in front a large mountain, set to climb it. In the vision he only had socks on, though he still wanted to try. The higher he climbed the more holes he got in his socks, until he was left barefoot. Each step along the way hurt from all the sharp stones in his path. He suddenly found himself at the entrance to a cave. He knew he had to go inside to explore. In the darkness of the cave he stepped on even sharper stones without being able to see them, causing enormous pain. Unable to bear it anymore, he sat down. Feeling around with his left hand, he discovered a treasure chest by his side. He tried opening it but wasn't able, and when he dug in with his fingernails, they fell off. In the end he managed with his teeth. Inside were countless small, sparkling rock crystals; they slowly drifted out of the chest and illuminated the cave, which proved much larger than Edi had initially imagined. It looked like an entire universe, with myriads of glittering stars.

The vision contains many allusions to Edi's personal life. Growing up poor in Albania, he moved to Switzerland at twenty-three, where he took a job in construction. He was a skilled and dedicated worker, leading his superiors to value and promote him. Pursuing professional development courses and working his way up the ladder, Edi soon had a group assigned to him and was eventually overseeing entire construction sites. All this drew the envy of his coworkers, and twice he was hassled and bullied so badly that he took ill psychologically and had to leave work. Being unable to work was a serious trauma for Edi, since it meant his dream of making something of himself in Switzerland—the dream that had driven him to take on the many risks and trials of emigration— had failed. In his psilocybin fantasy the sharp stones, visible at first then later invisible, were the workplace bullying he had experienced, which shifted from crude jokes about his origins at first to more subtle attacks conducted behind his back. During his first stay at the hospital, his doctor at the time had described him to a nurse as "a poor little thing" (the literal term in German is "a poor sock.") This offhand comment from the doctor landed as a heavy blow and likely explains the hole-filled socks he was wearing in his vision. His fingernails falling off recalled a nail fungus he once had.

Despite the many personal references to Edi's life, his vision wasn't entirely personal. The trope in which a person must climb a difficult path or endure a harrowing situation to find treasure is age old, showing up in any number of fairytales. In "The Star Money," a story collected in the Brothers Grimm, a treasure falls into the maiden's lap after she has proven her generosity and compassion along an arduous path. Heroes in fairy tales generally must withstand trials through courageous or magnanimous acts; if they succeed, they are rewarded with treasure. Just like Edi, Hansel and Gretel also receive precious gems after a difficult turn; in alternative versions it is a golden donkey, a magic table, or a prince. Whatever the case, the reward usually overcompensates for the initial deficit.

This is the basic pattern, or archetypal structure, that brought Edi to Switzerland in the first place. His lack of trust in his own archetypal journey is partly to blame for his illness and subsequent therapy. Rock crystals, as they appeared in Edi's vision, were and are commonly used as a means of healing, showing up in ancient Greece, Rome, and among Arabic peoples. The Christian mystic Hildegard von Bingen also worked with healing stones, while shamanic healing traditions (in Siberia and Peru, for instance) consider stones to be stars that detached from the heavens and fell to earth, where they continue to exert cosmic medicinal properties. Edi knew a fair amount about rock crystals from his childhood in Albania. Yet in his wonderful variation on "The Star Money," the treasure doesn't fall around him—he returns it to its original place in the cosmos instead.

Edi and I went back and forth about his psychedelic experiences in multiple sessions. Called "integration sessions," these meetings aim to help patients integrate their psychedelic experiences psychologically. Edi brought a large rock crystal with him to our sessions, underscoring just how important the crystal fantasy had been for him. We came to understand the vision as an attempt to draw strength again from the archetypal source of the crystals. Out of doubt in the strength of the crystal (a metaphor for his own roots and his development) emerged a notion that the stones were returning to their cosmic origin to recharge their healing powers. Thanks to our sessions, after a long spell of invalidity Edi finally managed to regain his footing in the professional world.

This type of therapy occurs in a different time than academic psychology or psychoanalysis. In doing so it transcends simple cause-effect relationships—it is an experience in inhabiting and thinking in cycles. In ancient Greek, *arche* means both "origin" and "dominion," referring to a powerful primary source. "Archetype," then, describes a formidable original model or type. Jung's idea is that archetypes emerge from the collective unconscious cyclically, i.e., over and over again, and largely rule over our lives. Through the archetype we are able to connect to a transpersonal origin and time becomes transparent, the origin ever present. This kind of archetypal vision is familiar to us from myths, fairy tales, dreams, and hypnotic states, and is something psychedelics in particular seem to foster. By weakening our perception of short-term, linear-causal relationships, they allow us to recognize larger temporal cycles. In terms of our neurobiology, this is in part because the regions of the brain that respond the most strongly to psychedelics (i.e., those with the highest concentration of the necessary 5-HT2A receptors) have the longest and slowest connections to other regions of the brain, which means they integrate information over longer periods of time.[59]

Archetypal concepts are common throughout culture and religion. Indian saint Ramana Maharshi described the connection to the source as follows: "The ocean, being the store of all waters, evaporates, clouds are formed, and rain falls, giving rise to rivers which as soon as formed become restless,

---

59 Rita Kočárová, Jiří Horáček, and Robin Carhart-Harris, "Does Psychedelic Therapy Have a Transdiagnostic Action and Prophylactic Potential?," *Frontiers in Psychiatry* 12 (July 19, 2021)

as it were, course along as if to find their origin and repose only after being discharged into the ocean. Similarly, the individual emanating from the Heart is restless and becomes eager to find his own source. The way is the trail of the 'ego' into the Heart."[60]

The cyclical conception of time is a great deal older than its contemporary, rationalized, and linear counterpart. Romanian religious scholar Mircea Eliade writes that in the past people did not experience the power of archetypes sporadically, as we do, but lived lives that were largely shaped by them.[61] To give one example, the Scandinavian settlers who first arrived in Iceland and cultivated the land didn't regard their act as one of original creation, the zero point on a timeline that then proceeded in linear fashion. Rather, their work repeated the gods' original work of creation. They identified themselves with the gods who gave form to chaos. In a similar vein, the ancient Israelites who built Jerusalem didn't view themselves as founding a city, but as recreating heavenly Jerusalem. Ancient Indian cultures built every royal city as replicas of the heavenly city from the Golden Age. Experiencing cyclical time in this way can be a tremendous source of resilience and steadiness. It is no wonder that people longing for transformation or healing seek out their origins, their navel, inner child, lost paradise, or transpersonal archetypes for help in reconstructing their sense of self.

Earlier eras of human history gave conscious archetypal form to every aspect of everyday life, giving them transpersonal and deeply meaningful resonance. Sowing, harvesting, hunting, sexuality, festivals, games, dances—all were embedded in cyclical time, experienced as a repetition of the original act of creation. The mundane business of daily life was imbued with sacred meaning, removed from linear time. Just like Edi restoring the cosmos during his psilocybin session, every significant act was archetypal, the restoration of an original time. Cyclical time shows that nothing is irrevocable—not pain, misfortune, injustice, illness, even death. Any time a present situation worsens it is a sign of the coming revival, which must follow, cyclically speaking. From a very early point in our history, humans have used psychedelics to directly experience originary time and the perennial renewal of the source. Groups indigenous to the Amazonas, for example, would take ayahuasca to return to the source of all

60 Arthur Osborne, ed., *The Collected Works of Ramana Maharshi* (S. Weiser, 1970).

61 Mircea Eliade, *The Myth of the Eternal Return: Cosmos and History* (Princeton University Press, 2021).

things—the womb—and witness the creation of the universe, the animals, the first human couple, and the social order.[62] Rather than in list form as in modern medicine (lists of symptoms, protocols, lists of medications, etc.), shamanic medicinal knowledge in Native American cultures is configured intuitively in concentric and overlapping circles that describe the cycles of the body, the cosmos, and spiritual forces.

The *Rig Veda* also emphasizes the special relationship psychedelics (in this case soma) bear to cyclical time, with the moon standing as the central symbol for soma in the text. Passages describe the moon as containing soma, and attribute its waning to the gods drinking the soma. Each month the moon fills little by little with soma, growing in the process. Soma's connection to the source, or origin, is emphasized throughout: "The psychedelic plants were born in the ancient times, three ages before the god," and it is described further as abolishing the order of time: "Those that are in the future they say are in the past; and those that are in the past they say are in the future."[63] Each of these qualities speak to the extraordinary transpersonal sense of time psychedelics instill, and their effect in fostering experiences of broader cycles or peering through the veil of time. This is what I mean when I refer to the "archetypal effect" of psychedelics.

In the words of one patient, "Now I'm beginning to see that it's not so easy. Thinking strictly in terms of cause and effect can lead me astray. Cause and effect can blend. I'm able to understand things more deeply now, be a child and adult at the same time, control and be controlled at the same time.... I got used to the idea of seeing my mother as the cause and myself as the effect. Now I can see that it was more like oscillations between us that weren't always good."

In his book *How to Change Your Mind*, Michael Pollan describes an impactful experience of his own with cyclical time while on psilocybin. The experience revolves around family, in particular his son, Isaac, and grandfather, Bob. "I watched a swiftly unfolding biopic of Isaac's life to this point—his struggles as an exquisitely sensitive boy, and how those sensitivities had turned into strengths, making him who he is."[64] Pollan's vision leaves him feeling deeply connected to his son: "I felt something on

---

62 Ralph Metzner and Jace C. Callaway, *Ayahuasca: Hallucinogens, Consciousness, and the Spirit of Nature* (Thunder's Mouth Press, 1999).

63 Doniger, *The Rig Veda*.

64 Pollan, *How to Change Your Mind*.

my eyeshades and realized I had wet them with tears. I was already feeling wide open and undefended when it dawned on me that I wasn't talking to Isaac, or not only to him, but to myself as well." He later thinks of his grandfather Bob, realizing a deeper unity also exists with Bob than what he had perceived before. Looking in the bathroom mirror, Pollan's face begins to melt into Bob's until they share the same elderly face, which for Pollan resembles "a human skull, but for the thinnest, palest layer of skin stretched over it, tight as a drum." Pollan's experience of cyclical time left him with a stronger sense of belonging in his family, creating a link between his own personal lifespan and the transpersonal cycle of his family that in turn helped him sort out his feelings regarding aging and death.

The experience of cyclical time has always played an important role in Indian philosophy. The Ājīvikas, for example, predecessors to the Buddhists, closely observed the periodicity of plants as a path to peace, freedom, and immortality.[65] Identifying with plants in this way appears in many Indian schools of thought, including yoga and Buddhism. The Buddha underwent a transition from conceiving of time in linear fashion to a cyclical view shortly before his awakening. In the Bhayabherava Sutta, a discourse in the Pali language, it is said that during his first nocturnal vigil on the evening of his awakening, the Buddha encountered all his countless previous lives in detail—a linear conception of time. This was followed during his second vigil by another vision, this time seen through his "divine eye," in which the Buddha saw the death and rebirth of countless creatures according to the law of karma—a cyclical conception of time. In the end, he succeeded in freeing himself from the cycle of rebirth once and for all. Understanding *samsara*, the Sanskrit term for the cycle of recurring events, was a precondition for awakening. The influential Tibetan Buddhist Chögyam Trungpa's description of LSD as a sort of "super Samsara" is intriguing in this regard; the substance strengthens certain samsaric tendencies that might advance one on the spiritual path of tantra.

An altered experience of time also lies at the heart of Hakuin Ekaku's experience of enlightenment, one of the most influential masters of Japanese Zen. After a long period of extreme asceticism and meditation Ekaku succeeded in breaking through time:

---

65 Eliade, *Yoga: Immortality and Freedom.*

> During the spring of my twenty-fourth year...I practiced assiduously. I slept neither by day nor by night, and forgot both to rest and to eat. Suddenly I was overcome by the Great Doubt. I felt as though [I was] freezing in an ice field extending thousands of miles.... This state continued for a number of days until the night while hearing the striking of the temple bell I experienced the transformation. It was like the smashing of a layer of ice, or the pulling down of a crystal tower. As I suddenly awakened and came to my senses, I felt myself to be like Master Yen-tou (Gantō), who all through the three times (past, present, and future) encountered no suffering. All former doubts were fully dissolved like ice which melted away. With a loud voice I called out, "How glorious, how glorious!" We need no escape from the cycle of life and death, nor need we strive after enlightenment. The seventeen hundred kōan exercises are not worthy of being posed.[66]

Hakuin's greatest moment of tension as a student of Zen dissolved in the moment that he saw through time, in an ecstatic state of liberation that bears many similarities to psychedelic states.

As described above, samsara bears a positive connotation in the *Rig Veda*. It is the joy taken in the soma moon, the container or embodiment of the sacred soma, that fills over and over again once the gods have drunk from it. In the later development of Indian philosophy, the word *samsara* acquired increasingly negative overtones and now refers, in Buddhist thought, to a cycle of suffering one endeavors to escape. Stanislav Grof devoted a great deal of time to negative cycles of this sort, eventually coining the expression "Systems of Condensed Experience" (or COEX systems for short) to capture one of the ways in which the human brain condenses experience. The term plays an important role in Grof's psychotherapy, and consists of a cycle of related experiences that arrange themselves around a highly emotional "root experience." A COEX root arises from a powerful and emotionally charged experience imprinting itself on the neural structures of the brain (also taking the shape of a transpersonal archetype or in epigenetic form, capable of being passed on from generation to generation). Subsequent similar experiences are then filed away with the original imprinted experience, in time forming neural "experience onions" that can generate strong patterns of avoidance, among other things. In Grof's experience,

---

66 Yu-Hsiu Ku, *History of Zen* (Springer, 2016).

psychedelics can help patients gain awareness of these systems and work with them.

One patient who came to me in search of psychedelic treatment suffered from a similar kind of negative cycle. Her mother had never felt she was in the right place; she felt always alone, or betwixt and between. Seeing this, my patient had done everything in her power to have a better life than her mother. She married an older reliable man who she truly loved and with whom she ran a restaurant. They had a daughter and spent many happy years together. One day, my patient suddenly took ill with a severe skin allergy, leaving her unable to work. She was then blindsided by her husband's death in a riding accident, followed by her daughter moving out. Now a widow and invalid, my patient felt like her mother—betwixt and between. When her daughter mentioned feeling she couldn't find her place in life after a failed romance, my patient began to believe that some evil power of fate was holding her family in check. Psilocybin helped her realize that this "power of fate" was related to how she perceived things—she was extremely mistrustful for instance, reacting to any feeling of tenderness or pleasant bodily sensation with extreme cynicism and dismissal. She realized that she wasn't allowing enough positivity into her life.

Cyclical time plays an important role in Western traditions as well. The most important and largest festival in ancient Greece, the Eleusinian Mysteries, celebrated the cycles of nature. The myth revolved around Demeter, the goddess of fertility and life, and explained how the seasons originated. US ethnomycologist Robert Gordon Wasson argues that festival participants were given a drink containing a psychedelic.[67] The festival was intended to impress on young Athenians that life was like a plant, born from death, an unavoidable period of time spent in the darkness of earth.

At international conferences, especially in the Anglo-American sphere, I have been struck by how the current psychedelic renaissance is tied into a rediscovery of Nietzsche's philosophy. One phrase from *Thus Spoke Zarathustra* is particularly well loved in revving an audience up for a lecture on psychedelics: "You must be ready to burn yourself in your own flame; how could you rise anew if you have not first become ashes?"[68] Yet the lines don't track with my own experience as a therapist. Nietzsche's

---

67 R. Gordon Wasson, Albert Hofmann, and Carl A. P. Ruck, *The Road to Eleusis: Unveiling the Secret of the Mysteries* (North Atlantic Books, 2023).

68 Friedrich Nietzsche, *Thus Spoke Zarathustra: A Book for None and All* (Penguin, 1978).

biting disdain for the down-and-out, for compassion and charity, make him less than ideal as a psychedelic figurehead. Even so, Nietzsche was full of contradictions and dealt extensively with topics that are absolutely of value as they relate to psychedelics in psychotherapy.

In his book *Untimely Meditations*, a key essay—translated as "On the Use and Abuse of History for Life"—Nietzsche emphasizes the importance of forgetting and starting over again to human creativity (a topic I address more thoroughly in chapter 7 on right identity). In his best-known work, *Thus Spoke Zarathustra*, Nietzsche judges people according to their regression or progress in linear time. This line of thought leads him to the concept of the "Übermensch.", i.e., the life-affirming, self-determined human being that Nietzsche regarded as an ideal image of human development. Psychedelics unfortunately appear as a regular topic in pseudo-Darwinist discussions about the next step in human evolution that are often linked to racist or radical right-wing concepts. It cannot be emphasized strongly enough, therefore, that Nietzsche juxtaposed his linear model of humanity's future to the cyclical time of the cosmos, the eternal recurrence of the same, a notion he borrowed from the Greek stoics and the Indian tradition. Nietzsche casts the idea in an explicitly ethical light: We ought to live as though we would live eternally. In other words, only do the things you would also be fine doing in endless repetitions. Nietzsche stresses further that his idea of the eternal recurrence is more profound, and thus more important than his Übermensch utopia.

Linear time awakens the need to transcend borders, strike out elsewhere, lose oneself in boundlessness. Cyclical time, on the other hand, sets the emphasis on limitations and corresponds to a desire for the finite, maintaining what has been received, cultivating tradition. It shows that all content is ultimately the same despite its constantly shifting forms (the basic tenet of archetypes). Cyclical time's most powerful symbol is the ring. Psychedelics allow us to experience these two contrasting forms of time and to integrate them into an unending current of new images and feelings that appear eternally familiar. It is the reconciliation of being and becoming. About cyclical time, Nietzsche wrote:

> Everything goes, everything returns, the wheel of existence rolls forever. Everything dies, everything blossoms anew; the year of existence runs on forever. Everything breaks, everything is joined anew;

> the same house of existence builds itself for ever. Everything departs, everything meets again; the ring of existence is true to itself for ever. Existence begins in every instant, the ball There rolls around every Here. The middle is everywhere. The path of eternity is crooked.[69]

The thought is very Indian—they are the words of King Soma.

Cyclical Time, Music, and the Known Universe

It isn't just Nietzsche's *Thus Spake Zarathustra*; one of the most popular film franchises in the world, *Star Wars*, also grapples with the tension between linear and cyclical time. For the costume design, author and producer George Lucas—a careful student of Jung's psychology of archetypes—didn't hire a futurist but an expert on historical films. Drawing inspiration from Buddhism, the Middle Ages, and US superhero comics, together they invented a style and series of characters that were at once futuristic and bygone. The light saber is a good example—an age-old weapon whose laser technology makes it superior to the most modern methods of destruction. Cyclical time also appears in the fact that animals, people, and humanoid robots—beings that arose in entirely different epochs, in other words—work wonderfully together. That makes for the good, bright side of things, a force that sees through time, flowing far out into the sea of the future while staying connected with the sources of archetypal origin. The "force" so often conjured in the film is the psychedelic power to integrate time—an ability the dark side lacks. "The past must die! Kill it if it must be" is the Dark Side's motto. It is worth noting that in real life Carrie Fisher, who played Princess Leia on the good side of the force, suffered from severe depression and acknowledged undergoing successful treatment with LSD.

In psychedelic therapy the experience of cyclical time can be strengthened through music. Arvo Pärt's piece "Spiegel im Spiegel" is particularly popular. The title ("Mirror in the Mirror") alludes to an infinity mirror, a set of parallel mirrors that produces an endless set of reflected images. Musically, the same effect is created through minor variations on a three-note sequence that seem to repeat endlessly, as though reflected back and forth by self-facing mirrors. While the piece is composed in F major, the breezy,

---

69 Ibid.

vigorous mood typical of the key never appears, with the cycles evoking a kind of longing. Peoples' experiences of music while under the influence of psychedelics illustrate that music absolutely works on us in metaphorical ways and can prompt deep knowing beyond the simple passing of moods.

Bach's cello suites as performed by the US musician Yo-Yo Ma are also popular sources, recommended by Michael Pollan and other well-known psychonauts. In composing the masterpieces, Bach set himself the task of adapting to the cello the sort of polyphony that is possible in piano and orchestral pieces. He instructs the cello to play a note that the human ear can recall for about seven seconds and then renews the note at the exact moment that the memory of it dies out. By slightly varying the following note or unexpectedly omitting one, a lively cycle emerges that is woven into further note cycles. It is a sophisticated structure which, perhaps unsurprisingly, psychedelics help patients detect. After embarking on the experience of listening to the cello suites, one patient who described herself as "unmusical" commented that "the music gives you the confidence that everything that goes will later come back." Cyclical time will often take visual form as well, as rapidly evolving ornamentation, for example. Alan Watts described it as "the rhythmic beauty of detail which the drugs reveal in common things."[70]

In his investigation of the temporal structure of archetypes,[71] Carl Jung's *Synchronicity: An Acausal Connecting Principle* argues that while events can be thought of in terms of causal chains, they are also related to one another via indirect routes. In fact, he argues, it is these indirect connections that first give rise to archetypes and higher orders of meaning. Presumably they are also what psychedelics bring to light and make tangible. This yields a new definition for archetype that is akin to the Chinese term *tao*. Jung quotes Lao Tzu's Tao Te Ching: "There is a thing confusedly formed, / Born before heaven and earth. / Silent and void / It stands alone and does not change, / Goes round and does not weary."[72] Recognizing this principle bears practical fruit: Of a prince who understands the Tao, Lao Tzu says, "The Tao is always at ease. / It overcomes without competing, / answers

70 Watts, *The Joyous Cosmology*.

71 Carl Jung, *Synchronicity: An Acausal Connecting Principle* (Princeton University Press, 2010).

72 Lau Tzu, *Tao Te Ching* (Penguin, 1963).

without speaking a word, / arrives without being summoned, / accomplishes without a plan."[73]

Research in the neurosciences and pharmacology has given us an increasingly clear picture of the biological mechanisms at work in how psychedelics relate to our sense of time. As described above, psychedelics impact the serotonin system, which among other things regulates physiological cycles like the circadian rhythm of sleeping and waking. Since this regulation affects the entire body, it occurs via hormones that are produced in the pineal and pituitary glands and distributed through the blood. Pharmacological studies now show that psychedelics causes the release of a range of these regulatory hormones, among them cortisol, melatonin, prolactin, oxytocin, thyroid hormones, and growth hormones.[74] The effect is medically significant since disruptions to biological rhythms make up a risk factor in many illnesses—not only for neuropsychiatric illnesses like depression or cluster headaches, but medical afflictions like breast cancer, colon cancer, intestinal infections, cardiovascular diseases, and metabolic diseases.[75] Psychedelics could thus play a beneficial role in potentially restoring biological rhythms that have been disrupted.

Among other therapeutic effects, ketamine and other psychedelics have been shown to decrease daytime tiredness, improve circadian rhythm, and increase slow-wave activity in depressive patients.[76] Slow-wave activity is a measure of neuroplasticity during sleep, i.e., the brain's ability during a state of sleep to steady its hold on important memory fragments, erase what doesn't matter, and work out psychological conflicts. Traditional antidepressants provide insufficient relief for the disruptions to circadian rhythms that appear with many psychiatric illnesses and hamper neuroplasticity.

Cluster headaches are a neurological illness marked by strong recurring headaches on one side of the head, typically around the eye. They are often accompanied by watery eyes, a stuffy nose, or swollen eyes, with

---

73 Ibid.

74 Emmanuelle A. D. Schindler, Ryan M. Wallace, Jordan A. Sloshower, and Deepak C. D'Souza, "Neuroendocrine Associations Underlying the Persistent Therapeutic Effects of Classic Serotonergic Psychedelics," *Frontiers in Pharmacology* 9 (March 1, 2018)

75 Ravi Allada and Joseph Bass, "Circadian Mechanisms in Medicine," *The New England Journal of Medicine* 384, no. 6 (February 11, 2021): 550–61.

76 Christoph Kraus, Daniel Wasserman, Ioline D. Henter, Elia Acevedo-Diaz, Bashkim Kadriu, and Carlos A. Zarate Jr., "The Influence of Ketamine on Drug Discovery in Depression," *Drug Discovery Today* 24, no. 10 (October 1, 2019): 2033–43.

symptoms lasting anywhere from minutes to hours. As the name indicates, the attacks arrive in clusters that can drag on for weeks or months. The physical pain they provoke is considered the most intense known, not infrequently driving their victim to thoughts of suicide, which has earned them the dark name of suicide headaches. Finally, the regularity with which they appear—a specific time early in the morning for example—has led some to dub them "alarm clock headaches." The unique temporal features of the headache suggest a malfunctioning of the internal clock in the hypothalamus. In a fascinating turn, LSD and psilocybin seem able to put a stop to acute instances of pain and the periods of clusters, and to prevent them from arising.[77] While the findings are currently being pursued in larger studies, there is already a great deal to speak for psychedelics' therapeutic value not only regarding psychological disorders, but medical illnesses affecting the inner ear.

Summary

It isn't physics that produces time, but our brains. This in turn is a primary cause of suffering; impatience, fear, and problems with identity are all inconceivable without time. Psychedelics give us a wealth of time while directing our attention to the present, bringing deep relaxation and relief from pain. Psychedelics improve autobiographical memory, creating a narrative effect that enables patients to understand how their present feelings or relationships tie into past events. The archetype effect, meanwhile, ushers us into cyclical time, the time of music, where it becomes possible to attune oneself to transpersonal rhythms and access archetypal centers of power.

77 R. Andrew Sewell, John H. Halpern, and Harrison G. Pope, "Response of Cluster Headache to Psilocybin and LSD," *Neurology* 66, no. 12 (June 27, 2006): 1920–22.

Chapter 3
Right Reward: The Path to Unconditional Joy

"Exhausted, I then slept, to awake next morning refreshed, with a clear head, though still somewhat tired physically," Albert Hofmann wrote in April 1943, following his first self-experiment with LSD. "A sensation of well-being and renewed life flowed through me. Breakfast tasted delicious and gave me extraordinary pleasure. When I later walked out into the garden, in which the sun shone now after a spring rain, everything glistened and sparkled in a fresh light. The world was as if newly created. All my senses vibrated in a condition of highest sensitivity."[78]

While Hoffman had no way of knowing it at the time, the psychedelic effect he was describing has proven unique among all the other psychotropic drugs that have been discovered or developed since 1950. Today therapists have around one hundred different psychotropic substances at their disposal, though nearly every one incurs some kind of sedative effect on the brain rather than heightening sensitivity. Sedation by medication is a valuable strategy in emergency psychiatry, as in the case of unbearable auditory hallucinations, paranoid anxiety, or the tendency to violent outbursts. Still, it's important to note that some recently developed psychotropic drugs no longer have a general sedative effect but work in refined, targeted ways that even hold long-term benefits, like bringing psychological stability to patients with severe psychiatric diseases—schizophrenia, bipolar disorder, or depression anxiety—that are often accompanied by heightened sensitivity to sensations or sounds.

No such recourse exists by contrast for patients suffering from feelings of deadness or muteness—depressive listlessness for example, termed *anhedonia* in professional literature—or the apathetic states that frequently appear in the case of chronic psychoses. The condition doesn't lead to acute

78 Hofmann, *LSD, My Problem Child.*

psychiatric problems, true, though many patients who experience it over the long term do wish they felt more and had their former liveliness back. Emotional deadening and a loss of sexual desire are two of the most common side effects that lead to patients break off treatment with psychotropic drugs. What is more, excessive feelings of listlessness brought on by medical prescriptions or illness can result in long-term isolation, invalidity, a low quality of life, and increased risk of suicide.

When Hofmann carried on his self-experiments with similar psychedelic substances following LSD, he discovered that the experience of heightened positivity toward all that made life worthwhile and rewarding was more the exception to the rule. In the case of the lysergamide found in the Mexican ololiuqui plant (as opposed to lysergic acid diethylamide, or LSD), Hofmann entered an altered state of consciousness that aroused a repellent and empty sense of disquiet instead of a pleasurable sense of well-being. The psychedelics I discuss in this book represent the handful of exceptions out of hundreds of psychedelic substances, the few capable of leading to positive and meaningful experiences, elevating their therapeutic potential.

The comparative ease of lowering sensitivity as opposed to attuning it more finely to what is positive or meaningful isn't a challenge unique to psychopharmacology alone; a similar line of development is visible in theology. On his journey around the world, the naturalist Charles Darwin determined that belief in the existence of cruel, malicious spirits was much more common than belief in a benevolent deity. In the Bible as well, God is initially characterized by an ill temper and his punitive, crushing interventions. Only later does he become the "sweet Lord" who plays a primarily supportive and rewarding role. Nietzsche describes a parallel tendency in Greek culture: "In order to be able to live, the Greeks were obliged, by the most profound compulsion, to create these gods. This process is probably to be imagined as taking place gradually so that, under the influence of the Apolline instinct for beauty, the Olympian divine order of joy developed out of the original, Titanic divine order of terror in a series of slow transitions, in much the same way as roses burst forth from a thicket of thorns."[79]

It is only over the course of the twentieth century that the rod and switch was replaced with showing students appreciation or encouragement. Approaches to healing have developed in the much the same way;

79 Friedrich Nietzsche, *Nietzsche: The Birth of Tragedy and Other Writings* (Cambridge University Press, 1999).

our predecessors primarily attempted to kill off or drive out whatever was pathogenic, evil, or demonic. There were various strategies for doing so: ripping or tearing, scratching, burning, even life-threatening methods like bleeding or trepanation, where the skull is bored into to drive out evil spirits. This must have made the introduction of shamanic techniques of ecstasy about as revolutionary as the introduction of resource activation or positive psychology were to the field of psychiatry, where previously patients were pacified by means of straightjacket or shock therapy. Through their use of peyote, iboga, ayahuasca, and other plants, shamans discovered parallel states of consciousness that can improve resilience and stimulate self-healing. These beneficial states were marked by feelings of ecstasy, the lightness of flying, vivid perception, visions, and experiences of the origin or centering—an increased sensitivity to positive sensations, in other words.

There is a simple reason for the parallel lines of development across such a wide range of fields: Our positive experiences of the world are generally more complex than our experience of the negative side of life. Rats, monkeys, and humans will all react quite similarly to electric shock, a laceration, or social isolation. Yet even members of the same family will react quite differently to favorable events: on weekends, the father tunes into auto racing, the mother to sunsets, the son to his manga comics, and the daughter to Pippi Longstocking books. During the week the family's capacity for enjoyment might look entirely different again, leaving the family dog Wolfie confused about where to begin with so many different kinds of positivity.

This means animal experiments are far less revealing for psychedelic research than they are for psychotropic drugs with a sedative effect. The effects of valium, an anxiety-relieving drug that strengthens the brain's inhibitory GABA system, are nearly identical in humans and animals for example. Hofmann's LSD experiments with animals, by contrast, didn't show any remarkable results. The psychedelic effects of LSD were only discovered thanks to the fact that self-experimentation was still common and permitted in 1943, leading to "roses bursting forth" in the field of psychopharmacology, to quote Nietzsche. Going forward, this means that psychedelics will remain both more complicated and more expensive to use than conventional psychotropic drugs. No one-size-fits-all solutions will be forthcoming; each course of treatment will have to be individually tailored to the patient and his or her present situation. Psychedelics also present complexity in finding the right dosage; in the case of ketamine infusions for instance, a very low dose of 0.5 milligrams per kilogram in bodyweight raises sensitivity to positive experiences by an optimal amount. Even the slightest bit more, 0.1 milligrams per kilo say, and the positive effect of the medicine lessens.[80]

US psychologist and psychedelics pioneer Timothy Leary introduced the concepts of "set" and "setting" as a way of exploring the broad range of psychedelic effects. "Set" is short for "mindset," referring to the mental constitution of the patient or consumer. "Setting," on the other hand, refers to the environment in which the substance is ingested. Leary worked off the assumption that a psychedelic's effect did not depend on the dosage alone, but critically on the patient's mood, thoughts, and expectations, as well as the context in which they took it and the impressions it raised for them. The notion has been proven correct in a great number of subsequent studies as well as clinical practice. Patients who have already experimented with MDMA in a party setting, for instance, often report an entirely different effects in the context of psychotherapy, where the impact is typically more emotional, introspective, intense, and meaningful. The therapist and co-therapist, also called "sitters," are an important part of the setting. Ideally, this means a patient will have their choice of different therapists or therapist pairs.

Shamanic cultures the world over understood the power "setting" centuries before it was clinically studied, crafting elaborate ceremonies and rituals that set the container for patients' plant medicine journeys. Many shamanic cultures also focus on "set": the Shipibo of Peru, for example, instruct journeyers with ayahuasca to adhere to a strict diet for up to two weeks before ingesting the ayahuasca brew. The "dieta" typically prohibits sugar, alcohol, and caffeine, as well as excess media use or violent imagery, and promotes a simple diet of vegetables, chicken or fish, and medicinal teas.[81]

---

80 Maurizio Fava, Marlene P. Freeman, Martina Flynn, Heidi Judge, Bettina B. Hoeppner, Cristina Cusin et al., "Double-Blind, Placebo-Controlled, Dose-Ranging Trial of Intravenous Ketamine as Adjunctive Therapy in Treatment-Resistant Depression (TRD)," *Molecular Psychiatry* 25, no. 7 (October 3, 2018): 1592–1603.

81 Debora Gonzalez, Jordi Cantillo, Irene Perez, Maria Carvalho, Adam Aronovich, Magi Farre, Amanda Feilding, Jordi E. Obiols, and José Carlos Bouso, "The Shipibo Ceremonial Use of Ayahuasca to Promote Well-Being: An Observational Study," *Frontiers in Pharmacology* 12 (May 5, 2021): 623923, https://doi.org/10.3389/fphar.2021.623923

Neuroscientific research has given us some idea of the mechanisms that make the impact of psychedelics especially dependent on setting. Traditional antidepressants, tranquilizers, and antipsychotic drugs inhibit the activity of the amygdala, which is responsible for our perception of emotional stimuli. The effect is to make the patient less dependent on environmental influences—a potentially significant advantage in the case of highly distressing situations. The downside is a general level of emotional dullness. Psychedelics by contrast, when used in the context of psychotherapy, actually *strengthen* our amygdala's responses to emotional stimuli on a lasting basis, while the predominance of negative stimuli decreases.[82] This complex suite of effects gives rise to a relaxed mood in which patients continue to respond to their environment.

Psychedelics and the Brain Reward System

In neuroscientific terms, heightened sensitivity to positive sensations means changes in the brain reward system, a complex network of neural pathways running from the brainstem through the middle of the brain to the forebrain. The archaic sections of our brainstem respond to instinctive rewards like sex, food, and self-assertion; the centers in the basal ganglia to longer-term rewards such as social belonging, social status, and self-worth. The parts of the reward system located in the forebrain, meanwhile, respond to rewards that are related to personal and suprapersonal growth: higher forms of love, self-realization, and spiritual peak experiences (about which I'll share more later). The overall system is governed by a range of messenger substances and hormones: Dopamine is responsible for the motivation to seek out and obtain rewards; oxytocin promotes social behavior; serotonin is involved in the experience and integration of the reward. The concept of "reward" or "rewarding" as it is used in this context refers to anything that is in some way worthwhile or fulfilling—anything positive that one experiences, not simply the reward for a given accomplishment. As

82 Leor Roseman, Lysai Demetriou, Matthew B. Wall, David J. Nutt, and Robin L. Carhart-Harris, "Increased Amygdala Responses to Emotional Faces After Psilocybin for Treatment-resistant Depression," *Neuropharmacology* 142 (November 1, 2018): 263–69; Franz X. Vollenweider and Katrin H. Preller, "Psychedelic Drugs: Neurobiology and Potential for Treatment of Psychiatric Disorders," *Nature Reviews Neuroscience* 21, no. 11 (September 14, 2020): 611–24.

British musician Sting described his own experience on psychedelics, "You can have immensely rewarding experiences, full of love and support, and a sense of buoyancy, and a religious sense of connection to the planet."[83] Sting's quote effectively summarizes the most important ways the brain reward system supports well-being, namely through feelings of love, support, effervescence, belonging, and spirituality.

The brain reward system is of decisive importance for staying healthy and resilient. Anyone still able to draw on positive feelings while in the throes of stress or trauma, whether that arrives as a sense of humor or gratitude, stands a better chance of overcoming their difficulties than those who feel exclusively negative feelings and can see only black. The brain reward system is capable of sedating the stress system, providing neuroscientific footing for the observation that esteem, social support, belonging to a culture, and a sense of purpose all offer protection against stress-related illnesses. Humans possess the largest reward systems of all living beings (relative to the rest of the brain). Humans are also the only living beings whose reward systems can form new nerve cells throughout life, making them extraordinarily adaptive and neuroplastic.[84] The degree of neuroplasticity means that true rewards give us wings—a first time artistic success, say—while false ones, as with substance abuse, can lead straight to the abyss.

Disruptions in the brain reward system are likely the leading cause of psychological disorders in general.[85] The core symptom of depression is anhedonia: a diminished interest in things that once brought joy, and an inability to experience or derive all kinds of pleasure. The state drives many depressive patients toward passivity, pessimism, and social withdrawal, which they experience as great sources of stress and torment. In the time I spent working at the US National Institute of Mental Health, I examined the neurobiological foundations of anhedonia. My team and I were able to show that even slight disruptions in the system—a reduction of the messenger substance dopamine, for example—set off a range of depressive symptoms

---

83 *Have a Good Trip: Adventures in Psychedelics*, written and directed by Donick Cary, Netflix, 2020.

84 Aurélie Ernst and Jonas Frisén, "Adult Neurogenesis in Humans—Common and Unique Traits in Mammals," *PLOS Biology* 13, no. 1 (January 26, 2015)

85 Gregor Hasler, "Can the Neuroeconomics Revolution Revolutionize Psychiatry?," *Neuroscience & Biobehavioral Reviews* 36, no. 1 (January 1, 2012): 64–78.

like listlessness, lack of drive, difficulties concentrating, and dejection.[86] Imaging studies have confirmed that depressed adolescents and adults exhibit dulled reward systems. Nor does the dulling appear only during acute phases of depression but lingers even after symptoms have subsided, raising the long-term risk that the depression will return and become chronic. Conventional antidepressants can inhibit the stress system, which is hyperactive during depression. This has the effect of reducing anxiety, sleeping disorders, and other stress symptoms, bringing great relief to many. Yet oftentimes the root issue—anhedonia—will persist, partly because of the stress system's inhibition. Patients with pronounced cases of anhedonia who don't suffer from the classic symptoms of stress thus show limited response to conventional antidepressants.

One of the most effective forms of psychotherapy against depression is behavioral activation, which aims to make patients more sensitive to positive stimuli by raising their overall level of activity. This works just fine when the case involves nothing more than a bad mood—after an unpleasant encounter with a colleague, when everything seems dark and stormy, a walk through the woods can work wonders. The walk demonstrates to the brain reward system that the world is more rewarding and positive than assumed; it is also an experience in self-determination, showing the person that it is possible to change their feelings through action. If the source of the dulling lies elsewhere, however—a pathology in neuroplasticity for example—psychological interventions are often to no avail.

For all these reasons, the discovery that low psychedelic dosages of ketamine were highly effective in patients suffering from chronic depression and pronounced anhedonia landed like a bomb in the professional community, thrilling even the conservatives and critics.[87] In 2018 the annual congress of the American College of Neuropsychopharmacology in Hollywood, Florida, gave the impression that the majority of contemporary psychiatric research revolved around the finding, with more than fifty studies presented on the therapeutic potential of ketamine. If pharmaceutical

86 Philipp Homan, A. Neumeister, A. C. Nugent, D. S. Charney, W. C. Drevets, and G. Hasler, "Serotonin Versus Catecholamine Deficiency: Behavioral and Neural Effects of Experimental Depletion in Remitted Depression," *Translational Psychiatry* 5, no. 3 (March 17, 2015)

87 Rejish K. Thomas, Glen Baker, John Lind, and Serdar Dursun, "Rapid Effectiveness of Intravenous Ketamine for Ultraresistant Depression in a Clinical Setting and Evidence for Baseline Anhedonia and Bipolarity as Clinical Predictors of Effectiveness," *Journal of Psychopharmacology* 32, no. 10 (September 5, 2018): 1110–17.

companies, universities, and national research funds are now ready to invest large sums in testing out psychedelics as a new class of antidepressants, it has much less to do with their mystical effects than their impact on the brain reward system.

Are Psychedelics Addictive?

Illnesses involving addiction constitute another disorder of the brain reward system. Addiction-forming substances like nicotine, alcohol, heroin, cocaine, and cannabis increase the amount of dopamine released into the reward system, leading to positive feelings, albeit temporarily. Over time the system may dull and undergo deep structural changes, diminishing interest in higher or longer-term rewards. The following terms describe how the brain reward system malfunctions with addiction:

Tolerance: Habitual consumption of the addictive substance means smaller and smaller doses of dopamine are released, so the substance must be consumed in steadily larger quantities to achieve the same effect.

Dominance: Drugs are relatively strong dopamine stimuli. The more a drug is consumed the less the brain responds to other rewards, which the drug makes seem relatively unimportant by comparison. People typically grow asocial over the course of addiction, only taking interest in people who have something to do with their addiction, neglecting their families, and losing interest in work. The neuroplasticity of the brain reward system diminishes significantly in the process, making it next to impossible to develop new interests.

Withdrawal: Our dopamine system makes us psychologically resilient, instilling interest, motivation, security and self-confidence. Drugs exhaust the dopamine system however so that after consumption symptoms of withdrawal like anxiety, insecurity, listlessness, an inability to concentrate, and lethargy appear. This creates a strong temptation to reach for the substance to put an end to the unpleasant state of affairs. The mere thought of withdrawal is often enough to

> drive a person to consume again, a negative motivation that becomes more prominent over the course of addiction. In time many addicts no longer even enjoy the source of their addiction and continue consuming simply to fight off withdrawal symptoms.

I provide such a detailed account of addiction since many patients and their relatives fear that psychedelics may become addictive. Addiction is in fact a key issue with "positive" psychotropic drugs that do not sedate but stimulate the brain. None other than Sigmund Freud was convinced of cocaine's suitability for treating depression, until a friend he treated with the drug died an agonizing death following from addiction. At present we are seeing millions of people engulfed in misery due to the opiates (heroin-like substances) doctors have prescribed them for pain. In the last ten years alone, more than half a million people have died from overdosing on pain prescriptions.

Treating addiction and substance abuse makes up a large part of what psychiatrists do, whether at the doctor's office, a hospital, or emergency care. Alcohol dependency ranks as one of the greatest psychiatric challenges that exists. As a psychiatrist with decades of experience in emergency psychiatry, psychiatric clinics, day hospitals, and outpatient clinics, I could put the question to myself: "Have you ever seen an addiction to psychedelics?" The answer is an unequivocal "no." I have also done psychiatric consulting for nearly ten years at the ER of the University Hospital of Zurich. This is especially relevant because Zurich is home to one of the world's largest techno parties, the Street Parade, which attracts over one million people. The ER is filled during that time with people who have consumed illegal substances, while the concentration of drugs in Zurich's wastewater ranks among the highest in the world. Yet even working in this capacity, I've never met a single person who reported an addiction to psychedelics. The same goes for other experienced colleagues. This is entirely worth noting since nearly all substances are potentially addictive when abused.

Pharmacological studies show that tolerance develops very quickly with psychedelics; the effect lessens by the second time, and after three or four times given on consecutive days they no longer have any impact. There is also a cross-tolerance effect: It isn't just LSD that no longer has an impact after taking repeated doses—psilocybin doesn't work either, even in very high dosages. This fact alone prevents addiction from forming. Ayahuasca is an exception with no tolerance forming, though there is no evidence of ayahuasca becoming addictive, either.

Dominance is in any event a more important factor where the development of an addiction is concerned. In his many experiments with LSD, Albert Hofmann never once experienced his interests narrowing; on the contrary, they expanded. This is the opposite of dominance. If even repeat consumption of LSD does not lead to dominance it means the brain reward system is not being dulled, as is typically the case with dependency on alcohol, cocaine, or heroin, though also with compulsive eating and gambling, which involve potentially grave consequences like depression or lowered social interest.

The neuroscience behind the lack of dominance is that psychedelics either have no or only a very slight effect on our dopamine system. Cocaine works primarily on our dopamine system by contrast, greatly elevating our attention and drive and creating a heightened feeling of self-worth. Psychedelics work instead on the serotonin system, with the opposite effect: Our focus broadens and our consciousness expands. Psychedelics also stimulate interest in things that aren't addictive—flowers or music, for example, colors, shapes, drinking water, or the folds in one's pants, in Aldous Huxley's case. Taking interest in simple, intrinsic rewards is a typical effect of serotonin.[88] At the same time, interest significantly declines in things that do have addictive potential such as sex, sweets, or money. A psychedelic state is comparable to the harmless, fulfilling happiness of contemplative mountain hikers or monks; it has nothing to do with the fast-paced dopamine rush of power-hungry managers. It provides a countermodel for happiness, explaining how it is psychedelics help people liberate themselves from addiction.

For millennia now people have used psychedelics for spiritual and healing purposes without their use leading to addiction. Repeat surveys and clinical studies with large sample sizes have confirmed the historical, clinical, and pharmacological finding that no known pharmacological addiction

88 Casper Schmidt, Nikolina Skandali, Carsten Gleesborg, Timo L. Kvamme, Hema Schmidt, Kim Frisch et al., "The Role of Dopaminergic and Serotonergic Transmission in the Processing of Primary and Monetary Reward," *Neuropsychopharmacology* 45, no. 9 (May 11, 2020): 1490–97.

to psychedelics exists.[89] Ketamine presents a special case, which is used in high dosages as a risky party drug and can provoke severe symptoms of withdrawal including physical maladies and depressive moods. When abused, daily dosage typically ranges from 300 to 900 milligrams; one gram or higher isn't uncommon in cases of habitual abuse. By comparison, a dosage of 0.5 milligrams per kilo body weight has proven effective when treating depression, 30 milligrams for a woman weighing 60 kilograms or about 132 pounds, for example. There are no known cases of addiction forming at this much lower dosage, which instead has an antidepressive and psychedelic effect. Pharmacologically, this is tied into the fact that a psychotropic drug's effects on the brain (at the receptors, for example) is strongly influenced both by the dosage and the way it is administered. The amphetamine MDMA constitutes a second special case, since the large amount of dopamine it releases within the brain reward system can also prove addictive. It is difficult to say for certain however, since MDMA is rarely consumed in its pure form when abused but is instead mixed in with other amphetamines with greater addictive potential.

Below I look to describe in greater detail two ways psychedelics impact our brain reward system that are of therapeutic value: their effects on positivity, and the peak experience effect.

Positivity

One meta-analysis of eight clinical studies on psilocybin showed that the vast majority of test subjects had found their experience pleasant, enriching, and nonthreatening.[90] Forty-nine percent of study participants had experienced the effects of psilocybin as very pleasant, 43 as pleasant, and just 8 percent as unpleasant. In analyzing thousands of reports on psychedelic experiences with my colleague Adrian Hase, we were able to show that

89 Matthew W. Johnson, Roland R. Griffiths, Peter S. Hendricks, and Jack E. Henningfield, "The Abuse Potential of Medical Psilocybin According to the 8 Factors of the Controlled Substances Act," *Neuropharmacology* 142 (November 1, 2018): 143–66.

90 Erich Studerus, Michael Kometer, Felix Hasler, and Franz X. Vollenweider, "Acute, Subacute and Long-term Subjective Effects of Psilocybin in Healthy Humans: A Pooled Analysis of Experimental Studies," *Journal of Psychopharmacology (Oxford)* 25, no. 11 (September 20, 2010): 1434–52.

the experience of positivity wasn't limited to psilocybin alone but held for all psychedelics.[91] With MDMA, positive experiences were even more frequent than with psilocybin or LSD. This came as a surprise, since patients suffering from psychosis or neurological illness nearly always experience the loss of abstract thought, changes in sensory perception up to the point of hallucination, and the dissolution of their ego as something highly unpleasant, threatening, and fear-inducing. In other words, without a pronounced positivity effect—an important component of the protective helioscope effect I describe in chapter 1—a psychedelic experience would be difficult to endure.

The term *positivity* forms part of US psychologist Barbara Fredrickson's well-considered and thoroughly researched concept of "broaden and build." "Broaden" refers to the capacity that positive emotions such as interest, joy, gratitude, connectedness, calm, hope, love, and confidence have for expanding our consciousness, perceptions, and scope of action. Negative feelings (fear, rage, or anger), by contrast, narrow our perception and consciousness, with the aim of ensuring survival in a threatening environment, as in fight-or-flight situations. The concept applies to psychedelic therapy since one long-term effect of psychedelics is to increase positivity. That includes taking greater joy in the natural world, music, or works of art, feeling greater self-acceptance, self-worth, and empathy for oneself, and experiencing a heightened sense of optimism, mindfulness, and connectedness.[92] Studies show that positivity also changes our social perceptions, leading us to see unity in place of division, the "we" instead of the "I." Racist prejudice diminishes, for example.[93] Positivity further aids physical health, improving sleep, reducing stress hormone levels, supporting the distribution of relationship and growth-oriented hormones (dopamine and endorphins), strengthening the immune system, reducing inflammation, preventing colds, easing pain, and lowering blood pressure.[94]

---

91 Adrian Hase, Max Erdmann, Verena Limbach, and Gregor Hasler, "Analysis of Recreational Psychedelic Substance Use Experiences Classified by Substance," *Psychopharmacology* 239, no. 2 (January 15, 2022): 643–59.

92 Jacob S. Aday, Cayla M. Mitzkovitz, Emily K. Bloesch, Christopher C. Davoli, and Alan K. Davis, "Long-Term Effects of Psychedelic Drugs: A Systematic Review," *Neuroscience & Biobehavioral Reviews* 113 (June 1, 2020): 179–89.

93 Kareem Johnson and Barbara L. Fredrickson, "We All Look the Same to Me," *Psychological Science* 16, no. 11 (November 1, 2005): 875–81.

94 Barbara Fredrickson, *Positivity: Top-Notch Research Reveals the 3-to-1 Ratio That Will Change Your Life* (Three Rivers Press, 2009).

The second term from Fredrickson's theory, "build," refers to the observation that positive feelings, which are usually passing and varying, tend to accumulate and mutually reinforce each other over time. Positivity thus leads to more positive activities, which in turn helps to establish an enduring sense of positivity. "Building" is another typical long-term effect of psychedelics; in the months following one ayahuasca ceremony, participants reported: "I spent more time in nature," "I pursued sport in healthier ways," "I stopped putting off some of my tasks," "I made contact with people who I hadn't spoken with in a long time."[95]

In a series of studies, Fredrickson found the balance between positivity and negativity (negative emotions, withdrawal, pessimism) to be decisive for the well-being of individuals, pairs, and work groups. The average proportion was 2:1, i.e., we experience twice as many positive feelings as negative. With a ratio of 3:1 or greater, positivity acquires an internal dynamic in the form of an upward spiral, encouraging expansion, flourishing, and growth. Ratios of less than 1:1 by contrast, where negativity outweighs positivity, can trigger downward spirals into crisis, blockages, or burnout. People with psychological disorders typically experience more negativity than positivity.

Whereas conventional psychotropic drugs like antidepressants, tranquilizers, and antipsychotics are capable of lowering negativity, psychedelics possess the unique ability to increase positivity. Though stimulants can be a blessing for many patients who don't respond to other medications, they are not consistently effective in depression (or as an antidepressant), possibly because they do not promote neuroplasticity to the same degree as psychedelics, meaning their positivity effects don't last.[96]

I'd like now to explore three different manifestations of psychedelics' positivity effects: the epicurean phenomenon, the entelechy phenomenon, and the kundalini phenomenon.

---

95 Maha N. Mian, Brianna R. Altman, and Mitch Earleywine, "Ayahuasca's Antidepressant Effects Covary with Behavioral Activation as Well as Mindfulness," *Journal of Psychoactive Drugs* 52, no. 2 (September 30, 2019): 130–37.

96 Calvin Ly, Alexandra C. Greb, Lindsay P. Cameron, Jonathan M. Wong, Eden V. Barragan, Paige, C. Wilson et al., "Psychedelics Promote Structural and Functional Neural Plasticity," *Cell Reports* 23, no. 11 (June 1, 2018): 3170–82.

The Epicurean Phenomenon

A surprisingly small section of our brain's reward system deals with the actual "consumption" of rewards—eating a chocolate, for instance. The larger part of the system is instead devoted to the anticipation of reward—the idea of eating chocolate in the near future. This can be illustrated with a simple neuroscientific experiment: Let's say we credibly inform a study participant that she'll receive a ten-dollar bill in an hour. This stimulates a remarkable amount of activity in the forebrain, experienced in the form of pleasant anticipation. Once the anticipation subsides and the study participant is actually paid the money, the actual receipt of the money hardly elicits a response. If the participant isn't paid, the stress system engages, whereas dopamine is released only if the sum is considerably higher than ten dollars. Technically, this means that it isn't the reward per se that determines the release of dopamine—and with it one aspect of the positive feeling—but the reward prediction error, or the difference between the expectation of the reward and the actual reward.

Most of our expected rewards are unconscious: When we flip a switch, we expect light to come on. When we turn on the faucet, we expect water to come out. We expect the radiant, warming sun to greet us in the morning. The unconscious nature of our expectations makes it impossible to enjoy entirely everyday things like light, water, and sunlight. In addition to being unconscious, many of our expectations are unrealistic; that our work colleagues will always be in a good mood for example, or that our friends will always be available. Inflated expectations are a primary cause of disappointment and embitterment, leaving it impossible to enjoy our own lives and life with other people.

The ancient Greek philosopher Epicurus was a true expert on the brain reward system. Through his observations, he became convinced that continuously lowering our expectations was the most effective way of achieving happiness. Intense pleasures raise expectations, and as such should be avoided. He determined further that slightly varying a flow of small pleasures broken up by periods of abstinence was an effective way of keeping expectations low. At his garden in Athens, Epicurus would host others interested in his way to happiness; above the garden gate stood the phrase: "Dear guest...a friendly host will welcome you with barley-meal, and serve you water also in abundance...this garden does not whet your appetite; but quenches it."[97]

Applying Epicurus's method has become quite difficult in our modern world, which is positively brimming with intense stimuli and tempting offers. More and more of us suffer from unconscious expectations that have been raised to fever pitch by consumer products purposely designed to addict. In other words, advertisements and social media increase our sense of anticipation at the expense of true happiness. Psychedelics decidedly lower our expectations by contrast, "resetting" or "rescaling" the brain reward system in the process. This is evident from the joy people typically find in small things while on psychedelics: a glass of water, the sun, or light, for example. Feelings of astonishment, rejuvenation, freshness, or a capacity for surprise are just as typical, and indicate the thoroughgoing nature of psychedelics' ability to reset our expectation. "I'm seeing everything for the first time again, like a kid!" I heard from one patient who had suffered years of feeling embittered and joyless. The REBUS theory I described in chapter 1 suggests that the ways in which the brain reward system loosens under psychedelics is part of a larger process in which our beliefs and assumptions about the world generally grow less fixed.

The *Rig Veda* offers a detailed description of the brain reward system's increased sensitivity under the influence of soma, stating for example that it is a "joy-winner," "reward finder," "gives birth to joy," brings "unfailing refreshment," and "works wonders and gives joy, moving on paths of gold."[98] German philosopher Arthur Schopenhauer recognized early on that people in modernity were increasingly borrowing happiness against the future. He compared us to donkeys in Italy, who were made to move more quickly by hanging a bundle of hay from a stick affixed to their heads that they forever hope to reach. Today we might speak of the "cravings" that dominate our lives. Yet in dissolving our expectations, psychedelics also make any sense of anticipation vanish along with them. This creates room in our emotional landscape to experience joy directly, whether in colors, shapes, music, or light. This true form of delight holds the advantage that it does not have to be paid for later with disappointment, a sense of dullness, or boredom. The

97 Lucius Annaeus Seneca, *Moral Epistles* (Harvard University Press, 1917).

98 Jamison and Brereton, *The Rigveda: The Earliest Religious Poetry of India*; Karl Geldner and Peter Michel, *Rig-Veda: Das Heilige Wissen Indiens* (Marix Verlag, 2008).

Rig Veda describes the effect of non-expectation succinctly: "Soma is not a seeker, but a finder."[99]

The impact psychedelics have on our brain reward system's neuroplasticity was a central part of psychedelic therapy for Stanislav Grof, where "some of the issues that might be discussed...[include] the wisdom of drawing one's satisfaction from ordinary things that are always available in life; or the absurdity of exaggerated ambitions and needs to prove something to oneself or to others."[100] They are the exact terms in which Epicurus conceived of his own life philosophy.

The Entelechy Phenomenon

Like Epicurus, Aristotle was an empiricist, basing his philosophy on sensory experience. Yet Aristotle did not place the happiness of low expectations at the center of his thought. A tutor to eventual kings like Ptolemy, Cassander, and Alexander the Great, what interested him was rather how politicians, businesses, and athletes might maintain positivity and resilience in uncertain, quick-paced, and dangerous times. He developed a notion of happiness that remained independent of the heights and depths of the world at large, and wasn't subject to external circumstance. Staying happy meant lowering expectations of one's social environment and context while at the same time elevating one's self-expectations and the possibility of happiness. Aristotle was well aware that this was no simple matter; pursuing gluttony, gambling, or sexual exploits were easy enough for the Athenian upper class, but didn't result in positivity or lasting happiness. Pursuits that brought pleasure, but did not grow addictive—contemplation and reflection, but also sports, a healthy diet, and artistic activities—were better suited to the purpose.

Expressed in more philosophical terms, Aristotle distinguished between two sorts of process: Those that were a means to an end, and those that carried the end within themselves. He regarded the latter as more valuable, referring to it as "entelechy": existing in a certain state (*ekhein* in Greek) that holds its own end (*telos* meaning "end, perfection") within itself (*en* meaning "within"). Modern psychology picked up on the notion, considering it

99 Michel, *Rig-Veda: Das Heilige Wissen Indiens.*

100 Grof, *LSD Psychotherapy.*

from a scientific perspective. Sources of motivation that carry their goal within themselves such as dancing, or music, are called "intrinsic," as opposed to those with "extrinsic" motivations, which are largely driven by external factors—be they money, Gucci purses, or the standing of the local soccer team. Academic research the world over attests to the importance of activities with an intrinsic motivation for resilience and well-being.[101]

One participant in Albert Hofmann's initial psychedelic experiments, Swiss Islamic scholar Rudolf Gelpke, had the following experience of entelechy after ingesting LSD: "I knew it was useless to lift a finger. On the contrary: Doing nothing was closer to knowledge, for the reason that willpower blocks out insight. A person without will lights up...it is the eros of self-reference. I was certain of my strength for the rest of time, even if my solar plexus did ache."[102] The eros of self-reference is a good image for intrinsic motivation, which makes us independent of our surrounding environment. Gelpke writes further that this form of eros makes it possible to withstand pain; our resilience increases, in other words. Finally, he finds that this psychedelic eros isn't based on any sort of active doing. Activity would only disturb it—direct, mindful perception of the world and oneself and visionary experiences are a pleasure in their own right, a form of enchantment that one might deem "erotic" in the broadest sense.

In his autobiography, Chilean psychiatrist Claudio Naranjo reports a conversation after an ayahuasca ceremony. When asked by the ceremony leader how he felt and what he had seen, Naranjo replied that "my answer was that I felt one thing, not a thousand things, and that thing was not something I could talk about other than to say that it was simply a state of happiness."[103] An inability to identify precise causes and factors is typical of a state of intrinsic happiness.

The *Rig Veda* discusses the phenomenon of entelechy under the influence of soma at various points, characterizing it as "drawing power from itself," a strengthening strengthener, a self-turning wheel. The notion of drawing power from oneself was further elaborated on in Indian culture: The *Brihadaranyaka Upanishad* describes a state in which "man himself becomes the light...There are no pleasures, joys, or delights there, but he creates the

101 Peter Schmuck, Tim Kasser, and Richard M. Ryan, "Intrinsic and Extrinsic Goals: Their Structure and Relationship to Well-Being in German and U.S. College Students," *Social Indicators Research* 50 (May 2000): 225–241.

102 Hofmann, *LSD, My Problem Child.*

103 Naranjo, *My Psychedelic Explorations.*

pleasures, joys and delights."[104] The *Chandogya Upanishad* maintains that a "person who finds pleasure in themselves, who flirts with the self, who mates with the self, and who finds bliss in the self—he will become entirely his own master, he will obtain complete freedom of movement throughout all worlds."[105] The text isn't referring to the Western ego, the selfie-enamored self, dependent on feedback and likes, but the harmonically breathing, living body that rests within itself and enjoys inner independence. It is this sense of resting in oneself that pharaonic sculpture, statues of the Buddha, or images of Christ Pantocrator in Byzantine mosaics radiate. Nor is this ideal of inner motivation by any means restricted to spiritual life in Indian tradition. In the Bhagavad Gita, one of Hinduism's central holy texts, the god Krishna instructs the prince Arjuna that he should continue to be active (i.e., refrain from asceticism), without making himself reliant on the fruits of his actions.

The notion of a self-contained and self-content eros appears across many different cultures. For Carl Jung, fully integrating the animus and anima—the male and female aspects of the personality, respectively—represented the highest stage of individuation, by which he meant self-realization or the emergence of an integrated, self-contained self. "Individual" originally comes from the Latin term for indivisible, *individuus*. Chinese philosophy meanwhile distinguishes between the yin, the female principle, and yang, or the male principle. Various Chinese meditation and healing practices like shadowboxing (tai chi) seek to integrate yin and yang as a way of cultivating the self, allowing mental calm and silence to emerge.

Entelechy isn't the exclusive domain of humans either; many animals are likewise able to experience joy without external motivation. Konrad Lorenz, an Austrian biologist and Nobel laureate, observed in blackbirds that they sing their most complex and beautiful songs only in marginal states of arousal and when they are singing for themselves. When they are singing for another blackbird or as part of a courtship display, by contrast, the songs become simple repetitions of the same theme. This seems to take part in an age-old strategy for making oneself less dependent on the surrounding environment—one which continues to function even under extreme stress. Concentration camp survivors recounted that reciting poetry or solving

---

104 *The Brihadaranyaka Upanishad with the commentary of Sankaracarya* (Advaita Ashrama, 2008).

105 Patrick Olivelle, *The Early Upanishads: Annotated Text and Translation* (Oxford University Press, 1998).

mathematical problems helped them to endure the horrifying physical and psychological hardships to which they were subject.

One patient of mine, Roland, felt he was constantly taken advantage of, even exploited by others, a feeling that was closely related to a strong desire to be loved and "carried" by others. These feelings initially increased during his LSD session. "My hunger for love is insatiable," he said, "even if everyone loved me it wouldn't be enough. And this hunger turns me into a slave. I would do anything to be loved more. My dependence brings a kind of stress that is more and more unbearable." Later in the same session he experienced a kind of love that he called "spiritual." It was a form of self-love, he said, that he felt ashamed about. His issue, described at the start of the treatment under the blanket term of "stress," became ever more transparent. It was a sense of shame at self-love that drove him into depending on others. In our follow-up sessions we were at last able to work through this dynamic and develop strategies to lead Roland out of dependency. Those included *metta*, or loving-kindness meditation, which helps to foster self-perception, self-acceptance, and self-love.

Another patient suffering from a mild eating disorder and obesity had a literal experience of how psilocybin can help external rewards become internal rewards. "You don't need to play any music, Mr. Hasler," she told me. "I'm already listening to very beautiful music. I don't need the chocolate I brought along as an emergency provision either. I carry the mysterious, sumptuous, bitter power of the chocolate beans I love so much inside myself. At the moment I can feel them more intensely than if I were to eat the chocolate."

Pronounced experiences of entelechy tend to subside once the acute effects of the psychedelics have worn off. Still, many patients can recall them, and some are able to enter back into them without taking psychedelics again. Joy that isn't dependent on context must be learned and practiced on a repeat basis, so that we are able to draw on it in times of loss, emergency, or existential crisis. Many patients report psychedelic therapy giving them greater independence. This in turn supports the notion that psychedelics support this learning process through direct experience, and by increasing neuroplasticity.

Carl Jung didn't just see entelechy as a mere factor in resilience, but recognized it as the primary goal of individuation. "It is of the utmost importance for one to be real in this world," he argued in a talk on kundalini yoga, "for one to truly fulfill one's entelechy, the germ of life that one is."[106]

The Kundalini Phenomenon

"Gregor, you need more positivity in your life," a US colleague at the National Institute of Mental Health once told me. While he meant that I might benefit from acting somewhat nicer and more grateful, the psychedelic positivity effects that I'm describing here often come in the form of deep-rooted, holistic, physical, at times transformational experiences. They are qualities in which the kundalini phenomenon plays an important role.

Freud observed that modern civilization leaves individuals increasingly alienated from certain instincts and drives, as they are necessary to suppress in order to coexist peacefully. This alienation, he predicted, would bring on an epidemic of neurotic suffering, characterized by superficial feelings and conformity to social expectations, a sense of uprootedness, and a lack of meaning. He further anticipated that repressing our sexuality would prompt immature forms of sexuality that could lead to instinctual outbursts or sexual violence to an extent that has become frightfully clear in the context of the Me Too movement. We also see this phenomenon in churches and religious communities that advocate sexual repression, with scandals around sexual abuse coming to the public's attention.

Aldous Huxley put this civilizational problem as follows: "All that the conscious ego can do is to formulate wishes, which are then carried out by forces which it controls very little and understands not at all. When it does anything more—when it tries too hard, for example, when it worries, when it becomes apprehensive about the future—it lowers the effectiveness of those forces and may even cause the devitalized body to fall ill."[107]

Stanislav Grof believed that psychedelics can help us come into contact with unconscious instinctual energies. In this context he saw broad similarities between psychotherapy with LSD and kundalini yoga, as both techniques can suddenly release an enormous amount of energy that then allows for deep-seated change.

---

106 Carl Jung, *The Psychology of Kundalini Yoga: Notes of the Seminar Given in 1932* (Princeton University Press, 2012).

107 Huxley, *The Doors of Perception*.

In Indian spirituality, kundalini is the embodied consciousness of *prana*, or life energy, which takes the form of a serpent that lies coiled at the base of the spine. Kundalini yoga looks to rouse kundalini and draw it up along the spine through the chakras into the crown chakra, or our higher self. *Chakra* is the Sanskrit term for "wheel or circle," and designates a physical center of consciousnesses that is often depicted as a lotus blossom. An ascending kundalini is thus equivalent to a step-by-step expansion in consciousness. The highest level is *samadhi*, the Sanskrit word for "total self-collection." *Samadhi* is a state of elevated focus in which the body encounters ultimate reality. Another method for awakening kundalini is uniting *prana*, the upward-flowing life force, with *apana*, the downward-flowing life force; this unity is experienced as a powerful warmth in the breast or belly. Kundalini energy bears similarities to the mystical image of a living or purifying fire; alchemical, transformative fire; as well as the all-encompassing fire energy that many traditions regard as the foundation for all therapeutic and spiritual change.

The Indian mystic Gopi Krishna popularized the notion of kundalini in the West through his arresting autobiography *Kundalini: The Evolutionary Energy in Man*. Krishna gives a stirring account of how he discovered Kundalini energy while meditating:

> During one such spell of intense concentration I suddenly felt a strange sensation below the base of the spine, at the place touching the seat, while I sat crosslegged on a folded blanket spread on the floor.... I recalled that I had read long ago in books on Yoga of a certain vital mechanism called Kundalini, connected with the lower end of the spine, which becomes active by means of certain exercises, and when once roused carries the limited human consciousness to transcendental heights, endowing the individual with incredible psychic and mental powers...It was stated that Kundalini represents the cosmic vital energy lying dormant in the human body which is coiled round the base of the spine a little below the sexual organ like a serpent, fast asleep and closing with her mouth the aperture of the *Sushumna*, the hair-like duct rising through the spinal cord to the conscious centre at the top of the head.[108]

108 Gopi Krishna, *Kundalini: The Evolutionary Energy in Man* (Ramadhar & Hopman, 1967).

The expansion in consciousness Gopi Krishna experienced through his kundalini awakening bears a fascinating similarity to the changes in consciousness brought on by psychedelics. As Krishna writes, "The only thing I was aware of was a progressively expanding field of consciousness and a slowly increasing brightness of the external and internal objects of perception, which in course of time brought the idea irresistibly home to me that though outwardly one with the restlessly active mass of humanity I was a different being inside, living in a lustrous world of brilliant colour of which others had no knowledge whatsoever."[109]

From a neurological perspective, kundalini might be understood as a force that helps us connect and integrate the evolutionarily diverse elements of our brain reward system: the instinctual, reptilian brain; the limbic system, which regulates our emotions; the goal-oriented dopamine system; and the higher rational and intuitive holistic centers of our conscious forebrain. Reconciling natural drives with higher motivations is the central aim of depth psychology. Jung, for example, regarded kundalini as the instinct toward self-realization. In this connection Gopi Krishna writes, "The whole science of Kundalini is fundamentally based on the assumption that it is possible for one to rouse to activity a mighty dormant power in the human body...the idea of stirring to activity a dormant vital force in the body, examined in the light of modern knowledge, can only signify the development or generation of a new type of vitality or life energy which clearly implies a recasting of the nervous system."[110]

I see the neuroplastic effects of psychedelics with a likely role to play in this transformation. Research in neuroscience has shown psychedelics to promote communication between regions of the brain that normally show little reciprocal influence, especially in area below the cortex. Communication increases between the basal ganglia, where older parts of the brain reward system are located, and higher cortical regions, the gray cerebral cortex of the limbic system, for example.[111] It is this sort of integration that presumably underlies the kundalini phenomenon.

Lora, a patient I treated with MDMA who had suffered sexual abuse during her childhood, was mired in drinking problems and eating binges.

109 Ibid.

110 Ibid.

111 Felix Müller, Patrick C. Dolder, André Schmidt, Matthias E. Liechti and Stefan Borgwardt, "Altered Network Hub Connectivity After Acute LSD Administration," *NeuroImage Clinical* 18 (January 1, 2018): 694–701.

She reported only being able to experience desire and pleasure orally or in her throat, leaving her mostly fascinated with things that entered through the mouth, whether it was prosecco or cheesecake. Her intellectual interests were equally limited to the same subject; she liked to read cookbooks, restaurant guides, and magazines about trends in wine culture. She was completely indifferent to psychology or spirituality; terms like *chakra* or *kundalini* meant nothing to her. Even her dreams revolved around food and drink—a Coca-Cola bottle that opened by itself, for instance. Under the influence of MDMA however, she saw that the gullet wasn't the only source of pleasant feelings. Rather, she experienced a sense of well-being throughout her entire body, and for a short while a feeling of warmth in her lower abdomen. This came accompanied by sexual feelings, erotic sounds—of kissing, for instance—or the feeling of being touched softly on the belly. The energy rose along her spine, spreading a feeling of warmth across her chest. As the feeling spread, a deep sense of empathy came over Lora for a friend who suffered from depression and drinking problems and had taken her own life. Tears trickled from between her closed eyes. The energy at last rose to her throat, and she felt a slight hunger. She removed a single strawberry from a bowl that I handed her and ate it slowly and attentively: She thought it was the best strawberry she had had in her life. A single strawberry left her so satisfied that she no longer felt hungry and lay back down. Next the heat rose to her head and she had a vision of lying in a tipi at night, looking at through a hole in the top at a sea of stars shining brilliantly and pulsating warmth. Her face and body were completely at ease.

Therapeutically, it was important for Lora to experience an expansion of physical desire and pleasure, in other words to expand her physical awareness. In doing so she had a direct experience of Epicurus's insight that healthy rewards must involve all or most parts of the body. The same applies for nonphysical gratification—receiving praise for an accomplishment for instance—which according to Epicurus always promote a feeling of overall physical well-being and prevent a sense of insatiability or addiction from arising. From a spiritual perspective, Lora's complex physical experience could be understood as ascending kundalini energy. Her erotic feelings were the activation of her root and sacral chakras, which lie close to the perineum and sex organ. The deep sympathy she felt for her deceased friend suggests an activation of the heart chakra, while her vision of warmly glowing stars suggests an activation of the chakra in the forehead, which Indian texts associate with visionary experiences and the notion of the third eye.

While Lora's erotic sensations were short-lived, it is possible for feelings like this take up a great deal of space. Nearly without fail, it is a kind of eroticism that does not entail a need for sexual intercourse or masturbation. This means that anxiety around sex or feelings of shame and guilt decrease without naked lust emerging, which is often a product of fear and tension. In its place a holistic erotic experience can take root. In the experience of Claudio Naranjo this experience is particularly frequent with ibogaine, a substance originally found in Africa and used as a stimulant and for its hallucinogenic effects. Naranjo describes one patient he treated with ibogaine for feeling sexual dissatisfaction. In the therapy session, and under the influence of ibogaine, she pictured having intercourse with her boyfriend. As a result, strong sexual energies spread throughout her body, before flowing out into the entire cosmos. She herself wrote about her experience:

> I saw how that energy that I had received from the earth through my vagina in the conscious sexual act could be physically pleasurable, but that it also transformed into more subtle energies. When it reached my heart, I sensed it fill me with a feeling of deep, immense, total love. Not only for my partner whom I was making love with, but for the whole world. As the energy kept going up to my head and beyond it, I felt like I was making love with God, with the whole. I could see that my partner was God, and myself at the same time. I understood spiritual ecstasy.[112]

It isn't uncommon for sexual feelings to transform into spiritual visions under the influence of psychedelics. As a neuroscientist, I account for this by the improved functional connection between sections of the brainstem guided by instinct and the higher, cortical layers in the brain reward system.

Integration of this sort is also an important concern in shamanism. Within shamanic healing traditions, journeys into the animal realm, or identifying with wild and fearsome animals, are intended to help better integrate vitality, spontaneity, and our instinctual nature. The Maya and Aztec cultures are both familiar with the god Quetzalcoatl, or "feathered serpent" in Nahuatl.

---

112 Naranjo, *My Psychedelic Explorations*.

Quetzalcoatl is a striking symbol for an integrated brain reward system that pairs the forms of a bird and serpent, or the buoyant mental and spiritual forces of a bird with the earthly, instinctual energy of a serpent. In psychedelic therapy, visions of snakes combined with feelings of buoyancy can indicate a process of integration. This is particularly common in connection with other medicinal plant mixtures from Mexico and Central America—ayahuasca. If one follows the *Rig Veda*, where medicinal plants are both older and closer to the source than the gods themselves, it is easy to imagine ayahuasca prompting or enabling visions of a shining plumed serpent.

Based on years of clinical experience, Claudio Naranjo proposed a scheme for classifying psychedelics according to how they activate chakras, with each substance working on a different chakra.[113] He paired ibogaine with the root and sacral chakras, ayahuasca with the navel chakra, MDMA with the heart chakra, psilocybin with the forehead chakra, and LSD with the crown chakra. I find the classifications intriguing from a clinical perspective since they may prove useful to evaluate in studies. Grouping and classifying psychedelic substances scientifically would doubtless help in applying them in a targeted manner to a patient's problems and preferences.

The kundalini phenomenon, which one might speak of just as easily in terms of expanding or transforming desire, helps people free themselves from addiction by transmuting short-term, immediate forms of arousal into more holistic, longer-term interests. Smaller-scale, provisional studies have already demonstrated the positive effects of psychedelics in treating addictive illnesses;[114] early leaders in psychedelic research even considered it to be their primary function. One of the co-founders of Alcoholics Anonymous, Bill Wilson, responded well to a round of LSD therapy himself. He described the positivity effects he encountered in a letter to the philosopher Gerald Heard: "I am certain that the LSD experience has helped me very much. I find myself with a heightened color perception and an appreciation of beauty almost destroyed by my years of depression.... I do feel a residue

---

113 Ibid.

114 Collin Reiff, Elon E. Richman, Charles B. Nemeroff, Linda L. Carpenter, Alik S. Widge, Carolyn I. Rodriguez et al., "Psychedelics and Psychedelic-Assisted Psychotherapy," *The American Journal of Psychiatry* 177, no. 5 (May 1, 2020): 391–410.

of assurance and a feeling of enhanced beauty that seems likely to stay by me."[115]

Confidence, motivation, and esteem are typical of this effect. Unfortunately, the ban on psychedelics in the US in Wilson's era made studies with larger sample sizes impossible.

US psychedelic pioneer James Fadiman observed in studies of his own that regular consumption of psychedelics in low doses (10 to 20 micrograms of LSD instead of the 100–200 micrograms usually administered in therapy sessions) promotes positivity.[116] The author Ayelet Waldman joined one of Fadiman's studies, later writing about her experience with microdosing in her book *A Really Good Day*:

> This morning I took LSD.
>
> The table I'm sitting at right now is not breathing. My keyboard is not exploding in psychedelic fireworks, lightning bolts shooting from the letters "R" and "P." I am not giddy and frantic, or zoned out with bliss. I feel no transcendent sense of oneness with the universe or with the divine. On the contrary. I feel normal.
>
> Well, except for one thing: I'm content and relaxed. I'm busy, but not stressed. That might be normal for some people, but it isn't for me . . .
>
> The individuals whose reports Fadiman presented in his book experienced "joy and gratitude," increased focus, better mood. I wanted that. They reported rarely losing their tempers, becoming more fun to be with. I really wanted that. They experienced that most seductive and elusive thing: a really good day.[117]

The book gives a striking account of psychedelics' positivity effects, illustrating that they are still possible at a dosage where no other psychedelic effects occur (such as changes in perception, an altered sense of time, or an altered experience of oneself). Studies that used a placebo for comparison's

---

115 Don Lattin, *Distilled Spirits: Getting High, then Sober, with a Famous Writer, a Forgotten Philosopher, and a Hopeless Drunk* (University of California Berkeley, 2012), 193.

116 James Fadiman, *The Psychedelic Explorer's Guide: Safe, Therapeutic, and Sacred Journeys* (Park Street Press, 2011).

117 Ayelet Waldman, *A Really Good Day: How Microdosing Made a Mega Difference in My Mood, My Marriage, and My Life* (Anchor Books, 2018).

sake are still yet to show microdosing as having any clinically significant effect, though this may have to do with the fact that positivity wasn't specifically tested for, or the placebo effect was especially strong. Even as a medication in name only, placebos are still capable of prompting positive expectations and increasing positivity.

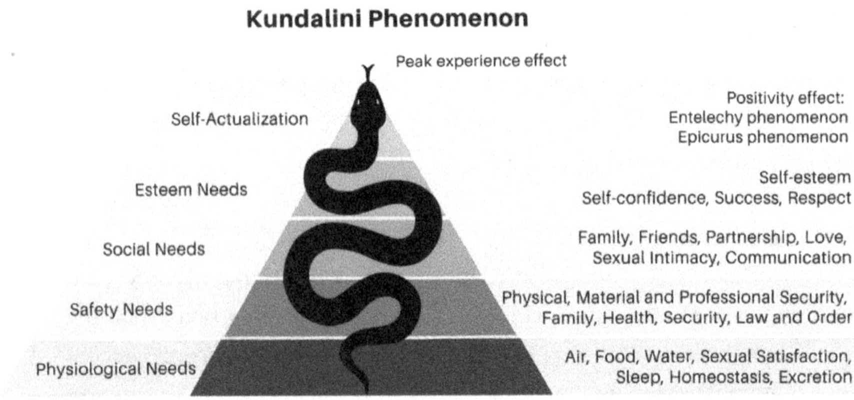

Kundalini phenomenon and peak experience effects related to the Maslow pyramid

Peak Experiences

US psychologist Abraham Maslow saw needs and rewards as an essential lens through which to perceive human well-being. His famous diagram reflects the insight that our needs are arranged hierarchically—at the lowest, or most basic level are physical needs for breathing, sustenance, sleep, and vitamins. One level up is our need for safety as it relates to the body, family, and place of work. Next come our social needs like connection, love, and sexuality. The following level concerns individual needs—our desire for freedom, independence, and esteem. The top of the pyramid is self-realization, exhausting one's potential or finding one's purpose, which Maslow also termed "entelechy." Maslow's hierarchy of needs are easily put into dialogue with the chakras in Indian thought: Our need for safety corresponds to the root chakra; connection and sexuality are linked to the sacral and navel chakras; love and self-worth with the heart chakra; and self-realization with the chakras at the throat and forehead.

Maslow recognized that if we are unable to satisfy our needs at one level, our motivations remain stuck there as a potential source of psychological disruption. A child who never feels loved, for example, will find love a struggle throughout life. In general, a brain reward system that has gotten stuck or remains fixated at a particular level of need is a frequent cause of psychological issues. It isn't uncommon as a therapist to encounter a patient who was disregarded or neglected during childhood now posting dozens of selfies daily in order to gain recognition, since their needs have remained stuck at a childhood level. It is just as common to find in the prehistory of patients with a sweet tooth that their parents pacified them with sweets instead of love and affection early on, leading to a physiological fixation. The neuroplastic effects of psychedelics can help loosen fixations of this sort in the brain reward system. Together with the epicurean phenomenon, this might help change a patient's expectations of his or her environment—the expectation that only food will pacify, for example. The entelechy phenomenon can further help patients attain the level of self-realization in Maslow's schema, while the kundalini phenomenon makes the various levels of the pyramid more permeable, allowing greater integration between lower and higher levels.

Maslow further recognized that satisfying one's needs was a never-ending process even for psychologically healthy people, since satisfaction at one level prompted other higher needs to emerge. The minute our hunger is stilled, we will long for love—once we are loved, we will strive for higher social status, and so on. Within the chain of development our needs are always defined by a lack—what we don't have.

This insight made Maslow curious about people who were happy but weren't driven by needs or states of deficiency—those on a spiritual path, for instance. He observed in them that achieving certain altered states of consciousness marked by intense joy, flow states, feelings of ecstasy, or euphoria helped them to find a way out of the dynamic established by the hierarchy of needs. He termed these states "peak experiences," describing them as "rare, exciting, oceanic, deeply moving, exhilarating, elevating experiences that generate an advanced form of perceiving reality, and are even mystic and magical in their effect upon the experimenter."[118] Maslow believed that every person was capable of peak experiences in principle, and that under the right circumstances, psychedelics such as LSD or psilocybin could elicit peak experiences in certain people.[119]

Peak experiences have specific characteristics, which I describe below. Each aspect is perceived as part of a unified experience, bringing an overall sense of vitality, prosperity, and wholeness. Peak experiences may involve simple activities or intense, complex events—it isn't the "what" of the experience that matters so much as the feeling of bliss it elicits.

Maslow determined that intensely positive experiences of this nature have the potential to shift our values, creating needs that transcend those of his original pyramid that were all defined by their absence. He termed this new category "being needs" or "being values," including states connected with higher forms of well-being and fulfillment such as truth, goodness, wholeness, fairness, playfulness, and self-sufficiency.

Peak experiences can alter our values, Maslow argued, by leading us to revise our attitudes and help us to see things from a new perspective and different center point. From a neurological point of view, peak experiences present a window of opportunity in which our brain reward systems are extremely neuroplastic and capable of operating at a higher level. Childhood and adolescence are critical phases in the development of our social reward system, for example, periods in which any number of things can go awry that are quite difficult to correct later in life. I've already discussed a lack of recognition from one's parents, or receiving food instead of love as possible risk factors. An especially large body of research exists on people who have been subjected to extreme and prolonged bullying as adolescents; the experience leaves them at a heightened risk of social withdrawal and depression for the rest of their lives. Animals experience these same critical phases of development. The social brain of mice is at its most open and sensitive when they are young; social isolation during this period leads to enduring anxiety and social withdrawal. In a groundbreaking article published in 2019 in *Nature* magazine, the US neuroscientist Gül Dölen and her team were able to show that a single dose of MDMA was enough to make the brain reward system in a grown mouse as flexible and neuroplastic as that of

---

118 Raymond Corsini and Alan Auerbach, eds., *Concise Encyclopedia of Psychology* (J. Wiley, 1998).

119 Abraham Maslow, *Religions, Values, and Peak Experiences* (Penguin Books, 1978).

a young mouse.[120] This in turn made it possible to reprogram impairments to the brain reward system through positive social experiences in a way that made social behavioral disorders disappear.

Maslow stressed that peak experiences brought on by psychedelics hold the same value as those prompted by other sources like meditation, a peak athletic performance, or an overpowering musical experience. He was convinced that psychedelics allow us to guide peak experiences to a certain extent, so that we don't have to wait for them to come along by chance.

Psychedelic experience can share the following characteristics with peak experience:

- Intense feelings of positivity, enthusiasm, ecstasy, and bliss.
- Perception grows more receptive and is less prejudiced than normal.
- An altered sense of time, instilling a sense of universality and unity.
- Everything is fully accepted as it is.
- Fears and worries fade away or dissolve.
- Tension and conflicts in life tend to be transcended or resolved.
- Emotions like astonishment, reverence, admiration, humility, and devotion increase.
- A feeling of physical warmth arises, tied to a pleasant sensation of vibrations radiating out from the center of the body into the limbs.
- Perception is relatively self-forgetful and selfless.
- One does not strive for anything, wishes nothing, needs nothing.
- Peak experiences give life itself a meaning; they show that life is worth living. In this way they can prevent suicide.
- Peak experiences are perceived as an end in themselves rather than a means to an end.
- Peak experience can lead to an acceptance of death.

It is easy to spot the common ground that peak experience shares with the psychedelic effects I have discussed so far. The mindfulness effect for example, which opens us to direct perception and acceptance; the archetype

---

120 Romain Nardou, Eastman M. Lewis, Rebecca Rothhaas, Ran Xo, Aimei Yang, Edward Boyden et al., "Oxytocin-Dependent Reopening of a Social Reward Learning Critical Period with MDMA," *Nature (London)* 569, no. 7754 (April 3, 2019): 116–20.

effect, which generates feelings of unity and universality; the kundalini phenomenon, which creates feelings of warmth; or the entelechy phenomenon, which calls attention to the intrinsic value of lived experience. I discuss the aspect of self-dissolution in greater detail in chapter 6. Intensely positive feelings such as bliss, which are totally unrelated to desire since they don't aim at a specific reward, are relatively specific to peak experiences. Peak experiences also differ from more straightforward experiences of positivity in their temporal structure, culminating in a high point of pitched intensity.

Maslow's interest in peak experience was preceded by that of the influential psychologist William James, who called them "mystical experiences." James recognized moments of intense bliss or love of the world as an important source for values to develop. In the same way that a person's love elevates the perceived value of the beloved, mystical states of love or trust can elevate the perceived value of the entire world. Just as love casts the beloved in an entirely new light, the entire world appears in a new light for the mystical lover. This love grants access to compassionate or altruistic values, and which overflow the boundaries of egotistical desires or mere prudent morality. The "mystical experience" makes the world a more lovable place, and at the same time reinforces our trust in our own ability to love. James suffered from severe depression and derived his theory of value from his experience with laughing gas, a substance that acts like a psychedelic and helped free him from his depression to gain a new experience of positive values. Values, in the way James understood them, can be rediscovered or developed. Patients will often discover previously buried values in the course of psychedelic therapy; as Nietzsche wrote in *Thus Spoke Zarathustra*, "For all his possessions are well concealed from the possessor; and of all treasure pits, one's own is the last to be digged...man is difficult to discover, most of all to himself." Peak experiences can help us discover the treasures that lie buried within ourselves.

Blissful states are not unique to Christian mysticism; they occupy an important role in many spiritual traditions. Shamanic ecstasy shows close parallels to the concept of peak experiences, for example, and may include flights of the soul beyond the earthly home of one's physical body out into the broader cosmos, leaving limited, conditioned existence to enter total freedom.

Peak experiences also played a central role in the life of the Buddha. The Buddha's spiritual path began with a crisis in values and rewards. Though he came from a good, prosperous family, he was plagued early on by dissatisfaction with normal life. He sensed that the love of his father, mother, and friends wouldn't provide an eternal source of happiness or satisfaction. At the same time, he began to doubt in the effectiveness of ablutions, Brahmanic sacrifices and appeals to the gods, even coming to doubt in the Vedic gods themselves. Had these gods really been the ones to create the world? The Buddha's doubts led him to found a new teaching in which the traditional rewards (Vedic sacrifices, for example) were irrelevant. The new path consisted of looking within by means of meditation to discern the true nature of mind. In doing so, the Buddha had to overcome five obstacles, or hindrances: desire, aversion, sloth and torpor, restlessness and fear, and doubt, all expressions of our archaic brain reward system. The Buddha realized that a mind disturbed by these forces would never achieve clarity or peace. By concentrating and remaining collected, the Buddha succeeded in achieving a peace that was neither disturbed by inner needs or external influences. The state recalls the effects of the entelechy phenomenon or Epicurus's notion of "ataraxia" (a state of serenity), bringing on intense forms of joy that are in turn comparable to peak experiences.

The Buddha identified five levels of rapture, which he called *pīti*:

- Slight joy: "Raises the hairs of the body"
- Momentary joy: "Comes like repeated flashes of lightning"
- Descending joy: "Washes over the body again and again and then subsides"
- Transporting joy: "Has the power to lift the body into the air"
- Suffusing joy: "Pervades the whole body touching every part and is likened to water flooding into a rock cave."[121]

For the Buddha, this intense form of rapture was a part of waking up, which among other things can be seen as a radical revaluation of values and perspectives. Similar states frequently appear under the influence of psychedelics.

The *Rig Veda* credits the psychedelic substance soma with giving birth to joy and bringing people to a place where there is an abundance of joys. Among its creative and ecstatic effects, it is described as:

- the semen of the stallion bursting with seed
- thought fertilizer

121 Rupert Gethin, *The Foundations of Buddhism* (Oxford University Press, 1998).

- smashing asunder obstacles to progress
- making wide spaces
- a bringer of abundance
- the cosmic power of fertility
- drilling wellsprings and setting the waters to flow[122]

In the *Rig Veda*, soma is described as a fertilizer—not in the agricultural sense, but as a form of cosmic nourishment that animates the world. It is what makes plants grow, poetry flow, and life itself flourish. During Vedic rituals, soma juice was poured and consumed, its flowing motion symbolically linked to rain and seminal fluid—both ancient emblems of fertility and renewal. These layered descriptions highlight soma's power not merely to enhance joy or vitality, but to awaken new forms of joy, creativity, and insight. In a modern register, soma can be seen as supporting neuroplasticity in the brain's reward system, fostering openness, renewal, and transformation.

I had my own experience of intense joy and love while on MDMA under the guidance of Swiss psychiatrist Peter Oehen. Before the psychedelic took hold, Peter guided me into a mindful meditative state with a body scan, a tried-and-true mindfulness practice. My mind felt quite open as I tried to stay focused on my breath and surrounding environment without judging them. It was a September morning, and I lay on my back in a large, beautiful room with tall ceilings. It smelled like fall, and a soft light drifted through the window into the room. Only as the MDMA gradually took hold did I realize how I was controlling my perception through judgements. *It smells good,* I thought. *It's a nice temperature. The blanket has a pretty white-yellow color. Peter is a good companion. I feel a little unwell, but it's not a bad thing*. I became aware of these automatic judgements because the MDMA was making it more and more difficult for me to maintain them; in the end I gave up, exhausted by the effort. My sense that the MDMA was peeling away my judgements prompted some fear but also relaxed me physically, something I especially felt in the neck. My head sank lower in the pillow.

Freed now from any sort of judgement, the floodgates to an enormous reservoir suddenly opened and a warm wave of an exceptional joy flooded me from head to toe. I melted like snow in the rush of feeling. Peter noticed

122 Doniger, *The Rig Veda*; Jamison and Brereton, *The Rigveda: The Earliest Religious Poetry of India*; Olivelle, *The Early Upanishads*.

that I had entered a different, overpowering state and placed his hand on my chest. "Keep your breath calm and focus on the area around your heart," he advised. Following the initial surge, my thoughts returned. The final words of Jesus crossed my mind: "It is accomplished." Had he been referring to a passage from the judging, condemning world to the realm of unconditional love? In my relaxed state, it further occurred to me that envy made no sense whatsoever. Why should another's happiness lessen my own? There was such an excess of happiness that there simply couldn't be any issues with its distribution. There was so much happiness, in fact, that I could scarcely cope with it as an individual; I could only be happy if others were able to share in it. The Christian principle of abundance came to mind; Jesus had said: "I came that they may have life, and have it in abundance."[123] The principle seemed to cast all the other Christian teachings—which in a sober state came across as somewhat exaggerated and irrational—in a fully logical, rational light. In the presence of such abundance, this flood of love, not loving one's enemies or only loving those who loved you became an absurd act of miserliness.

Later I recalled a poem I had encountered as a teenager, which at the time had struck me as overly meek and pious: "Lord! send what Thou wilt / Pleasure or pain / I am content that both / Flow from Thy hands."[124] Now, however, the poem made complete sense. The principle of abundance turned everything into a reward, a source of joy and happiness. I felt certain that the person I was in this state stood much closer to Jesus and Buddha than the one from several hours before, the man worried about starting and ending his MDMA trial punctually so he still might answer all the emails he had received that same day.

I don't mean to argue that my experience with MDMA made a better person of me, but it did let me understand the kinds of experiences and perspectives that lead one to generosity, altruism, and a higher life. It also gave me a direct bodily experience of how the brain reward system counteracts the stress system. In a state of abundance, any difficulty, illness, or unwelcome twist of fate is taken as a source of enrichment and elicits deep gratitude instead of a stress reaction. Finally, I understood how even given their tendency to expand our horizons and soften our hearts, to dissolve the self or let things fall, arise, or melt away—all of which are associated with

123 John 10:10.

124 Edward Mörike, "Prayer."

insecurity and a loss of control—psychedelics do not provoke psychotic fear but joy and a deep sense of peace instead. It is much the same as when the aching feet, swollen limbs, or frozen fingers of a mountain climb give way to bliss once the peak has been attained.

Peak experiences are not a common event in psychotherapy; multiple sessions are often required for such an experience to surface. Nor are they always as overwhelming as the one I myself had. One patient described a long-lasting peak experience she had—Maslow describes them as "plateau experiences"—as follows: "I saw my situation very clearly during my LSD session, my loneliness, the disappointments in my private life, the rejection and conflict at work, the meaningless disputes with my father. Yet all these experiences and insights were somehow filled with a loving and peaceful feeling. I didn't have any negative feelings like hatred, rage, fear, annoyance—nothing like that. If I really think about it, I was grateful for my life for the first time."

The deep sense of joy psychedelics instill can be seen as a sort of "post-traumatic stress effect in reverse," where a positive experience brings lasting positive change and sense of well-being.

Summary

Depression, like many other psychological disorders, is often accompanied by deadened emotions and an inability to sense the beauty in life. Unfortunately, conventional psychotropic drugs cannot restore this sensitivity and may often even exacerbate emotional numbness. Psychedelics, by contrast, possess a unique ability to make our brain reward systems more sensitive. The resulting positivity effect increases the interest, joy, gratitude, hope, and love we feel, expanding our consciousness and capacity for action in the process. Aspects of the positivity effect include finding joy in small, daily things (the epicurean phenomenon), the unconditional joy we feel in doing something we like to do (the entelechy phenomenon), and heightened psychological-physical energy (the kundalini phenomenon). Psychedelic peak experiences, meanwhile, describe states of ecstasy that can help individuals to become conscious of their deepest values and attitudes, and integrate those values in their lives.

Chapter 4
Right Meaning: The Path to a Purposeful Life

The importance of Michael Pollan's 2018 book *How to Change Your Mind* for the psychedelic renaissance can hardly be understated. A bestseller in the US, the book rescued psychedelics from the mire of hippie culture and military interrogation techniques by providing a clear and accessible summary of what we know of their history, pharmacology, safety, and therapeutic potential. It is interesting to note in this regard that Pollan drew inspiration for his audacious book from a scientific article published in 2006 by US psychopharmacologist Roland Griffiths, entitled "Psilocybin can occasion mystical-type experiences having substantial and sustained personal meaning and spiritual significance."[125] "What was most remarkable about the results reported in the article," Pollan writes,

> is that participants ranked their psilocybin experience as one of the most meaningful in their lives, comparable "to the birth of a first child or death of a parent." Two-thirds of the participants rated the session among the top five "most spiritually significant experiences" of their lives; one-third ranked it *the* most significant such experience in their lives. Fourteen months later, these ratings had slipped only slightly. The volunteers reported significant improvements in their "personal well-being, life satisfaction and positive behavior change," changes that were confirmed by their family members and friends.[126]

---

125 Roland R. Griffiths, W. A. Richards, U. McCann, and R. Jesse, "Psilocybin can occasion mystical-type experiences having substantial and sustained personal meaning and spiritual significance," *Psychopharmacology/Psychopharmacologia* 187, no. 3 (July 7, 2006): 268–83.

126 Pollan, *How to Change Your Mind.*

These are astonishing results, and they tally with earlier findings. In a survey taken of people who had consumed LSD in a therapeutic setting, 72 percent responded to the question "Have you noticed a change in the significance of things or events" with "Yes, very clearly." Sixty-two percent responded similarly to the question: "Did you feel part of a larger unity?"

Aldous Huxley similarly called attention to a heightened experience of meaning while on mescaline in *The Doors of Perception*, describing how he found his own breath reflected back in the breathing of the environment, leading toward "deeper to ever deeper meaning."[127] As the US Zen instructor Sean Murphy recalled in an interview about psychedelics and Buddhism, "Basically what I saw was that the world was incredible, deeply significant; that reality was amazing. Deeply significant, deeply meaningful, it deeply mattered, it was all unified. That's what drugs showed me."[128]

Meaning and Psychotherapy

These findings are significant within the context of psychotherapy. Feelings of significance, meaning, and connection have steadily declined in the West, weakening resilience and exacerbating the risk of psychiatric problems in the process. One survey conducted of 140,000 people from 132 countries showed, as expected, that people in wealthy countries like Denmark demonstrated greater satisfaction with their lives than people in Africa or South America.[129] Yet when it came to leading a meaningful life, the results were reversed. People in Spain, France, and Austria experienced significantly less meaning in life than people in Senegal, Togo, or Ecuador. Further analysis showed that people who lack meaning in their lives commit suicide much more frequently than people who felt they were leading a meaningful life. No such connection was found, by contrast, between feeling satisfied with life and the rate of suicide. This explains why suicide is a relatively common occurrence in Western countries, and underscores

127 Huxley, *The Doors of Perception*.

128 Douglas Osto, *Altered States: Buddhism and Psychedelic Spirituality in America* (Columbia University Press, 2016).

129 Shigehiro Oishi and Ed Diener, "Residents of Poor Nations Have a Greater Sense of Meaning in Life Than Residents of Wealthy Nations," *Psychological Science* 25, no. 2 (December 13, 2013): 422–30.

the psychological importance of building the capacity to imbue life with meaning.

Nietzsche captured the importance of meaning for the psyche in memorable terms, writing that "he who has a why to live for can bear almost any how."[130] In his book *Man and His Symbols*, Carl Jung wrote that a person "can stand the most incredible hardships when he is convinced that they make sense."[131] Based on his experiences as a psychiatrist and Holocaust survivor, Viktor Frankl developed a form of psychotherapy he called "logotherapy," which taken literally means "healing through meaning." Frankl wrote:

> According to logotherapy, this striving to find a meaning in one's life is the primary motivational force in man. That is why I speak of a will to meaning in contrast to the pleasure principle (or, as we could also term it, the will to pleasure) on which Freudian psychoanalysis is centered, as well as in contrast to the will to power on which Adlerian psychology, using the term "striving for superiority," is focused.[132]

Frankl maintained that people were capable of finding meaning even in hopeless situations or life-threatening crises, a capacity he termed "tragic optimism." Tragic optimism speaks to our potential as humans to transform our suffering into a source of accomplishment, and feelings of guilt into meaningful action. "We must never forget," he continued, "that we may also find meaning in life even when confronted with a hopeless situation.... When we are no longer able to change a situation—just think of an incurable disease such as inoperable cancer—we are challenged to change ourselves."[133] According to Frankl we are not born with an innate sense of meaning; rather, we must locate one in the concrete experiences of daily life, investing whatever space we have happened to wind up in with meaning. Therefore, finding meaning in things isn't dependent on external circumstance alone, but also on our ability to notice our experiences and imbue them with significance.

---

130 Friedrich Nietzsche, *Twilight of Idols and Anti-Christ* (Penguin UK, 1990), p. 42.

131 Carl G. Jung and Marie-Luise Von Franz, *Man and His Symbols* (Doubleday, 1988), p. 311.

132 Viktor Frankl, *Man's Search for Meaning* (Washington Square Press, 1985), p.98.

133 Ibid., p. 111

Our experience of meaning is linked to our sense of time. Higher realms of meaning are often associated with larger windows of time; we hold eternal truths to be especially meaningful, for example.[134] Religions typically operate against a vast temporal horizon that allows them to attach great value to everyday acts, like a single gesture of generosity toward a stranger. Setting events within a large, even eternal temporal context lends them a purposeful, and thus meaningful, role within the greater whole. By contrast, a life led day-to-day without a greater awareness of time's arc is often perceived as lacking meaning.

This is where psychedelics enter the picture, granting us a heightened experience of meaning by weakening our short-term linear-causal thinking and letting us recognize larger temporal cycles. This awareness does not remain solely captive in the present-moment psychedelic experience; the intellectual and emotional associations that arise within an expanded sense of time continue to reverberate after the trip. Neurologically, this is because the brain regions that respond most readily to psychedelics have the longest and slowest connections to other regions in the brain, and thus process information dealing with larger stretches of time.[135] The neuroplastic effects of psychedelic substances mean that these longer connections can establish themselves permanently, linking seemingly meaningless events in a larger, unifying temporal context.

Yet meaning is not only bound up in temporality; it also depends on social factors and the actual content of our experience. We can picture meaning as a web of ideas and relationships. Emotions that exist outside the web would be nothing more than pleasant or unpleasant experiences of physical stimulation. For many people, engaging with art, literature, nature, spirituality, or community generates meaning by setting their social, emotional, and intellectual worlds in dialogue; experiences are placed in a meaningful context through a certain lens. By calling forth alternative states of consciousness, psychedelics can alter the normal pathways along which information flows, leading to new associations between thoughts and lived experiences. A shift in perspective provides a new angle from which to view possible connections.

---

134 Roy F. Baumeister, *Meanings of Life* (Guildford Press, 1991).

135 Rita Kočárová, Jiří Horáček, and Robin Carhart-Harris, "Does Psychedelic Therapy Have a Transdiagnostic Action and Prophylactic Potential?," *Frontiers in Psychiatry* 12 (July 19, 2021)

This explains in part why creative people have taken psychedelics as a way of finding new solutions. Steve Jobs, the founder of Apple, and Doug Engelbart, the inventor of the computer mouse, hypertext, and networked computers both report that psychedelics gave them important insights in their work. Psychedelics also helped the Beatles continue to develop and incorporate different traditions and styles into their music. Their album *Revolver*, for example, is a direct result of their experiences on LSD, especially the song "Tomorrow Never Knows," which combines classical avant-garde composition, electro-acoustic sound manipulation, and traditional Indian music. LSD has also played an important role in scientific discoveries. Francis Crick, the Nobel Prize laureate and founder of modern genetics, discovered the double helix structure of DNA under the influence of LSD. This is especially fascinating because the underlying data did not originate in Crick's laboratory but with other research groups. Crick's genius "merely" consisted in giving a new interpretation to existing data—he combined it anew. In other words, he gave it a different, higher meaning, a process in which LSD seems to have aided.

Meaning and Self-Understanding

Aside from helping us better understand the world, a proper sense of meaning can also help us better understand ourselves. Making sense and finding connections within our own life stories, needs, feelings, and thoughts makes it easier to make the right decisions, act with purpose, and handle our emotions. Developing an internal sense of meaning also confers a sense of self-assurance and confidence; thus, developing internal meaning is a central task in clarification-oriented psychotherapy like psychoanalysis or psychodynamic treatment. Finally, a sense of meaning helps us to understand our relationship to the world, i.e., the relationship between inside and outside. Under certain circumstances we may feel we have transcended ourselves, that our "small ego" has dissolved into a greater whole, or that we have achieved a sense of unity with the universe. All of these are typical of psychedelic experience which, as Griffiths' studies show, strengthen our capacity for assigning meaning in a way that allows it to devolve not simply at the personal level, but the transpersonal level as well.

Meaning is not simply something that is recognized; it can also be actively created. Italian astronomer Galileo Galilei named the small dots he spotted with his telescope near Jupiter "moons," a revolutionary act, since previously the term "moon" hadn't been an astronomical concept but referred exclusively to our own moon. Galilei's creative act of reinterpreting the term may have made us feel smaller, but it also gave us a stronger connection to the cosmos. In the end, the act contained the tremendous realization that other solar and planetary systems similar to our own existed—the vantage point from which humans regarded the universe shifted. Psychedelics help people to perceive these sorts of analogies and similarities, leading to a feeling of connection with the wider world and even the cosmos.

The feeling of connection plays an important role in meaning. Ancient Indians developed a series of symbols under the influence of psychedelics that retain tremendous integrative force to this day. The *Rig Veda*, for example, likens the effects of soma to a wheel spinning quickly without growing hot. In subsequent Vedas, the wheel became an important symbol linking human life to the order of the cosmos, among other reasons because the stars spin in the heavens as if on a wheel. The Buddha adopted this symbol while giving it new meaning: The Buddhist terms *dukkha* (pain, suffering) and *sukha* (happiness) can be traced back to the image of a wheel that has been improperly or properly placed on a wagon axle, respectively. Jung, for his part, interpreted the wheel as an archetype of the self. Also related is *mandala*, the Sanskrit term for circle. In recent times, the English word *hub* has acquired a host of new technical meanings: In aviation a "flight hub" designates an airport connecting short- and long-distance flights, while in computer science a hub is an important node within a network. The popularity of this psychedelic symbol from the *Rig Veda* comes as little surprise, serving as an archetypal image for connection, integration, meaning, and life itself.

Meaning and Resilience

In clinical psychology, the ability to detect and create meaning is often dubbed a "sense of coherence." The phrase comes from the Israeli-US stress researcher Aaron Antonovsky, and contains three aspects:

Comprehensibility, or the degree to which life events make sense and are understandable.

Meaningfulness, or the extent to which people feel that life has emotional meaning.

Manageability, or the extent to which people perceive that they have sufficient available (internal and external) resources to satisfy their needs.

People with a strong sense of coherence suffer less frequently from stress-related illnesses like burnout or PTSD and are in a better position to handle severe physical illness.[136] Psychedelics can improve the first two aspects of our sense of coherence directly (comprehensibility and meaningfulness); the third they strengthen indirectly by improving self-awareness and a personal sense of coherence. Our sense of coherence becomes especially weak when we experience a crisis in meaning. It is little wonder, then, that psychotherapy supported by psychedelics has proven especially effective in these cases—a younger patient suffering from an aggressive form of cancer, for instance. "Why me?" many of these patients ask themselves. "Why should I be the one to have this illness? Did I do something wrong? What meaning does my life have if I have to say good-bye to my family and all my unrealized projects and plans?" Crises like these come with a heightened risk of suicide and "hasty death" when potentially effective therapies aren't taken into consideration.

Up to 90 percent of cancer patients report existential and spiritual subjects as being very important to them during therapy, with an improved sense of spiritual well-being contributing significantly to their general well-being.[137] Psilocybin has proven capable of improving the process of end-of-life care; according to multiple placebo-controlled studies, a single

---

136 Monica Eriksson and Bengt Lindström, "Validity of Antonovsky's Sense of Coherence Scale: A Systematic Review," *Journal of Epidemiology and Community Health* 59, no. 6 (June 1, 2005): 460–66.

137 Michael P. Bogenschutz and Stephen Ross, "Therapeutic Applications of Classic Hallucinogens," in *Current Topics in Behavioral Neurosciences* (2016): 361–91.

dose can significantly reduce fear of death and depressive feelings.[138] The effects endured for 80 percent of patients, instilling a greater sense of well-being and optimism. There were various psychological mechanisms at work in the way patients changed; some left with a stronger sense of faith that their consciousness existed as part of a larger consciousness that wouldn't vanish upon death, while others began to see death not as an irreversible disaster but an opportunity for their consciousness to expand. During his last moments on earth, Aldous Huxley had his wife inject him with 100 micrograms of LSD in order to broaden his consciousness in what she described as the "most serene, the most beautiful death."[139]

Patients suffering from depression are especially prone to crises of meaning. These often emerge in connection with anhedonia, as discussed in the previous chapter, though they can also arise independently. One patient I treated for depression underwent treatment with LSD as a way of rekindling meaning in her life, largely seeking it in terms of concrete information: whether she should pursue further professional training, for example, or take a trip around the world. She had previously given a great deal of thought to her purpose in life and made several changes to experience a greater sense of meaning. Two hours after taking the LSD, she reported that her questions about meaning had vanished completely, and with them her depression. In fact, she gave a cheerful, upbeat impression: "I don't experience any special sort of meaning," she said. "My life makes sense if I look at it that way, which means searching for meaning is no longer necessary. Before meaning was something abstract to me; I imagined that others had already found a purpose at some point or another. But now I see that meaning is a gift you receive, and that answers all your questions at once."

The example illustrates how a deficit of meaning can be the driving force behind a depressive disorder. It shows too that with a certain degree of connectivity and interchange, the brain is capable of recognizing meaning even without having to pursue especially meaningful activities. This heightened perception of and sensitivity to meaning likely owes to the way

---

138 Roland R. Griffiths, Matthew W. Johnson, Michael A. Carducci, Annie Umbricht, William A. Richards, Brian D. Richards et al., "Psilocybin Produces Substantial and Sustained Decreases in Depression and Anxiety in Patients With Life-Threatening Cancer: A Randomized Double-Blind Trial," *Journal of Psychopharmacology* 30, no. 12 (November 30, 2016): 1181–97.

139 Shaun Usher, ed., *Letters of Note: Correspondence Deserving of a Wider Audience* (Canongate, 2021): 180.

psychedelics promote neural connectivity and neuroplasticity. After the treatment feelings of meaninglessness did return in part for the patient, but the experience had demonstrated to her that the exhausting search for meaning wasn't the only possible solution to the problem—and that meaning can also be a state of mind. LSD showed her that we must first be able to experience meaning before we seek it out.

Psychedelics will often lend greater significance to certain things even among patients who aren't in the throes of crisis. I find music to be an especially fascinating case, something that is given a higher meaning in every culture. I have had any number of patients tell me during their preparatory sessions that certain styles of music mean nothing to them and are therefore unpalatable. Even so, I will often play such "meaningless" music, at least for a short while, knowing that psychedelics alter our perception of music. During one psilocybin session a patient who typically felt nothing from Bach's compositions suddenly found herself thrilled by them; it was all she wanted to listen to. This proved an important experience for her since her father loved listening to and playing Bach on the piano. The experience helped her better understand her father, and subsequently to reestablish contact with him. Music sung in a language the patient doesn't understand has also been useful in elevating the depth of their experience, as the specific meaning of the lyrics remains open. One track that is especially well-loved among my patients is "Ipmilin hálešteapmi" sung by Mari Boine, a Sami woman from Norway.

A crisis or deficit of meaning will often take the form of boredom. Workplace stress regularly turns out to be a case of insufficient challenge, imprisonment in meaningless inactivity, or monotony. Answering fifty emails a day mostly becomes stressful when those emails contain boring subjects or trivial requests; if emails from Rihanna, Roger Federer, or Angela Merkel were landing in our inboxes, the burden would not weigh as heavily. Psychologically speaking, many burnouts are really bore-outs in disguise. Boredom is a widespread problem in individualistic societies that lack any sort of cultural or spiritual center of gravity, with only a personal or individual sense of meaning remaining. This means that the minute we cease to actively pursue our own set of interests we lose any sense of meaning and grow bored. Boredom is significant in a clinical context because it comes with an increased risk of eating binges, overconsumption of television, aggression, and drug abuse.

The dangers of boredom are observable at the beginning of every psychedelic session. Once the patient has taken the psychedelic I bring them into the consultation room, where we wait for the effects to take hold. In the sessions leading up to treatment I always advise patients to bring some reading material in case they grow bored. I also stress that it can be worthwhile not to distract oneself during the initial period of waiting, but rather allow themselves to enter a meditative state, with my guidance, so as to consciously experience the onset of the psychedelics.

Existential philosophers like Søren Kierkegaard or Martin Heidegger spent a great deal of time thinking about boredom. Both viewed it as an opportunity since it confronted a person both with themselves and existential matters, i.e., the question of meaning. This is critical, since today our selves and our identities are among our core sources for meaning. In terms of existential philosophy, we might call the expectant, often-bored state of consciousness that precedes psychedelic effects a "being-in-advance," with a new openness that reshapes one's sense of self as it unfolds. In this case it is the meaninglessness itself that becomes meaningful, as we come to understand ourselves differently through it. "I see things coming that are still meaningless, but which point toward meaning, which carry potential meanings," one patient reported as the LSD began to take effect.

One depressive patient who suffered from chronic boredom and routinely broke off psychotherapy for the same reason feared that the same would occur with psilocybin. That proved not to be the case, however: "The trip was really exciting. The colors and movements of the wall, the music, and my inner state all being related, that was really, really exciting." Here, too, it becomes clear that seeing the connections between internal and external states is a helpful method for circumventing boredom. The patient laughed out loud on multiple occasions throughout his session on psilocybin, something he found remarkable since he never laughed otherwise. It was a heartfelt laugh, bubbling up out of astonishment at all the meaning and connections he hadn't thought possible. This isn't at all rare with psychedelic therapy; one could even call it "the psychedelic laugh." In concert with my patients, I've been able to identify the following reasons for this sort of response:

Laughter is a sign of being overwhelmed in a positive sense, because no habitual or rehearsed behavior exists in response to the new sense of meaning.

Laughter is ironic and arises in response to a meeting point between different levels of meaning. "The self laughs about the small I," as Nietzsche described it.[140] In the words of one patient, "[I feel] that I am open, borderless, timeless, suspended, free, and at the same time I'm sitting here in your office. All I can do is laugh out loud at the contradiction."

Laughter is a response to fear. Fear is a natural reaction to new meanings, and to the mind and heart opening. Laughter is an opportunity to transform fear into courage.

Laughter is a sign of freedom or liberation. Psychedelics increase neuroplasticity, allowing nerve cells to form new connections and patients to experience new types of meaning, which may include a feeling of freedom.

Laughter may signal the distance a person has gained from him or herself. This type of laughter harkens back to the laughter of the gods as Homer describes it, who are free to laugh about themselves and the world. As one patient described it to me, "I see myself now from the outside, worrying about my appearance, my weight, about eating right, all these worries and awkward self-awareness, and all I can do is laugh. It's a liberating laugh, a good laugh."

Laughter can come in response to our consciousness expanding. The ways in which time and space can merge under psychedelics is quite funny or odd at times. "I can't say for sure whether it was yesterday or on the fifth floor," as German comedian Karl Valentin quips.[141] One of the *Rig Veda*'s authors makes light of his own experiences on

---

140 Nietzsche, *Thus Spoke Zarathustra*.

141 Karl Valentin, *War es Gestern, oder War's im 4. Stock: Sprachclownerien* (Piper, 1996).

> soma, writing: "One of my wings is in the sky; I have trailed the other on earth. Haven't I drunk Soma?"[142]

> Laughter is a way of responding to contradictions. In this sense, psychedelics' effects can operate like a joke that juxtaposes opposing, contradictory, or foreign elements, as with the comedian pair Laurel and Hardy. It also recalls Schopenhauer's observation that "humor arises when we suddenly notice the incongruity between a concept and a perception that are supposed to be of the same thing."[143] In this context, laughter represents the triumph of our actual perceptions over abstract thought, much like Immanuel Kant's theory that laughter arises from the sudden dissolution of an expectation.

> Laughter is a spiritual force, an indication of wisdom and harmony between oneself and the world. The Dalai Lama is quick to laugh.

It is a beautiful sight to behold severely ill people laughing heartily again after years without laughter. Viktor Frankl described humor as "another of the soul's weapons in the fight for self-preservation.... It is well known," he continued, "that humor, more than anything else in the human make-up, can afford an aloofness and an ability to rise above any situation, even if only for a few seconds."[144]

With certain psychological disturbances it is not too little but too much meaning that is the issue. The classic symptom is mania, which typically appears in schizophrenia and other psychotic illnesses. Mania consists of an unalterable conviction that is not shared by others and does not match reality. With physical mania, for instance, an itch might be a sign that the secret service is sending the patient electric stimulation. A patient suffering mania cannot separate themself from their beliefs or entertain any kind of psychedelic laughter about themself. The way psychedelics affect our sensory perceptions and sense of meaning can lead to manic experience only growing stronger, making them unsuitable for people with psychotic disorders. Even if a patient isn't psychotic themself but has blood relatives who are, they

---

142 Doniger, *The Rig Veda.*, p. 132

143 John Morreall, "The Philosophy of Humor" in *The Stanford Encyclopedia of Philosophy*, 2023.

144 Viktor Frankl, *Man's Search for Meaning* (Washington Square Press, 1985).

are still currently excluded from psychedelic studies and treatments based on the genetic risk that consumption will trigger psychosis. Time will tell whether these guidelines are appropriate, or over-restrictive.

This danger became apparent in the case of a patient I treated for PTSD. While on LSD he became paranoid and mistook my secretary for a work colleague he accused of torturing him systematically for years. At moments the patient grew so agitated that I had to restrain him. While the symptoms eventually subsided, the subsequent integration sessions and a series of conversations with relatives and other therapists confirmed my suspicions that the patient's trauma had more to do with his paranoia in processing stressful social interactions. We steered clear of any more LSD sessions after that.

The experience showed me that a fear of psychedelics triggering psychotic states isn't pulled from thin air—there can be real dangers. However, I remain convinced of psychedelics' therapeutic potential for treating mania by disrupting our experience of meaning and making us more psychologically and spiritually flexible. The conviction rests on my experience working with patients with severe compulsory disorders who were suffering from delusional beliefs. One patient, for example, regarded any object her mother touched as poisonous and dangerous. Unlike psychotic patients, however, she was able to keep a certain distance from her fears, feeling them to be exaggerated. Her fears didn't grow any stronger while on psilocybin; on the contrary, she was able to see her mother in a more positive light and gained greater distance from her fear of poisoning. In short, she was able to assess her situation differently.

Reevaluating stressful events, also called reappraisal, has been made the subject of countless studies. Alongside acceptance, a topic I discussed in the first chapter, reappraisal is without doubt one of the most important factors in psychological resistance. Research into reappraisal has shown that over time it is possible to give a stressful incident a different meaning or even to strip it of meaning, whether to soften or put an end to a physiological stress response.[145] Aside from the way they affect our sense of meaning, psychedelics are also able to transform stressful, excessive amounts of meaning, calming the stress system. Albert Hofmann gives several different examples of this in his book *LSD, My Problem Child*. Werner Stoll, the first psychiatrist to take LSD, responded to criticism of his appearance and

145 Nook et al., "Emotion Naming Impedes Both Cognitive Reappraisal and Mindful Acceptance Strategies of Emotion Regulation," 187–98.

his altered body image as follows: "The supervisor emphasized my own wretched appearance. He seemed remarkably graceful. I myself had small, finely formed hands. As I washed them, it was happening a long way from me, somewhere down below on the right. It was questionable, but utterly unimportant, whether they were my own hands."[146] In other words, while on LSD Stoll didn't attach any meaning to criticism of his body or the changes in how he perceived it, since he no longer identified with his body. Normally this type of reappraisal is only available to people who have attained a high level of spiritual awareness.

Another example in Hofmann's book come from a young ad salesman who experienced a form of synesthesia while on LSD: "With my eyes open, the radiant colors flooded the room, folding over on top of one another in rhythm with the music. Suddenly I was aware that the colors *were* the music. The discovery did not seem startling. Values, so cherished and guarded, were becoming unimportant."[147] In this case too, the salesman's ability to withstand dramatic changes in his sensory perception proceeds from "cherished and guarded values," or fundamental assumptions about reality, losing any and all meaning.

These striking examples illustrate that reappraisal while on psychedelics often occurs from a bird's-eye view. The *Rig Veda* describes this phenomenon well: "We have drunk the Soma; we have become immortal; we have gone to the light; we have found the gods. What can hatred and the malice of a mortal do to us now, O immortal one?"[148] Another term for overcoming the earthly world is *transcendence*. The ability to transcend is a potent aspect of building resilience, since an outside perspective relativizes the experience of stress at a lower level, stripping it of its meaning. Shamanic flight is an archetypal image for this sort of experience. Certain spiritual traditions further relate transcendence to overcoming the sensory, temporal world and achieving a pure, eternal state of consciousness. Still, this is only *one* possible form of transcendence.

One extreme example of transcendence comes in Huxley's description of his self-dissolution: "To this new-born Notself, the behavior, the appearance, the very thought of the self it had momentarily ceased to be, and of other selves, its one-time fellows, seemed not indeed distasteful (for

---

146 Hofmann, *LSD, My Problem Child.*, chapter 4.

147 Ibid., chapter 5.

148 Doniger, *The Rig Veda*.

distastefulness was not one of the categories in terms of which I was thinking), but enormously irrelevant."[149] For Huxley, an existentially decisive event like the death of the self (ego death) did not produce any stress while under the influence of psychedelics. Anyone finding him or herself in such a state is truly incapable of suffering.

As a rule, reappraisal proceeds unconsciously; we find ourselves surprised by our indifference or a new sense of meaning only after the fact. Yet many people also report being able to reinterpret situations of their own will while on psychedelics. In describing her experience on LSD to me, one patient reported that she could "give new definitions to things, events, space, and time. I have access to places in my brain where these definitions are made. Redefine what is good and what is bad. It can even be dangerous. It depends on how you redefine, whether it feels good or bad. I don't have much practice yet in redefining or defining things anew. But I'm getting better with each session. The higher the dose, the greater the freedom to do so." I should qualify this last comment by saying that a higher dose is not always advantageous where reappraisal is concerned. There are patients for whom the psychedelic experience becomes meaningless or overpowering at higher doses, making it unsuitable for reappraisal.

Having described psychedelics' impact on how we experience meaning, which I have discussed in terms of reappraisal, laughter, and transcendence, I would like now to turn to two specific psychedelic effects with important therapeutic potential: revelations and visions.

Revelations

I encountered the biblical rule of abundance long before my own experience with MDMA. My father was an educated, well-read man who taught me a great deal. His views were strongly shaped by his education in the social sciences and economics. Social scientists, however, view the law of abundance through a capitalistic lens, where the mass production of goods—bread and wine in the Bible, for example—alleviates distribution problems. This was a view to which I also subscribed. My experience on MDMA, however, also let me see abundance as a state of consciousness

149 Huxley, *The Doors of Perception*.

that can help make the world more just. "Psychedelic" is composed of two Greek words: *psyche*, or soul, and *delos*, clear or evident. When combined the word literally means "the revelation of the soul," something that I experienced quite forcefully for myself.

Carl Jung, who struggled by his own account (like my father) with a tendency to regard things abstractly rather than emotionally, rightly saw a general issue of the modern era within his own difficulties: "Because in our civilized life, we have stripped so many ideas of their emotional energy, we do not really respond to them any more.... In this civilizing process, we have increasingly divided our consciousness from the deeper instinctive strata of the human psyche, and even ultimately from the somatic basis of the psychic phenomenon."[150] This recalls Aldous Huxley's championing of sensory, descriptive, and direct language in schools. It also matches my own observations of how patients unresponsive to psychotherapy often favor language that's detached from reality.

Psychedelics affect our relationship to language in a way that improves our understanding at the intuitive, emotional, and physical levels. I call this type of understanding "revelatory" because the knowledge that arises isn't new but has always been there, right beneath the surface—it is just the meaning that has expanded. From a religious perspective, "revelation" signifies the disclosure of a divine truth; generally speaking, "revelation" designates a profound sensory experience with potentially life-changing impact. Michael Pollan accurately described psychedelics as offering "a graduate education in the obvious," allowing even academics and cynical intellectuals for whom nothing is sacred to find new, profound meaning in banal sentences like "Love holds everything together" or "Love conquers all."[151]

Using language in a vivid, visceral way is an age-old healing technique. In an important article within psychotherapy circles, "The Mushrooms of Language," US author and shamanism researcher Henry Munn described the ceremonial use of psychedelic mushrooms among Mazatec shamans in Mexico as a way of renewing language to render it more lively, ecstatic, and meaningful.[152] This allowed the shamans to better communicate with

150 Jung, *Man and His Symbols*.

151 Pollan, *How to Change Your Mind*.

152 Henry Munn, "The Mushrooms of Language," in *Hallucinogens and Shamanism*, ed. Michael J. Harner (Oxford University Press, 1973).

the supernatural forces of the universe on behalf of their people. The rebirth that mushrooms are said to bring about is meant in a linguistic sense; they create the people and world anew through the ecstatic language they produce. Much like modern psychotherapists, the shamans regarded speech as medicine. Yet in contrast to modern psychedelic treatment, it was they, not the patients, who would take psilocybin to commune with the spirit world on behalf of their patient. The patient thus profited indirectly, with the psychedelic helping the shaman to express with language that would be meaningful to the patient:

> The shaman provides the sick woman with a *language* by means of which unexpressed and otherwise inexpressible psychic states can be immediately expressed. And it is the transition to this verbal expression—at the same time making it possible to undergo in an ordered and intelligible form a real experience that would otherwise be chaotic and inexpressible—which induces the release of the physiological process, that is, the reorganization, in a favorable direction, of the process to which the sick woman is subjected.[153]

As a method of healing this largely coincides with how depth psychology understands therapeutic change, where the linguistic skill of the therapist plays a decisive role.

The insight that revelation is critical to human development is equally ancient. For the Buddha, awakening wasn't simply a new experience but fundamentally a new way of understanding the world around him. Aristotle believed that every person sought the best for themselves, and that self-destructive behavior came from a false understanding of what that "best" was. This means that true, embodied understanding (or revelation) is essential in leading a good and happy life.

The correlation between lack of understanding and self-destructive behavior is on daily display in the doctor's office. The warning "Smoking is harmful to your health" often doesn't fully land with patients since they are unable to understand the full implications. "Health" and "harmful" are abstract terms, while the relationship between health and smoking is often presented as statistical, something that doesn't affect any one person directly. Our brain isn't especially adept at thinking in terms of probability and risk.

---

153 Ibid.

Unlike a scientific warning, revelation involves the apprehension of something that affects us unconditionally and holds a deeply personal and infinite meaning. In the case of smoking, revelation could look like an individual really feeling the harm it causes in every single pore, perhaps even picturing their cells being damaged. As a smoker once told me while on psilocybin, "Now I finally understand that smoking harms me. I no longer want to tar my lungs with smoke, or cover them in mucous." He did in fact quit smoking after the session. Revelation allows reality to shine forth from every apparent form; it makes the One and the True fully, completely, and boundlessly present in everything. The patient experienced unity and truth in all things. From this perspective of infinite love and truth, the revelation that smoking is harmful can be felt both viscerally and spiritually—the revelation emerges from within, rather than being prescribed by some external authority.

The revelations patients undergo under the influence of psychedelics may sometimes raise large topics—the health of an intimate relationship for example, or the meaning of life—though they regularly revolve around unwelcome medical or biological facts, as we have seen. But how do these revelations come about in the first place?

The simple explanation is that psychedelics stimulate our experience of meaning, imbuing a sentence like "Smoking is harmful to your health" with gravitas and truth. Revelation further allows us to understand things in a more holistic, intuitive, and visceral way. Patients' revelations are often articulated in vivid terms. In the example given above, smoking in general takes the concrete form of smoke itself, while the damage is vivified in the form of mucous and tar. Patients will often perceive an abstract or social situation as a physically palpable force, uttering sentences like "I can feel my mother gently choking me from behind," or "Now I feel it: At work, but also at home, there is an odd force pushing me to the side. I'm always standing there at the edge but never in the middle."

Thinking in terms of forces may come across as somewhat esoteric; patients have reported to me: "I feel a healing force, a beneficial force that connects everything and holds it together" or "Now I see. Everything is one. Love is the force holding everything together." This recalls Plato's definition of love as the desire and pursuit of the whole, an insight patients experience not abstractly but as a physical force. In modern neuroscience, physical force provides the grounding image for every connection we can conceive of; we begin to grasp its meaning even before birth. External forces like gravity and warmth, and internal forces like hunger or restlessness, act on our bodies, revealing the reciprocal relationships that exist between ourselves and our environments. This primal experience of connection in turn forms the basis for experiencing meaning later on. As children, we begin to understand that forces not only work on us, but that we ourselves can also be the source for forces that influence our bodies and external world. We learn how to move our bodies and influence others in such a way that we become centers of power. We develop better and better strategies for manipulating our environment, reaching for a toy, raising a cup to our lips, or moving our bodies through space. We encounter obstacles that exert force on us, and discover that we can also exert force, whether by going around, over, or through the objects that stand in our way. Sometimes we are frustrated, defeated, or powerless in our exertions, sometimes we succeed. In this way we gradually expand the meaning of "force." For US philosopher Mark Johnson, these original experiences of force form the building blocks for our language.[154] "You can" means that your own force is neither hemmed in or blocked. "You must" indicates an external force forcing us in a specific direction, while "you may not" is an immovable object that blocks our force. The multifaceted meanings of *stress*, *resilience*, and *balance*, common terms in psychotherapy, derive their meaning from these sorts of physical experiences.

Psychedelics give us a second opportunity to experience and speak in this original language, with the advantage that many more regions of the brain understand the connections we are expressing in this fashion. Such was the result of one neuroscientific study that researched the brain's activity when grasping the meaning of sentences. The sentence "She had a hard day," for instance, activates the sensory-motor cortex, a part of the cerebral cortex that is responsible for integrating abstract and physical information.[155] The sentence "She had a bad day," by contrast, does not provoke the same effect; no intellectual-physical integration occurs, and the meaning of the sentence remains abstract.

---

154 Mark Johnson, *The Body in the Mind: The Bodily Basis of Meaning, Imagination, and Reason* (University of Chicago Press, 1992).

155 Simon Lacey, Randall Stilla, and K. Sathian, "Metaphorically Feeling: Comprehending Textural Metaphors Activates Somatosensory Cortex," *Brain and Language* 120, no. 3 (March 1, 2012): 416–21.

Authors and effective public speakers make deliberate, if subtle, use of revelation by using physical metaphors in their work: "I leapt out of my skin" or "We nested down on the sofa." Metaphors are an essential component of psychotherapeutic language. The most influential and popular metaphor for conceiving of psychological problems comes from Sigmund Freud, who interpreted neuroses as childlike experience and behavior. For Freud, a star lawyer who rants and raves at home because his wife is on the telephone is expressing the hurt of his defiant inner child, who feels powerless when his mother is talking with his father. The young woman who would like nothing more than to merge with her boyfriend is making up for her father's lack of presence. While these interpretations are scientifically dubious (psychoanalysis greatly overestimates childhood wishes to merge), they can still prompt a feeling of revelation, helping the patient understand and overcome neurotic behavior. Freud's rich assortment of childhood metaphors created a therapeutic language that allows us a better understanding of our brains. Psychedelics allow us to understand and experience our problems in a similarly childlike, physical fashion. Here one might use Freud's term "regression," i.e., a temporary retreat to an earlier stage of personality development or, as I see it, linguistic development. In the therapeutic context it is the experience of revelation that strikes me as important; a deeper, more intuitive and visceral understanding of a present-day psychological or social problem.

A series of studies now show experiences of revelation under the influence of psychedelics to have lasting effects.[156] Roughly half of patients succeeded in improving health-related behaviors following psychedelic treatment, specifically consuming less tobacco, alcohol, and coffee. Physical activity increased, they spent more time outside, and they paid better attention to their sleep. A number also reported losing weight. One study examined twenty patients six months after a single psilocybin session; all had suffered from severe depression and remained unresponsive to conventional therapy. The authors summarized the changes in health-related behaviors as follows: "As a result of these lessons [the revelation of manifest truths during treatment], there were some major lifestyle changes; nearly half of the sample reported improvements to diet, exercise, and cutting down on drinking alcohol. One described the improvement to his diet

156 Pedro J. Teixeira, Matthew W. Johnson, Christopher Timmermann, Rosalind Watts, David Erritzoe, Hannah Douglass et al., "Psychedelics and Health Behaviour Change," *Journal of Psychopharmacology* 36, no. 1 (May 29, 2021): 12–19.

that happened after the dose as 'life-changing,' although he was not sure how these changes came about as he did not receive direct 'lessons' about diet."[157]

Revelatory effects are especially adept at deepening psychotherapeutic processes and making them physically tangible. Claudio Naranjo describes one patient for whom ibogaine transformed a years-long psychotherapeutic journey into a moment of revelation: It was "the way to integrate all that I have done so far. It was lovely to see how in a single experience I was able to see the process I am going through, the work of many years, finding things and events that I was very clear about in my head and that I had not been able to bring down into the body, and almost everything materialized in a single structure."[158]

Spanish psychotherapist Asunta de Hormaechea reports a similar experience, with ayahuasca helping her to understand her training in psychotherapy: "The first experiences revealed to me with great clarity and depth all that I had understood in my personal therapy work. Expressed in this way, it does not seem to be very significant, but it was highly transcendent, as what I already 'knew' became a deep understanding that went far beyond the understanding I had until then. I could say that understanding was embodied, became alive, cellular, and organic. 'The verb was made flesh' was a phrase that came to me at that time and that faithfully described what I was feeling."[159]

Revelatory experiences are not a common topic of discussion in medical circles, during consultations, or in standard psychotherapy. Even writers have difficulty finding the language for them. As Virginia Woolf put it, "What is the meaning of life? That was all—a simple question; one that tended to close in on one with years. The great revelation had never come. The great revelation perhaps never did come. Instead, there were little daily miracles, illuminations, matches struck unexpectedly in the dark; here was one."[160] In my experience, psychedelics function like matches that can ignite revelations, strengthening and illuminating the course of therapy.

---

157 Rosalind Watts, Camilla Day, Jacob Krzanowski, David Nutt, and Robin Carhart-Harris, "Patients' Accounts of Increased 'Connectedness' and 'Acceptance' After Psilocybin for Treatment-Resistant Depression," *Journal of Humanistic Psychology* 57, no. 5 (June 19, 2017): 520–64.

158 Naranjo, *My Psychedelic Explorations*.

159 Ibid.

160 Virginia Woolf, *To the Lighthouse* (Vintage, 2019).

Visions

Most people associate the terms "imagination" or "vision" with artistic activity, dreams, and fantasies. The view can be traced back to the Romantic period, as reflected in former German chancellor Helmut Schmidt's sarcastic comment that "people with visions had better go to the doctor's."

Yet the faculty of imagination has much broader significance, one that the great philosopher of reason himself, Immanuel Kant, considered in depth.[161] According to Kant, imagination first allows us to give meaning to our experiences, without which we would never fully apprehend reality. Imagination and visions, in other words, are a precondition for ordering experience.

In his *Critique of Judgement*, Kant distinguishes between "reproductive" imagination and "productive" imagination. The former is necessary for understanding a thing the way it is. Concretely, this means arranging and composing our views so that they hew as closely to reality as possible. This faculty corresponds with our capacity for revelation, where new connections are established between previous, manifest experiences to give them deeper personal meaning. "Productive" imagination, by contrast, constructs a new image out of the broad diversity of our perceptions or views. Productive imagination also lays the groundwork for our awareness of time, as new images arise out of the old and broaden our notions and ideas, disclosing new potential meanings by arranging them in different orders. Symbols are one impressive result of this visionary capacity, promoting reflection in terms of images that generates new insights about the object being symbolized. Seen in this way, the symbol points beyond itself and into the future.

Great suffering and serious illnesses cannot usually be processed or endured in a rational manner. The reproductive imagination, Kant argues, isn't sufficient on its own in such cases; people undergoing serious life crises need a vision that will stabilize them and show them how to proceed. In this context, visionary experiences are a built-in resilience factor.

The visionary experiences that psychedelics elicit may be dream*like*, but they aren't dreams. Unlike with dream states, psychedelic consciousness is characterized by its exceeding wakefulness. The scenes that play out before us, often journeys through imaginary landscapes, do so over a much longer period of time than is normal in dreams. Psychedelic visions are also highly

161 Immanuel Kant, *Critique of Judgment* (Hackett, 2007).

specific and full of color, while dreams are usually vague and without color. Even while I perceive myself as a river, or feel my consciousness in everything, I have not lost my sense of reality. Rather, one gets the impression that different realities exist; I am looking into a different reality, but without leaving the everyday world. This is what makes terms like "hallucination" or "hallucinogen" inappropriate—they refer to an altered order of perception that is experienced as reality—a loss of reality, in other words. We don't lose our sense of reality under psychedelics, however, but rather have it expanded by an inner seeing. As with dreams, visions can make wishes and conflicts visible and let us "see" feelings. Among other things, this helps us to describe our dreams in vivid language, to better understand and guide them along. Or as US linguist and ethnobotanist Terence McKenna put it, "What 'psychedelic' means is: Getting your mind out in front of you (by whatever means necessary) so that you can relate to it as a thing in the world, and then work upon it."[162]

Visions are creative accomplishments in their own right. They might include unusual, illogical, or "impossible" things in playful combinations; they can also give concrete, concise form to ideas and feelings. They are proof of the wealth of our inner lives, raising our self-esteem. Yet visions are more than simply a "product" of the brain—they are also receptive to things outside us that would have remained hidden without them.

One example of this sort of creativity and receptivity came through a patient who had been quite ill for a long time already when she was referred to me for clinical treatment. Confined to life in a rocking chair, she rarely spoke and was suspected of suffering from early onset dementia, a blank slate without any fantasy or imagination. Under the influence of LSD, she had a vision of an "opalescent light," in which she perceived me as a combination of the physicist Stephen Hawking and the artist Andy Warhol. The accompanying clinician was in a state of shock, saying that she "had no idea that the patient was so imaginative and had such a broad vocabulary, or any familiarity with artistic or scientific celebrities." In subsequent integration sessions, the patient demonstrated a wish for an "opalescent" form of therapy, which combined scientific and creative elements.

Visions like these that strengthen and stimulate the therapeutic process are relatively frequent events. Another patient of mine endured a difficult

162 Terence McKenna, "Empowering Hope in Dark Times," read by the author, Wilshire Ebel Theater, June 2, 1991.

childhood in which her parents were forever letting her know how little money and time they had for her, and that it would have been better had she been aborted. She succeeded in becoming a world-famous opera singer despite such a cruel lack of love, but before every performance, and even while onstage, she was assailed by bouts of fear that she would fail. Her parents had told her that she shouldn't even exist, after all, so how could she be expected to survive in front of a live audience? She undertook LSD therapy in an effort to rid herself of her fears. At one point during her trip she had a vision of an endless stretch of weeds. "I am the weeds, Dr. Hasler," she told me. "I love weeds. They're incredibly strong. They're healing, nutritious, and they decide when they come and go."

A third patient suffered from her family constantly fighting. Every Christmas or birthday was choked with tension and ended in open hostility. The presents for the children weren't age-appropriate and potentially harmful, the food too rich, the meat undercooked, the Christmas tree too small, the candles too dangerous. While on psilocybin, her resentful family transformed into a dance troupe. "Maybe that's how I have to look at our life together going forward," she said, "We aren't fighting, we're dancing!"

Psychedelic visions can also impact our awareness of time, changing our relationship to burnout or other stress-related illnesses in the process. People suffering in this way typically find themselves at the end of one story and need to narrate over the course of many therapy sessions how it is they burned out. Often, they're missing any perspective on the future. This clinical impression tallies with studies in neuroscience showing that nearly every psychiatric problem is accompanied by mental myopia.[163] The same applies in reverse: An orientation toward the future is an important factor in resilience, offering us protection from stressful states or psychological disorders.[164] All this points toward the importance of excessive focus on the short term as a contributing factor to stress and psychological suffering. In short, a truncated, restricted, or nonexistent horizon makes us more susceptible to stress. One consequence is that patients will significantly

---

163 Michael Amlung, Emma Marsden, Katherine Holshausen, Vanessa Morris, Herry Patel, Lana Vedelago et al., "Delay Discounting as a Transdiagnostic Process in Psychiatric Disorders," *JAMA Psychiatry* 76, no. 11 (November 1, 2019): 1176.

164 Lei Zheng, Sonia Lippke, Yidi Chen, Danyang Li, and Yiqun Gan, "Future Orientation Buffers Depression in Daily and Specific Stress," *PsyCh Journal* 8, no. 3 (April 4, 2019): 342–52.

overestimate the scope of short-term problems, leading to impulsive reactions like outbursts or substance abuse.

Psychedelic visions can help to expand our horizons or give us new ones to work with. As one patient put it, "What I can say for certain is that this session [with psilocybin] has shown me that there is a light at the end of the tunnel. That's something I haven't seen over the past few months. I did have some hope, otherwise I wouldn't have come to you, but now that hope is much more concrete." The light at the end of the tunnel represents the merger between the patient's restricted, stress-oriented horizon line and the vision of a broader horizon brought on by the psychedelic. The *Rig Veda* describes this psychedelic effect as giving us "wide-gazing thoughts and insights" or "inspiring good thoughts and joyous expansiveness to the extreme."[165]

This is to say that wishes or dreams taking on concrete form through psychedelic visions can constitute a step toward their realization.

Neuroscientific research has shown that psychedelics operate directly on our sense of sight, which is made up of the retina, the optic nerve, the thalamus, and the visual cortex (the gray matter of the occipital lobe). Under the influence of psychedelics the thalamus, which filters visual stimuli, becomes more permeable, while blood flow to the visual cortex increases significantly. These effects become especially apparent with closed eyes and are comparable to sleeping or waking dreams.[166] Yet they last much longer, allowing the brain to create extensive visions with vivid details, a great sense of spaciousness, and iridescent color. Nor do the psychedelic effects on our visual system matter only in a psychological context, but in a medical sense as well. People who struggle to perceive color or space experience objective improvements in their visual functioning.

Aphantasia is the medical term for an inability to imagine or create mental images. When asked to close their eyes and picture an animal, nearly 70 percent of people do not immediately see an animal, which could be sign of aphantasia. They may think of the names of animals, but the corresponding images do not come to mind. People who experience aphantasia also have a short visual memory; they would find it difficult to replay sequences

165 Doniger, *The Rig Veda*.

166 C. Kieran, R. Fox, Manesh Girn, Cameron C. Parro, and Kalina Christoff, "Functional Neuroimaging of Psychedelic Experience: An Overview of Psychological and Neural Effects and Their Relevance to Research on Creativity, Daydreaming, and Dreaming," in *Cambridge University Press eBooks* (2018): 92–113.

from a movie in their minds' eye after a trip to the cinema. Aphantasia can occur in varying degrees of severity, usually emerging early in life. While it isn't regarded as an illness but a normal variation, it can still leave people at a significant disadvantage, especially those in creative professions, or when creatively picturing and managing the stress that nearly all of us experience. Aldous Huxley himself suffered in part from aphantasia, as he writes, "I am and, for as long as I can remember, I have always been a poor visualizer. Words, even the pregnant words of poets, do not evoke pictures in my mind. No hypnagogic visions greet me on the verge of sleep. When I recall something, the memory does not present itself to me as a vividly seen event or object."[167] As an author this greatly impaired Huxley and was one of the main reasons he took mescalin—to improve his visual fantasies. It should be noted as a caveat that psychedelics only address partial antaphasia. Psychedelics seem not to have any effect on a complete inability to develop mental images.[168]

Visions can also have social functions, helping a community to bond. According to Michael Harner, a US shamanism expert, shamanic visions deliver profound knowledge about the meaning of life and death, as well as our place within the human community and the greater whole.[169] Carlos Castaneda's books further confirm the importance of visions in shamanistic culture, with his teacher Don Juan repeatedly stressing that being a visionary warrior allows us to find, or better yet see, the underlying structure of life.

Visions also play an important role in Buddhism. The Sanskrit term *avidya* is often translated as "ignorance," which literally translates to an inability to see or have visions. Upon being asked by a student what the blessing of meditative concentration was, the Buddha replied: "Vision and knowledge in accordance with reality."[170]

Visions and symbols occupy a central place in Jungian psychology. "For the sake of mental stability and even physiological health, the unconscious and the conscious must be integrally connected and thus move on parallel lines," Jung writes in *Man and His Symbols*. "If they are split apart

167 Huxley, *The Doors of Perception*.

168 Olivia Tween, "Investigation into Aphantasia: Neurological, Functional, and Behavioral Correlates" (master thesis, Beloit College, 2019), doi:10.31237/osf.io/q7v2k.

169 Michael Harner, *The Way of the Shaman* (Harper & Row, 1990).

170 Joseph Goldstein, *Mindfulness: A Practical Guide to Awakening* (Sounds True, 2016).

or 'dissociated,' psychological disturbance follows. In this respect, dream symbols are the essential message carriers from the instinctive to the rational parts of the human mind, and their interpretation enriches the poverty of consciousness so that it learns to understand again the forgotten language of the instincts."[171] Jung further recommends visionary experience as a means of combatting banal intellectualism or a loss of meaning:

> Today we talk about "matter," we describe its physical properties. We conduct laboratory experiments to demonstrate some of its aspects. But the word "matter" remains a dry, inhuman, and purely intellectual concept, without any psychic significance for us. How different was the former image of matter—the Great Mother—that could encompass and express the profound emotional meaning of Mother Earth. In the same way, what was the spirit is now identified with intellect and thus ceases to be the Father of All. It has degenerated to the limited ego-thoughts of man; the immense emotional energy expressed in the image of "our Father" vanishes into the sand of an intellectual desert.[172]

Psychedelic visions—experienced in waking consciousness, and thus more precise and more easily encoded in our memories—are even better positioned than dreams for making sense of messages from the subconscious and imbuing the world with meaning.

US anthropologist Clifford Geertz also wrote of the important role visionary symbols play in our sense of well-being. Religions for Geertz were systems of symbols aimed at evoking strong, all-encompassing, and enduring moods. Psychedelic-assisted therapy has demonstrated that it is also possible to access personal or archetypal symbols which lend strength to their seers—the weeds in my patient's vision, for example. The Griffiths study I discussed at the outset of this chapter further raises the prospect that visions induced by psychedelics can be experienced in a spiritual context, even as ultimate reality. Experiencing a psychedelic vision of ultimate reality, while remaining aware our own reality, is another example of transcendence.

---

171 Jung, *Man and His Symbols*.

172 Ibid.

Aldous Huxley recognized the great healing potential of psychedelics in modern life, where visionary experience is in strong decline. In pre-modern times, infections, untreated mental illness, extreme physical exertion, insufficient vitamins, and undernourishment all led to altered states of consciousness that were ripe for visions. Many people also deliberately subjected themselves to mortification, periods of fasting, ceremonial ingestion of entheogens, or other exercises intended to subjugate their physical needs and further encourage receptivity. The lack of CO_2 brought on by hyperventilation during shamanic singing, repeated recitation of psalms, or funeral mourners lamenting for hours on end could also trigger psychedelic visions.[173] Psychedelics are an excellent remedy for alleviating the poverty in the visions of our modern medicine and culture—they are doing so already.

In concluding this chapter I would like to share the experience of Ralph a patient I treated with psilocybin for severe depression. After his wife and children distanced themselves from him when they were no longer able to take his hypersensitivity, put-downs, and pessimism, his relationship to Buddhism grew increasingly important. He had belonged to a Buddhist community for many years, but as his depression progressed, he also began to doubt his own experiences, insights, and the group. He had been shocked when the disappearance of one member of the community was barely acknowledged after he reported it. The concept of karma had also begun to weigh on him more and more heavily. He came to me in the hopes that psychedelic treatment might give him a new lease on life.

Ralph was quite sensitive to psychoactive drugs, so in the first session I only administered 10 milligrams of psilocybin. Yet even a small dosage gave Ralph a vision of wandering for hours in a slum somewhere in South America. Though he had never been to a slum or South America, everything was pictured in great detail: He saw collapsed homes, earthen streets covered in puddles, mountains of different-colored plastic sacks, dried vomit and blood, broken glass, and everywhere the foul stench of decomposition, decay, and feces. The slum was completely empty of people. During the integration session Ralph expressed disappointment at the experience; while he could clearly recall his vision of the slum, he found it lacked meaning. I myself had several interpretations. For example, the Buddha's insight that

---

173 M. N Havenith, M. Leidenberger, J. Brasanac, M. Corvacho, I. C. Figueiredo, Leonie Schwarz et al., "Decreased CO2 saturation during circular breathwork supports emergence of altered states of consciousness," *Commun Psychol* 3, no. 59 (2025), https://doi.org/10.1038/s44271-025-00247-0.

people suffer because they want to possess and hold on to things that are by nature impermanent. I felt hesitant to offer this sort of spiritual interpretation, however, recalling US psychologist Mark Epstein's warning against easy readings in his book *Advice Not Given: A Guide to Getting Over Yourself*. Epstein, whose work combines Buddhism with psychotherapeutic approaches, bases his advice on spiritual grounds: "The Buddha, in getting over himself, did not vanish. In fact, his presence became even more powerful, his 'being' a vehicle of transformation for those around him. In this way, he became a true expression of advice not given."[174]

Despite Ralph's disappointment, three months later he called about a second session. "This time with fifteen milligrams," he said. Despite a supposedly meaningless experience, he had an intuition that another session might help him. His vision in the second session hardly differed from the first—he was back in a slum devoid of people. This time, the sight of a broken teapot and a black plastic rice bowl told him that he wasn't in South America but Asia. Here too, Ralph again found the vision meaninglessness. "It's always the same. The misery looks the same everywhere." Yet he didn't give up and continued exploring possible meanings. Peering in through the window of a hut he glimpsed a miniature statue of a Buddha seated on a small wooden altar with a relaxed expression, projecting an air of calm. In that moment, he grasped a core Buddhist insight: that suffering is not the exception, but the universal condition of existence. The sight shook Ralph to the core. "Now I understand," he said, starting to cry.

Summary

Throughout countries in the West, people complain increasingly of a lack of purpose. This is worrisome, since meaning constitutes an important pillar in psychological resilience. Psychedelics can help us to see and experience our personal problems inside of a larger context, allaying cancer patients' existential fears, for instance. For some, this expanded perspective includes a felt connection to a greater field of consciousness—or even to God—which can provide a deep sense of belonging and existential reassurance. Psychedelics' revelatory effects draw our attention to the things that are directly before us, giving them meaning and making them physically

174 Mark Epstein, *Advice Not Given: A Guide to Getting Over Yourself* (Penguin, 2018).

tangible—the harm smoking causes to our health, say. This can bring lasting changes in lifestyle, and strengthen the meaning we find in life. Psychedelic visions, in turn, allow unconscious images and symbols to become conscious. Visions further help us endure great suffering that would otherwise overwhelm rational thought.

Chapter 5

Right Relationship: The Path to Liberating Shelter

Understanding the world necessitates connection with it. The connection may be positive or negative and it may strengthen or weaken our resilience. One of our primary modes of understanding the world is through language. Signs, symbols, words, and sentences find resonance in the world, determining in large part how we understand and interact with it. The Latin word *nectere*, which provides the root for "connect," can mean "to fasten" or "to connect," but it can also mean "to bind." While binding in the sense of being trapped is a form of existential stress, a close emotional connection to family, friends, or a culture is indispensable to our well-being. We can become entangled or ensnared in these webs precisely because we are so dependent on them in our personal and professional lives. The Latin verb *ligare* (also meaning "to connect," or "tie") simultaneously serves as the root for *ligament*, the connective tissue linking our bones; *obligation*, or the duties that bind us to others; as well as the word *religion*, which addresses our ties with the eternal and the divine.

Human beings have never been more bound or connected to one another than they are today, whether through language, culture, business, technology, political and economic structures, or social media. Global economic crises and pandemics serve as frightening but impressive evidence of our interdependence. In a famous experiment, US psychologist Stanley Miller demonstrated that we are much more closely bound to one another than we think, not only in a technological or cultural sense, but a direct personal sense. The experiment showed that on average, two randomly selected people on the planet are separated by only five other people. Study participants were asked to try and contact a complete stranger, a veterinarian living in Australia say, by finding someone they knew who might be more closely connected to the veterinarian. On average, it took just six linked individual through their networks to establish a connection to the stranger.

Despite our extreme (and increasing) proximity to one another, it is more and more common for people to feel lonely. A recent study reported that a full 76 percent of California residents felt a medium to extreme sense of loneliness, and that the feeling impacted their physical and mental health negatively. People who were in touch with a sense of intuitive wisdom, openness, and spirituality, by contrast, felt much less lonely.[175] The growing issue of loneliness is widespread and pressing enough that the British government created a Minister for Loneliness tasked with developing strategies to combat the issue.

Loneliness isn't just an interpersonal problem. People also feel more and more cut off from their bodies, as though the mind were increasingly alien to the body, despite the thousands of connections linking it to the body, brain, and broader environment, whether through the blood, lymph, nerves, hormones, our immune systems, metabolism, or sensory organs. This kind of cerebral loneliness takes the form of a psychological dualism: On the one side there is the body with its normal daily functions, on the other the brain, which is always elsewhere, forever thinking, criticizing, and commenting. The effect is that our mental language is only loosely connected with the realities of the body; the mind has taken on a life of its own and created its own world. The price we pay is a distanced, disconnected, and inauthentic life, where we proceed for proceeding's sake.

Our lack of contact at the social and material-physical level is perilous, depriving us of a sense of our needs and vulnerabilities as well as those of the people and environments on which we depend. This type of remove doesn't represent a scientific or rational perspective, since it overlooks the very real contact and relationships we have with our body and environment. The damage wrought to our overall health and the ecosystems we inhabit is typical of this dualism.

Aside from the social, technological, and cultural factors, personal factors also contribute significantly to our pervasive loneliness. Cultivating a relationship to ourselves and the world is something we learn to do in childhood. British pediatrician John Bowlby discovered that as children

175 Ellen Lee, Colin Depp, Barton W. Palmer, Danielle Glorioso, Rebecca Daly, Jinyuan Liu et al., "High Prevalence and Adverse Health Effects of Loneliness in Community-Dwelling Adults Across the Lifespan: Role of Wisdom as a Protective Factor," *International Psychogeriatrics* 31, no. 10 (December 18, 2018): 1447–62.

we develop an inner "working model" which subsequently guides how we shape our relationships. People who experience a great deal of uncertainty, loneliness, emotional neglect, or physical abuse during childhood tend to be uncertain and ambivalent in relationships later in life and will have a hard time embarking on deeper relationships. As a psychological strategy, this caution and uncertainty works to shield the person from further traumatic relationships. Over the course of an entire life, however, this protective mechanism can become a burden, leaving the person incapable of building trusting, stable relationships.

Genetic factors also feed into our current loneliness epidemic. Throughout most of history humans lived as nomads in small communities, with tightly bound and egalitarian relationships. Nomadic life doesn't allow for private property or hierarchy, since everyone is equally dependent on everyone else. It was only as human settlements began to form ten thousand years ago that income disparity emerged and rigid hierarchies developed—a system for which we were unprepared, genetically speaking. British psychologist John Price pioneered an influential theory that holds the constant struggle for possessions and status responsible for the vast rise in depression, where 20 percent of the population now struggles with depressive disorders. Price argues that through slow speech, bent-over physical posture, downcast eyes, pessimism, and a lack of enthusiasm or joy, a depressive person indicates he no longer poses a threat in the struggle for status.[176]

Alongside differences in status, the increasing specialization of global society and economies also dampen our ability to find satisfaction in life. People complain more and more frequently of losing a relationship to themselves by being forced to play the same role on a constant basis. Existentialist philosophy dealt extensively with this topic; Heidegger wrote about the "real dictatorship of the They," i.e., external control by way of social expectation, through sentences like "*We* don't do that; that's how *we* do it." This form of outside control prevents any sort of real self-determination or existential sense of "mineness" from developing. French philosopher Jean-Paul Sartre, for his part, wrote that "hell is other people," meaning others' expectations and gaze determines what we can be, robbing us of our freedom. In this context, psychotherapy aims to help people in Western

176 John Price, L. Sloman, R. Gardner Jr., P. Gilbert, and P. Rhode, "The Social Competition Hypothesis of Depression," *British Journal of Psychiatry* 164, no. 3 (March 1, 1994): 309–15.

countries gain access to themselves, discover their true, authentic being, and realize their full potential.

The previous chapter showed how psychedelics help us establish stronger connections to our bodies, traumatic experiences, feelings of positivity, life histories, archetypes, and visions, and how these connections bring meaning to our lives. The feeling of connection psychedelic therapy fosters will often linger for weeks or even months afterword. As one fifty-two-year-old patient expressed it after a psilocybin session, "This sense of connection, it just feels good...this feeling of connection, that we are all linked to each other." This experience occurs quite frequently with psychedelics. Following psilocybin treatment, the change most frequently attested to is from a state of disconnection to one of reconnection;[177] a similar feeling is typical of MDMA. One patient suffering PTSD told he had "never felt such a loving connection to the world before as I did today. I can't say for sure whether I'll achieve it again without MDMA, but I'm not hopeless about my chances. Maybe it's like having an aerial map, so that I know there's a way now."[178]

The *Rig Veda* contains early references praising the social effects of soma, describing it as a "comrade who thrusts away affliction and insults" and a "compassionate friend"; when it is taken "our words flow together like rivers, made clear by deep understanding within the heart," "like a comrade for a comrade."[179] The passages are significant from a psychiatric perspective because loneliness, a lack of connection, and feeling cut off or insulated from the world are major problems in depression and other psychological illnesses. Sylvia Plath gives a piercing account of the feeling in *The Bell Jar*, a novel in which the bell jar represents the narrator's unwanted and painful separation from the world: "To the person in the bell jar, blank and stopped as a dead baby, the world itself is the bad dream," she observes, writing from personal experience.[180] Nor does the bell jar offer any protection—on the contrary, it leaves the person locked inside on

177 Watts et al., "Patients' Accounts of Increased 'Connectedness' and 'Acceptance' After Psilocybin for Treatment-Resistant Depression," 520–64.

178 Michael C. Mithoefer, *A Manual for MDMA-Assisted Psychotherapy in the Treatment of Posttraumatic Stress Disorder* (The Multidisciplinary Association for Psychedelic Studies, 2017).

179 Doniger, *The Rig Veda*; Jamison and Brereton, *The Rigveda: The Earliest Religious Poetry of India*.

180 Sylvia Plath, *The Bell Jar* (Harper Collins, 2005).

display. Within the jar the person remains out of touch with themselves and the world, while others are able to observe the painful dissociation with a critical eye.

Is the psychedelic feeling of connectedness just an illusion, a sort of chemically inspired fantasy? Considering the genetic, familial, social, cultural, economic, and ecological ties that bind us all, psychedelic connectedness actually seems a closer match to reality than the supposed truth that we exist completely independent of the world. In this regard the psychedelic state is both more realistic and rational than the daily experience of those who feel lonely. One of the learning goals in Buddhism is to see the world in terms of relationships. Everything that exists arises and passes away—it never exists for itself alone, but always in relationship. Ultimately, relationships are all that exist. Psychedelic experiences can help us reach this insight.

A current philosophical debate about loneliness casts further doubt on whether feelings of loneliness themselves are grounded in reality.[181] There may be moments, the argument goes, in which the inner life of others seems opaque and unreachable, but it would be false to conclude that it is invisible and unattainable forever. In a state of loneliness, one's mental life is exclusively internal. A state of connection, on the other hand, means that our minds are not something just on the inside, cut off from our bodies and the world around us. It is not so much empathy or compassion that leads us out of loneliness, as an empathetic mind is still a very private mind. A better means of combatting loneliness is acknowledging the existence of a common mind and world where we live alongside others. The transpersonal effects of psychedelics can help us perceive this. Gary, one of the many US Buddhists who have remained open to psychedelic experiences, described the effects as follows in a book on Buddhism and psychedelics: "When you are high, you have that experience; you see the energy, you see the connection between yourself and the other phenomena around you; you see the interaction of the energy between yourself and everything else going on around you; you see the interdependence of everything. So that makes it easier when I am focused on developing compassion."[182]

181 Sean Gallagher and Dan Zahavi, *The Phenomenological Mind* (Routledge, 2012).

182 Douglas Osto, *Altered States: Buddhism and Psychedelic Spirituality in America* (Columbia University Press, 2016).

Indigenous Cultures and Pro-Sociality

Entheogenic plants support community bonds in many indigenous cultures, strengthening identity, improving relationships, and promoting reconciliation. One example comes through the Native American Church (NAC), founded in 1880 at a point when the indigenous peoples of North America were teetering on the edge of destruction. The church considers peyote, the mescaline-containing cactus, their sacrament. The Native Americans Michael Pollan interviewed for his book *This Is Your Mind on Plants* found that their peyote ceremonies had done more to help heal the wounds from genocide, colonialism, and alcoholism than anything other method of healing. The NAC considers peyote to be an all-knowing spirit that can see through peoples' facades and knows them better than they know themselves. This gives the plant the power to expose an individual's errors and confront them with those errors. In the life of church members peyote functions a bit like a higher self, a spirit with an inner view and voice. Parents tell their children that the spirit of peyote continues to watch them even when they (the parents) are absent. In this way, the medicine helps to preserve social norms and moral codes of conduct, strengthening the community in the process.

James Slotkin's anthropological work highlighted the way in which peyote's prosocial impulses transcend thinking in terms of tribe, more important than ever in our interdependent and troubled world. "The Peyotists are supposed to have a feeling of brotherly love for one another," Slotkin observes. "This is expressed during the rite by means of elaborate forms of courtesy, respect, and honoring, as well as gift giving. Such brotherhood is also extended to Peyotists of other tribes. There is much intertribal visiting when a meeting is held; in fact, I never attended a rite when there were not present Peyotists from at least two other tribes."[183]

Psychedelics play a similarly important role in facilitating encounters between different communities in the Amazon region. The mind- and heart-opening effects of ayahuasca ceremonies helps ease exchange between people from distant geographical regions, build cultural and economic networks, and bridge the divide between insider and outsider. Shamans also use ayahuasca's psychoactive effects as a quick means of gauging the viability

183 James Slotkin in David Ebin, *The Drug Experience: First-Person Accounts of Addicts, Writers, Scientists and Others* (Grove Press, 1965).

of social relationships with strangers regarding their trustworthiness, common interests and values, and the potential for conflict.[184]

A recent study of ayahuasca ceremonies with Israeli and Palestinian participants shows that this ancient method of building peace retains its value in our own era. In particular, the ceremonies fostered a sense of social unity, intercultural exchange, and a common effort to process trauma. One participant commented that "we really experienced this place in which the connection is not Israel-Palestinian, it is human, the human tribe."[185]

English musician Sting also attests to the social and moral benefits of psychedelics: "It has [transformed] my ability to navigate the world, to be in a family, to relate to my children, to relate to my wife, to my colleagues. It teaches me about community and it teaches me that the core of all religious thought ought to be: Let me treat others the way I want to be treated myself."[186] Stanislav Grof described LSD's social effects as "typically accompanied by a definite shift from a competitive orientation toward synergistic behavior patterns."[187]

The social effects of psychedelics, which do not appear with conventional psychotropic drugs, reveal themselves through changes in patients' use of language. In a review of 2,947 firsthand accounts of experiences with psychotropic substances, my colleague Adrian Hase and I found that reports on the effects of LSD, MDMA, and psilocybin included a much higher number of social words like *we*, *us*, or *our* than those on antidepressants.[188] Other studies reached the same conclusion. In patient interviews, MDMA increased the use of positive social language—words like *friend, support, relationship, trust,* and *compassion*; words connected with peoples' intimate sphere like *love, erotic, uncertain, closeness,* and *death* also increased. The emotional register of the statements was evident through a halting flow of speech due to the effects of the MDMA. Amphetamines had no such

---

184 Françoise Barbira Freedman, "Shamans' Networks in Western Amazonia," in *Ayahuasca Shamanism in the Amazon and Beyond*, eds. Beatriz Caiuby Labate and Clancy Cavnar (Oxford University Press, 2014), 130–58.

185 Leor Roseman, Yiftach Ron, Antwan Saca, Natalie Ginsberg, Lisa Luan, and Nadeem Karkabi, "Relational Processes in Ayahuasca Groups of Palestinians and Israelis," *Frontiers in Pharmacology* 12 (May 19, 2021)

186 *Have a Good Trip,* Donick Cary, 2020.

187 Grof, *LSD Psychotherapy*.

188 Hase et al., "Analysis of Recreational Psychedelic Substance Use Experiences Classified by Substance," 643–59.

effect, by comparison. On the contrary, they seemed to dampen the emotional content of patients' language and increase the rate of speech, making it plausible that amphetamines (and not MDMA) be used as a means of boosting performance.[189]

Psychedelics' impact on language has been particularly well researched among Mazatec shamans.[190] In the ecstatic state, internal and external forces speak through the shaman; he will say, for example, "I am the one who speaks with mountains, with the tallest mountains. Speak with the mountains, say it. Speak with the stones, say it. Speak with the atmosphere, say it. Speak with the spirit of the day, say it." For the Mazatec, mountains are sites where divine forces reside, and speaking with them means contact with the living spirit of the natural world. In this state, the shaman becomes both a sender and receiver of healing messages.

The sense of connection that psychedelics instill can be so strong that people report encounters with transcendental beings—allies that possess intelligence and agency to act—such as plant spirits, Mother Ayahuasca, helpers, angels, or elves. Encounters with God have also been described.[191] These beings are often described as powerful, wise, and loving, and contact typically elicits positive feelings of joy, trust, surprise, love, friendliness, and friendship, though it may also cause fear. Encounters with entities are especially common in the case of DMT, a psychoactive agent contained in the ayahuasca brew. While not a focal point in modern Western mysticism, multiple other spiritual and religious traditions describe encounters with such beings, among them Jewish mysticism, the Bwiti religion of Gabon, and other shamanic healing cultures. Dietrich Bonhoeffer, a German theologian and prominent opponent of Nazism, described encounters with such beings in poetry written shortly before dying in a concentration camp in 1944: "By loving forces, truly and quietly sheltered / protected, consoled in a marvelous way.../ By loving forces wonderfully sheltered / we await with calm, come what may."[192]

---

189 Matthew J. Baggott, Matthew G. Kirkpatrick, Gillinder Bedi, and Harriet de Wit, "Intimate Insight: MDMA Changes How People Talk About Significant Others," *Journal of Psychopharmacology* 29, no. 6 (June 1, 2015): 669–77.

190 Munn, "The Mushrooms of Language," .

191 Anna Lutkajtis, "Entity Encounters and the Therapeutic Effect of the Psychedelic Mystical Experience," *Journal of Psychedelic Studies* 4, no. 3 (January 15, 2021): 171–78.

192 Dietrich Bonhoeffer, *Widerstand und Ergebung* (Christian Kaiser, 1998). Original translation.

Psychedelics have also been used for millennia in rites of passage, helping egalitarian communities maintain cohesion during the transition from childhood by integrating young adults into the social structures of the adults. Today many patients are unfortunately left alone with their psychedelic experiences, unable to talk about them among family, for example. Psychedelic experiences are frequently taboo in modern society, disrupting their integration. This is why, whenever possible, I involve the patient's immediate social circles in planning and integrating treatment, calling on other doctors, psychologists, and family members.

On a neurological level, psychedelics impact the fear network in our brain.[193] The amygdala, a central hub for processing fear, continues to respond to the environment but does so in a more refined way, making others appear less threatening and promoting feelings of trust and compassion. Psychedelics also have an anti-inflammatory effect.[194] This is significant for social behavior since inflammatory substances in the brain like cytokine trigger "lockdowns" that encourage social withdrawal, among other things, so as to minimize contact with pathogens. The image below shows what brings the feeling of connection: a greater degree of neuronal integration. Functional connections improve in the brain under the influence of psychedelics, as interactions across different regions increase.

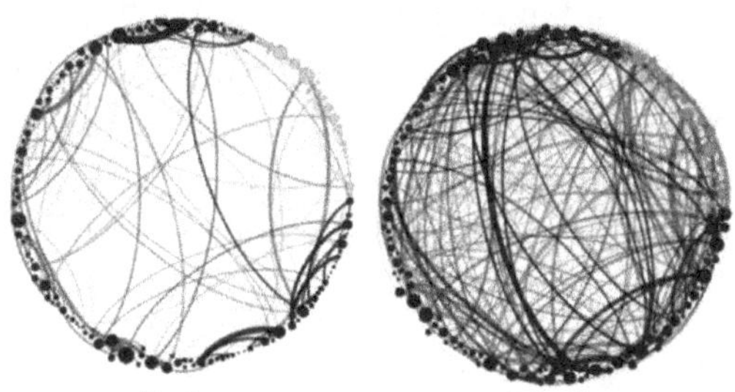

Fig. 5–1
Under the influence of psilocybin, regions of the brain that are otherwise unconnected to one another communicate with each other.[195]

193 Franz X. Vollenweider and Katrin H. Preller, "Psychedelic Drugs: Neurobiology and Potential for Treatment of Psychiatric Disorders," *Nature Reviews Neuroscience* 21, no. 11 (September 14, 2020): 611–24.

194 Thomas W. Flanagan and Charles D. Nichols, "Psychedelics as Anti-inflammatory Agents," *International Review of Psychiatry* 30, no. 4 (July 4, 2018): 363–75.

195 Giovanni Petri, P. Expert, F. Turkheimer, R. Carhart-Harris, D. Nutt, P. J. Hellyear et al., "Homological Scaffolds of Brain Functional Networks," *Journal of the Royal Society Interface* 11, no. 101 (December 6, 2014)

Relationships and Neuroplasticity

The social effects of psychedelics may be even more profound and lasting than previously assumed according to one striking study from US neuroscientist Gül Dölen published in *Nature* magazine.[196] Like humans, mice undergo a "critical period" of neuroplasticity during early age and adolescence in which they are especially receptive to their social surroundings, akin to Bowlby's observation that as children we develop an inner "working model" that guides our subsequent behavior in relationships. This critical period ends with adolescence, after which it becomes much more difficult to change our patterns of social behavior and learn new ways of relating. If we learned as children that social relationships were fundamentally based on achievement, abuse, or deception, such experiences will be difficult to shed, potentially leading to problematic relationships, social withdrawal, or isolation. It is now known that the end of this critical period for social learning is brought on by a dulling of our oxytocin nerve cells, making it useless to simply administer more oxytocin. What Dölen and her team discovered, however, was that MDMA increases receptivity to oxytocin among these same nerve cells in mice, effectively reopening the critical window for social learning. When MDMA was given to the mice within a socially stimulating, secure, and positive environment, their interest in social contact increased over the long term. Nor does the effect seem unique to MDMA. A handful of studies now show that LSD and other psychedelics promote prosocial behavior by enhancing neuroplasticity.[197] The findings hold great promise for psychiatry and psychotherapy given the long-term psychological impact that traumatic experience and childhood neglect (like depression or social anxiety) can have. The conventional substances used to treat these consequences remain generally unsatisfactory, with their psychotherapeutic potential significantly limited by the "critical period" of neuroplasticity having ended.

---

196 Nardou et al., "Oxytocin-dependent Reopening of a Social Reward Learning Critical Period With MDMA," 116–20.

197 Danilo De Gregorio, Jelena Popic, Justine P. Enns, Antonio Inserra, Agnieszka Skalecka, Athanasios Markopoulos et al., "Lysergic Acid Diethylamide (LSD) Promotes Social Behavior Through mTORC1 in the Excitatory Neurotransmission," *Proceedings of the National Academy of Sciences of the United States of America* 118, no. 5 (January 25, 2021)

Dölen's study also raises questions about the importance of setting in therapy. MDMA was only effective in a social setting, among a group of animals, not in isolation. In shamanistic cultures ayahuasca is rarely taken by a single person alone; in the Amazon, ayahuasca ceremonies are an occasion for group dancing and singing, while in the Peruvian Amazon, groups of men are known to stand on tree trunks with their arms and legs wrapped around the man in front of him in order to bolster feelings of community. In psychedelic group therapy, patients encounter each other in an altered state of consciousness, which can strengthen the transformative process. It is helpful if groups reach a state where participants are prepared not just to open themselves up, but to accept others' viewpoints and feelings as being of equal value. As one patient described it: "We then reached a point where we were capable of feeling a complete sympathy with each other. A form of communication arose that bordered on the telepathic." Some patients, by contrast, may come to feel isolated or lost within the group, or avoid contact with others, making individual accompaniment by the therapist more suitable. Alternatively, support during group therapy from an appointed point person can help group compatibility.

Psychedelics can also be used in couples therapy, especially MDMA, which strengthens social sentiment and expression. Patients supported by a therapist are still able to control their openness throughout, however, preventing confessions that might be regretted later. MDMA can help couples in a good, stable relationship confront problems and move towards connection and solutions. For couples who are facing a possible end to their relationship, a deeply emotional and intimate shared experience can help reestablish contact. People will often seek out couples therapy in order to come to terms with the fact that the relationship can no longer be saved. In cases like these, MDMA can help people accept the end of the relationship with clarity and mutual understanding—coming to the insight that the only thing holding the couple together is perhaps fear of the unknown, or other factors. The clarity and tenderness that MDMA encourages allows couples to change without causing unnecessary harm.

The Therapist-Patient Relationship

The relationship between a patient and their therapist is a defining factor in psychotherapy. British psychiatrist Humphry Osmond, one of the first to use LSD in the context of psychotherapy and the figure responsible for coining the term *psychedelic*, considered trust to be the most important element in a therapeutic relationship, arguing that "a minimal amount of trust is essential, how much we don't know, but absolute trust is desirable and essential for using the psychedelic experience fully."[198] Empathy, sympathy, sufficient time, esteem, candor, and respect are all factors in building trust. Ready availability is also important in a therapist. All of my patients have my private cell phone number so they can reach me at any time.

A solid therapeutic relationship becomes especially important when unpleasant emotions such as fear arise. One patient's account of their experience on psilocybin gives a dramatic example of this: "It really affected me...I was in the cargo hold of a ship out at sea. I was teetering back and forth. There was nothing—absolutely nothing that I could hold on to, nothing, no point of reference or anything, just lost in space, it was totally crazy, I was really scared. And then I remembered that Tony and Michelle [the therapists] were right there, and suddenly it became clear to me why it was so important that I had gotten to know them and they had gotten to know me. I reached out my hand just said, 'I'm so afraid.' And I think it was Tony who took my hand...and said, 'Everything's ok. Let it happen, just let it happen.' And so, I mean, that's what I did."[199]

Two key phenomena for describing the therapeutic relationship are *transference* and *countertransference*. Transference occurs when the patient transfers intense feelings from a different situation onto the therapeutic relationship. If a patient never really saw eye-to-eye with his father, for instance, and the therapist is busy explaining something complicated to him that he doesn't understand, the patient may suddenly grow angry. Psychodynamic therapy builds in a great deal of time and space for transferred

---

198 D. B. Blewett and N. Chwelos, *Handbook for the Therapeutic Use of Lysergic Acid Diethylamide-25 Individual and Group Procedures* (The Multidisciplinary Association for Psychedelic Studies, 1959).

199 Alexander B. Belser, Gabrielle Agin-Leibes, T. Cody Swift, Sara Terrana, Nese Devenot, Harris L. Friedman et al., "Patient Experiences of Psilocybin-Assisted Psychotherapy: An Interpretative Phenomenological Analysis," *Journal of Humanistic Psychology* 57, no. 4 (April 28, 2017): 354–88.

feelings, until the patient has understood and worked through them. In psychedelic-assisted therapy this isn't possible because patient and therapist are on a journey together, a hiking trip, and the mountaintop can't be reached if exaggerated feelings slow the team's efforts. Psychedelic therapy is much more productive if the patient doesn't transfer onto the therapist, i.e., remains realistic, or transfers positive emotions, viewing the therapist as an older brother who will protect him, for example.

Countertransference, on the other hand, designates feelings that the therapist may transfer onto the relationship. In this case too, a strong negative reaction to the patient isn't helpful, and is a sign that additional sessions are necessary in order to prepare for work with psychedelics. Therapists are often idolized and at times eroticized by their patients. In the therapist, this can lead to an overestimation or idealization of oneself, even feelings of being a guru. This is a critical juncture, since it means that caution, empathy, and consideration for the patient lessen, and the risk of abuse grows. It is essential for the therapist to have a solid background in psychotherapy and enough professional experience to recognize the countertransference and control it. Appropriate boundaries should also be discussed in advance of every session, including safety protocols if the patient grows paranoid or physically restless.

Current manuals on psychedelic psychotherapy strongly emphasize patient autonomy, regarding the patient as the pilot and the therapist as a flight attendant.[200] The metaphor looks to underscore the fact that the patient is the one leading the trip, with the therapist serving only in an auxiliary role. The image can also lead to misconceptions however, since the therapist typically has much more experience than the patient and is not merely accompanying the patient but is also responsible for their safety. A metaphor in which the patient is the pilot and the therapist is an air traffic controller is somewhat more precise, but casts the therapeutic relationship in a distant, indirect light. The patient doesn't just need a set of instructions after all, but practical and personal support during the flight. A third metaphor imagines the patient as the garden, the therapist as the gardener, and the psychedelic as a sort of mental fertilizer. This gets at the neuroplastic effects of psychedelics, though it may not be easy for every patient to picture themselves as a garden. The image of mountain climbing mentioned above can also be helpful. In this case the therapist is a mountain guide, while the mountain

200 Mithoefer, *A Manual for MDMA-Assisted Psychotherapy*.

symbolizes one's inner life and the patient's expanded consciousness. Yet another metaphor is the therapist as a midwife and the patient as a woman in childbirth. Like the therapist, the midwife is a professional, someone who has a great deal more experience dealing with childbirth and allows things to take their course while still intervening when necessary. As with a birth, new phenomena can arise during psychedelic treatment that must be received with openness. I will return to this metaphor in the last chapter on birthing effects.

Many ancient cultures place great value on the patient, or ceremonial participant, holding a direct relationship with the psychedelic. In the *Rig Veda* passages cited earlier, soma is addressed as a god or a force. Requests and gratitude aren't directed toward the person leading the ritual, but directly to the substance. In South America, ayahuasca is spoken to as a mother figure. A shaman once explained to me that the loneliness in the Western world is visible through the fact that we don't speak to our psychedelic plant spirits, and that it isn't possible to hold any sort of conversation at all with chemical substances like LSD or MDMA. This leaves many people feeling alone or lost while in psychedelic states, and in turn makes it challenging for a guide or therapist to accompany them. Experiencing Mother Ayahuasca as a counterpart thus doesn't just make cultural sense, but pharmacological sense. DMT for example, one of the active ingredients in ayahuasca, seems to encourage entities to appear more frequently than other psychedelics.[201]

The Tibetan Book of the Dead

Aldous Huxley's seemingly farfetched suggestion to use *The Tibetan Book of the Dead* as a guide on psychedelic journeys has had a significant impact on psychedelic psychotherapy, inspiring Timothy Leary to write a psychedelic version of the Tibetan book that he subsequently used as an accompanying manual for LSD trips. On his deathbed, Huxley's wife read him sections from Leary's book before giving him LSD per his request. Even contemporary instructions on serving as a companion for psychedelic journeys regularly contain ideas that can be traced back to *The Tibetan Book of the Dead*. Studies have also revealed near-death experiences and psychedelic states to have a great deal in common, meaning the book may

201 Strassman, *DMT: The Spirit Molecule*.

be useful in helping recognize, understand, and integrate these types of experiences. In what follows, I would like to briefly explore the model of spiritual companionship that *The Tibetan Book of the Dead* recommends, and the possibilities it offers the patient-therapist relationship.

First, it isn't a good idea to tell patients that as their psychedelic guide, you will be taking your cues from something called the *Tibetan Book of the Dead*. Many are shocked or confused, or find it macabre. In fact, the translated title of the book doesn't match the original meaning in Tibetan. It would be more accurate to call it the "book of transformation." The text itself is a Tibetan Buddhist work from the eighth century that describes the transition from one life to the next in terms of rebirth. For Tibetans, the transition represents an extremely delicate moment that can set a person on the path to enlightenment, thus exiting the cycle of rebirth or, depending on one's karma, reincarnation as a new being. This critical period is called *bardo* (intermediate state); the original book is called *Bardo Thödröl*, which translated literally means "Liberation Through Hearing During the Intermediate State." The title echoes the book's suggestion that people listen to their spiritual companions and accept their own feelings, thoughts, and visions in order to be free of them. Accepting in this way encourages enlightenment, or a favorable transformation into a more evolved being. In concrete terms it means not becoming enthralled to feelings or sensations but not avoiding them either, trusting in pure knowledge, and not seeking pleasure. This leads to a birth that is compared to being freed from a cocoon.

Jung understood the text as an "initiation process whose purpose it is to restore to the soul the divinity it lost at birth."[202] Leary in turn wrote that while the book "treats of the intermediate state between life and death, the esoteric aim...was to instruct adepts in changing consciousness. It is a book of the living, a manual for recognizing and utilizing ecstatic states of altered consciousness and applying the ecstatic experience in post-session life. *The Tibetan Book of the Dead* is an uncanny portrayal of states regularly encountered during psychedelic sessions. It is eminently practical, including detailed instructions for the guide and designed to be read by the subject before his experience."[203]

202 Carl Jung, contributor in *The Tibetan Book of the Dead*, ed. W. Y. Evans-Wentz (Oxford University Press, 1977).

203 Richard Blum, *Utopiates: The Use & Users of LSD-25* (Atherton Press, 1968).

This book differs from classic psychotherapeutic manuals in its emphasis on the autonomy and liberation of the "patient," who is at the heart of process. The text also holds out the possibility of existential and transcendental experience. In this context, the therapist becomes a companion responsible for set and setting, or the elements necessary for the process to run of its own accord. The intermediate state in the *The Tibetan Book of the Dead* and a psychedelic state bear the following similarities:

> The soul in the intermediate state is in an extremely variable position, bringing great clarity, mindfulness, concentration, and visionary capacity. Intuitive intelligence is increased ninefold. The condition acts as a spiritual catalyst. The same occurs in a psychedelic state.
>
> The consciousness of the intermediate state does not know death. For patients undergoing psychedelic treatment, we see a parallel in the fact that they do not directly perceive the transformative process while in a psychedelic state, but only afterward during the period of integration, which may continue for years afterward.
>
> A number of "divinities" are associated with the transformation of attachment and aversion in *The Tibetan Book of the Dead.* Angry gods represent energies that one must recognize and accept as one's own creative vision or traumatic memory; by doing so, they transform or vanish. In therapy this finds a parallel in the mechanism of acceptance as discussed in chapter 1. The peaceful gods are supportive, guiding us toward the light. They recall the positivity effects discussed in chapter 3.
>
> The book describes visions of various birthplaces over the course of a person's transformation: in utero, in an egg, in damp warmth, and in a lotus blossom. These visions all recall common psychedelic effects, likely because they belong to the originary time discussed in chapter 2.
>
> Clear light signals liberation from cyclical time, the progression from an individual to a generalized consciousness. The final chapter discusses this point in greater detail.

> Other important texts linked to *The Tibetan Book of the Dead* are called "Liberation Through Pure Seeing During the Intermediate State" and "Liberation Through Feeling During the Intermediate State." Liberation through direct perception is one of the basic tenets of psychedelic therapy, which when paired with increased neuroplasticity may create a new openness to experience, and room for new perspectives.

Given in the form of advice from a spiritual companion, the various concrete instructions *The Tibetan Book of the Dead* offers may prove equally helpful for psychedelic psychotherapy:[204]

> Allow the spirit to rest in its natural flow; clear, without restriction, unaffected, and relaxed.
>
> Realize now with full clarity that everything that now appears external to you...is without substantial existence.
>
> The pure [luminous] apparitions of reality itself will arise [. . .] Do not fear them! Do not be terrified! Do not be awed!
>
> So, recognize this to be the intermediate state! At this time, the aspects of the cycles of existence are reversed [into their own true nature].
>
> At that moment, abandon your fear of the yellow light, and recognize it as pristine cognition [. . .]! Let your awareness relax and abide directly within it, in a state of non-activity.
>
> Abandon pride! Abandon your habitual tendencies!
>
> If you recall this introduction, you will have confidence in the visions that have already arisen,
>
> Relax and abide in a non-referential state.

---

204 Timothy Leary, *The Psychedelic Experience* (Citadel Press, 2017).

> Do not be afraid! Do not turn away! Recognize these sounds and luminosities to be the naturally expressive power of your own awareness, manifesting naturally.
>
> [Due to the clarity, fluidity, and intelligence of the soul in the intermediate state] There is no doubt that even those with negative propensities can attain liberation at this point.[205]

Ralph Metzner, a psychology professor and pioneer in psychedelics, described his use of *The Tibetan Book of the Dead* during his own psychedelic experiments:

> When I saw fearful images, I remembered the admonition of the Bardo Thödröl that they were in my mind only, so I told them to go away. To my immense surprise, they did. Then, with an electrifying shock of insight, I realized that I could do this not only with these relatively trivial demons, but with all my fears...At that moment, I realized that not only my fear of him [one of his friends], but all my emotional reactions, positive and negative, toward him and towards anyone or anything, were all within me. In that moment my whole head opened up spherically in every direction simultaneously, 360 degrees, and I felt both serene and exhilarated as never before in my life. It was incredibly liberating.[206]

People who undergo psychedelic therapy as a way of preparing for death may also find the book both a practical and spiritual guide. Generally, the text can help us recognize the limited scope of our individual lives and begin to adopt a transpersonal perspective. Existentialist philosophy sees an opportunity in the finitude of life, our "being-toward-death" as Heidegger might phrase it, since in this way life reveals its singularity and inestimable value. This means "running toward death" provides a starting point for a self-defined, honest, full-fledged, and in Heidegger's words "authentic" life, one that doesn't take its cues from the yoke of the "they" of everyday society.

---

205 *Das Tibetische Totenbuch: Die Große Befreiung durch Hören in den Zwischenzuständen* (Goldmann, 2008).

206 Ram Dass, Ralph Metzner, and Gary Bravo, *Birth of a Psychedelic Culture* (Synergetic Press, 2010).

I would like now to turn to the ways psychedelics impact our sense of perspective and our sense of intimacy, two key aspects of our social mind that also hold special therapeutic value.

Perspective

For early and indigenous cultures, the world is a living being. Animals, of course, but trees and mountains too have spirits humans can address. In philosophical terms, people don't regard the world and the beings in it as objects, but accord them the status of subjects with their own interests, characters, and perspectives. In certain shamanic cultures humans can slip into the bodies other beings, directly experiencing the world from the perspective of a panther or a hawk. We would refer to this worldview as animistic. The earliest-known religions were animist, assigning every object (or certain objects) in nature a "personal" soul, a spirit that dwelled within them. Seen in terms of society, animism represents a form of egalitarianism. No omnipotent god or person exists; instead, each human, animal, or natural "soul" is dependent on the others. As children we pass through a phase of animism in which we personify our environments, glimpsing beings with intentionality and feeling everywhere we turn. Psychedelics give us a way to reactivate this perspective. Animism may not be helpful in running coal mines or slaughterhouses, but it can help us better understand and care for the world.

One patient of mine who suffered from increasing depression and had lost her creative spark had a cat named Mimi. For work the patient ran a shop online for cat-related products. Under the influence of LSD she turned into Mimi, experiencing her cat's fears and needs: the best hiding spots, which trees you could climb, good sources of food, a need for people to understand her and be able to read her body language, an urge to be free and the desire to get to know other cats. The patient's experience gave her a new lease on her energy and creativity, prompting her to develop a new set of products and services like an online course on communicating with your feline during the Covid pandemic. She also reported that her relationship with Mimi had improved. Arriving at a different outlook on oneself via psychedelics is a shift I call the "perspective effect." As the example shows, the perspective effect can improve our relationships and help us better understand our environments and the needs of others— a change that can also help us on our professional paths.

A second patient experienced a similar effect after a strong, tall, dark-skinned man moved into her apartment building. The woman grew so afraid of the man that she was on the verge of searching for a new apartment. She developed a habit of blaming him for all the unpleasant things in her life. Whenever she heard loud noises in the building or the newspaper didn't arrive, her new neighbor immediately presented himself as the cause. Under the influence of psilocybin, she became him, experiencing what it was like to be someone who was constantly under suspicion. Any loud word she spoke or sudden movement she made could be misinterpreted as dangerous or aggressive. Following her treatment, she saw that she had been doing her neighbor an injustice, and that her feelings were a form of racism. She initiated contact and invited him to afternoon tea. The man turned out to be a charming artist from the US who was on sabbatical in Switzerland. Since puberty he had suffered from others' projections about his dark skin and size, which among other issues showed up in constantly being stopped by police.

My patient's transformation reminded me of one of Ram Dass's psychedelic experiences. Ram Dass was still teaching at Harvard under his given name of Richard Alpert, at a time when people of color were by and large much more discriminated against and excluded than today. Alpert, a white man from a well-to-do home, practiced a noble sort of discrimination, tolerating the dark-skinned people he encountered in his professional and private life as "different," with a "very self-conscious kind of equality." Until, that is, he took an LSD trip with a black psychiatrist friend of his, which brought a shift in perspective: "And Madison and I turned on together and I looked at Madison, and there we were, the same human beings. It was just that he was wearing that skin and I was wearing this skin."[207]

Emma, a patient I treated over many years for depression, had a smoldering conflict with her mother, who lived in South America. She described her experience on LSD as allowing her "to describe every relationship with people who matter to me in a fraction of a second. All of my memories in the same second. Everything is clear. I'm blinking through time." Speaking about her mother, Emma shared, "I constantly felt the pressure my mother

207 Ram Dass, *Be Here Now, Remember* (Lama Foundation, 1971).

put on me as a kid to look pretty. Now I can feel the pressure I put on my mother because I was a special, different girl. LSD switches the perspective. I recognized for the first time who my mother really was: an old, worried woman." After her LSD session Emma grew more open toward her mother, and stopped avoiding difficult topics. She also become more open, more wild and lively with her partner. At first she was afraid people might take her for being crazy, but that wasn't the case—the response in her immediate social circles was positive.

Stanislav Grof observed that in working through difficult or traumatic experiences while on LSD, patients would take on the roles of everyone involved in the event, processing their trauma for diverse perspectives.[208] The variety of perspectives gave them a deeper understanding of the social situations that had given rise to whatever psychological issue was at hand.

At times the perspective shift induced by psychedelics may be so pronounced that it gives way to a fully animist experience. August, who was treated with psilocybin after a cancer diagnosis left her with existential fears, reported that it "was as if I was out in nature, and I could have stayed there forever—it was wonderful. There were all kinds of other things too, like the feeling of being connected with everything, everything in nature I mean. Everything—even pebbles, drops of water in the sea.... It was like magic. It was wonderful, and the point wasn't to talk about it, which turns it into an idea, it was like an experience instead. It was like being inside a drop of water, inside a butterfly wing or inside a leopard's eye."[209]

Claudio Naranjo observed marked, self-transcending perspective shifts under the influence of ibogaine, calling them the "eye behind the eye" phenomenon. As one of his patients described, "At one point, I felt that I had two eyes, and my physical eyes, my eyelids, were closed, but behind there were some other eyelids that were opening, like eyelids opening to the subconscious and to another dimension of reality. With these eyes, I could see my eye, my physical eye, my left eye...it got older, older and older, until it was very old people, and then went back to being, passing through different genders, like the eye of a man, like the eye of a woman, then of a man again,

208 Grof, *LSD Psychotherapy*.

209 Belser et al., "Patient Experiences of Psilocybin-Assisted Psychotherapy: An Interpretative Phenomenological Analysis," .

and of many women. My eye was in the body of many women and of many men in a kind of regression."[210]

Identifying with others at such a deep level allows us to see the world as an intricate web of subjects. Seeing the world through the eyes of a mother, a father, one's spouse, one's child, best friend, cat, or a stranger gives us a profound and empathetic understanding of social relationships and interactions. Incorporating the perspectives of trees, flowers, and butterflies helps us develop an ecological, holistic worldview with myriads of subjects all engaged in the great dance of mutual dependence and influence that we call "coevolution."

One hymn in the *Rig Veda* dedicated to human diversity and unity suggests that as different as we may appear, soma reveals us as all the same in our search for happiness, be it though water, wealth, or a woman's smile. Modern psychedelic experience would add that we are all alike in responding sensitively to rejection and being ostracized. In fact, patients often first become aware of this through psychedelic psychotherapy.

In this regard, psychedelics can help us experience directly William James's observation that "we are like islands in the sea, separate on the surface but connected in the deep."[211] James's insight is reminiscent of Jung's "collective unconscious," an innate mental structure made up of the universal lived wisdom of humanity as a whole—a plane of existence we all share, if only we can delve deeply enough into our consciousness.

One important therapeutic effect of this psychedelic shift in perspective is the reconciliation it offers, which is the opposite of alienation. According to Israeli philosopher Martin Buber, alienation and conflict belong to the "it-world," where human relationships are exploited the way one might an object. This stands in contrast to the "thou-world" of the relationships themselves. "It" and "thou" worlds always exist side-by-side, Buber wrote, though the balance shifts. Many of us are embedded in the it-world of possessing things and using people. To realize the thou-world, it becomes necessary to encourage participation and relationships in life as in therapy. To enter into relationships in the world we must cultivate our presence, which creates a space for true participation. Participation in turn allows us to recognize each other, which is required for reconciliation, be it moving past a

---

210 Naranjo, *My Psychedelic Explorations*.

211 William James, "The Confidences of a 'Psychical Researcher,'" *American Magazine* 68 (October 1909): 580–589.

conflict or out of a state of alienation. Reconciliation is a return to the world of thou, a journey to which psychedelics can offer considerable support

An inability to forgive oneself and others is an important cause of depression, fear, burnout, bitterness, and loneliness.[212] When we forgive, it decreases anger and resentment in our feelings, thoughts, and patterns of behavior while increasing the positive, well-intentioned feelings we hold toward ourselves and those who may have harmed us. Forgiveness rests on the ability to look at relationships in a balanced manner, considering one's own weaknesses and errors along with the strengths and talents of the other. This ability makes it possible to "patch up" relationships through forgiveness, lessening depression. Study findings indicate that the changes in perspective psychedelics offer us play an important role in their antidepressive effects.

It is not that psychedelics force one to forgive unconditionally, or in an unnuanced way. After being excluded and bullied by her older sister for years on end, one of my patients saw her in a positive light for the first time while on psilocybin, including the sister's vulnerability and fear of losing their mother's love. In a subsequent integration session, he explained, "I'm grateful for having had my sister's experience for once. I can understand her better now. But I've decided not to make up with her. The time isn't right for it."

Patients who live with autistic traits or autism proper often have difficulty putting themselves in another's place; they largely see the world from their own perspective. In children, this is visible in troubles imitating others. They'll repeat someone else's sentence mechanically for instance, without considering the feelings or particular situation of the person they are imitating. The identification with others remains on the surface, and lacks emotional and existential depth. In other words, in an autistic state, I perceive others only in relationship to myself, and not as people independent of me, manifesting in a lack of social emotions like empathy and guilt. Social anxiety is an important trait of autism, and it blocks social interests and skills from developing. Tentative findings now indicate that MDMA

212 John Maltby, Ann Macaskill, and Liza Day, "Failure to Forgive Self and Others: A Replication and Extension of the Relationship Between Forgiveness, Personality, Social Desirability and General Health," *Personality and Individual Differences* 30, no. 5 (April 1, 2001): 881–85.

loosens social anxiety among adults with mild forms of autism, strengthening their ability to identify with others and take on different perspectives.[213]

Intimacy

Intimacy refers to a close, familiar, and usually affectionate or loving personal relationship with another person that can involve emotional, intellectual, spiritual, and physical closeness. Intimacy is often associated with trust, vulnerability, and a deep sense of connection. It also presents a paradox in stress research: We have to allow vulnerability and weakness for intimacy to develop, and at the same time, intimacy turns out to be an important factor in resilience.[214] If a person constantly has their guard up against others, it will weaken their resilience over the long run as they grow lonely and alienated from themselves.

Often, people who aren't able to experience intimacy during childhood—if needs for closeness are regularly frustrated or abused, for instance—will have to learn intimacy later in life as a sort of second language through psychotherapy. They are frequently distant and avoid close contact, and often suffer a disrupted sense of self-intimacy, struggling to feel acceptance, concern, or love for themselves, or view themselves as worthy and deserving of love. Aside from a deficit in self-love, they lack experiences in mutual intimacy, whether through deep friendships or sexual relationships. They will often rely on sexuality instead, otherwise one of the peak experiences of intimacy, as a substitute for intimacy. For fear of being wounded by an intimate relationship they wrap themselves in protective armor, making any deeper sort of relationship next to impossible.

An ability to be intimate with oneself is an important precondition for achieving intimacy with others. Spiritual traditions the world over recommend practicing self-intimacy (or intimacy with God) as an important goal in coming of age. Profound personal experiences that one might call

---

213 Alicia Danforth, Charles S. Grob, Christopher Struble, Allison A. Feduccia, Nick Walker, Lisa Jerome et al., "Reduction in Social Anxiety After MDMA-assisted Psychotherapy with Autistic Adults: A Randomized, Double-Blind, Placebo-Controlled Pilot Study," *Psychopharmacology/Psychopharmacologia* 235, no. 11 (September 8, 2018): 3137–48.

214 Hasler, *Resilienz*.

religious or mystical are characterized by a high degree of intimacy; the Bible is filled with stories of people overcoming inner urges and outer distractions to discover higher forms of closeness or proximity. When in the Old Testament Jacob wrestles with a man out in the field at night, he is defending his intimacy with God in his tent. When Hannah goes to the temple and abandons all her familial relations—her beloved husband, the rival woman, her entire noisy clan—she does so in order to find intimacy with God. When Jesus feels alone and abandoned, he takes flight into intimacy with his father, i.e., himself, reinforced by his disciples falling asleep. Meditation is another form of intimacy; the Buddha's advice to acknowledge one's inner demons in order to be free of them serves to guard the intimacy of the act of meditating.

Psychedelics present one opportunity for experiencing intimacy within a secure context. Feeling vulnerable speaks to an increase in neuroplasticity, leaving our nervous system more open to environmental influences. In psychedelic psychotherapy, the helioscope effect I outlined in chapter 1 allows patients to set aside their protective armor in a finite, clearly defined, and safe context without having to take on greater risks. For many, this helps them experience intimacy for the first time in their entire lives. It is not intimacy with the therapist or the person attending their session (also called the sitter or co-sitter) that is the goal, but intimacy with themselves. The therapist's job first and foremost is to create and sustain a sheltered, respectful space where self-intimacy can develop. Developing self-intimacy becomes an effective way to experience intimacy with others, as the fears of coming into contact with oneself are often the same that keep us from coming into contact with others.

MDMA and other psychedelics are also called *entactogens*, a word composed of the Greek prefix *en* ("within"), the Latin *tactus* ("touch"), and the Greek suffix *gen* ("creating"). An entactogen thus refers to a substance that allows us to be touched from within—an important aspect of intimacy. Psychedelics look primarily to teach us about self-intimacy rather than intimacy with others, apparent alone from the fact that they often take patients through landscapes that are otherwise empty of people. These nonjudgmental landscapes help patients set aside their self-judgements and criticisms. The brooks and waterfalls, trees, and majestic, fog-enshrouded mountains they encounter along their journeys regularly call to mind the spiritually charged imagery of Chinese landscape painting. It is within the intimacy of these landscapes that patients find themselves confronted with their loneliness, their fear of not being loved or belonging, or of being left alone. In our everyday lives this fear can manifest as envy, jealousy, or a lack of social interest; lonely people will often avoid being alone so that they are not forced to confront it. Yet it is precisely an acceptance of fear and feelings of loneliness on which the capacity to love and participate in community is built.

The experience of intimacy on psychedelics will frequently elicit erotic feelings that don't end in sexual arousal. There is no better aid than Eros for humans, Plato says in his *Symposium*. Psychedelics allow us to see that Eros is much more than just sexual lust; it contains our drive to recuperate and become whole and healthy, to grow and transform, to learn, integrate, make meaning. Eros drives us to seek out ultimate truths. It is a profound form of openness—neuroplasticity par excellence. This explains why for many people, psychedelic self-intimacy is a much deeper and more striking experience than sexual intimacy. In Latin, *intimus* is the intensified form of *intra* ("inside"), meaning "the innermost," "most trusted," or "most secret." The point is to accept all of oneself and to feel accepted as one is. Intimacy is privacy at the existential level.

The intimacy that exists between patient and therapist should allow them to exchange thoughts, images, yearnings, fears, wishes, and hopes. The highly unique and personal quality of the psychedelic state makes the therapist's respect for the patient's alterity and altered consciousness essential. The word "respect" comes from the Latin verb *respicere*, which means "to look back again." Verifying, taking a second look, means we are taking something seriously. In this sense, the therapist must always look several times to understand what the patient is experiencing and wants, and what is appropriate for the situation.

Psychedelic intimacy can take different forms. Intellectual intimacy brings our deepest convictions to light; emotional intimacy confronts us with our deepest feelings, which are often of an erotic nature in that they communicate a longing to be whole. With social intimacy it is the give-and-take with the therapist that takes center stage, the urge to share one's deepest feelings and thoughts with another. With spiritual intimacy, a patient's existential privacy dissolves into an awareness of shared intimacy with all beings and even consciousness itself. This creates space for transpersonal thoughts and feelings and allows us to sense our way back to the One and recognize the depths to which we are connected to one another. All of these experiences of intimacy are of a nonsexual nature, though they will subsequently aid patients in their sexual intimacy, or help them consciously hold back from abusing sexuality as their sole source of intimacy, since alternative forms of intimacy now stand at their disposal.

At times, psychedelics' intimacy effects may be strengthened by the therapist touching the patient. Laying hands on a person is one of the oldest healing gestures that exists. Holding a patient's hand can help calm them and give them faith. Holding the agitated and trembling body of the patient—at the right moment and in the right way—can likewise support the therapeutic process. Physical touch should always be discussed as one possibility before the psychedelic session; female patients with a traumatic prehistory may be especially grateful to rule it out from the outset. Nor does physical proximity always have to include touch; a therapist might create a quieting, empathetic sense of connection simply by sitting down next to a patient in search of closeness, for instance. Any sort of touch whatsoever that could lead to sexual arousal is inadvisable.

Therapists should allow the patient space to explore the full spectrum of their human experience, whether they're feeling fear, peace, or an urge towards physical expression. They can do so by ensuring a peaceful and safe environment, and adopting an attentive, nonjudgmental attitude of calm non-activity. In principle, he or she should respond to the wishes of the patient. In the interests of their developing self-intimacy, I continually invite my patients to focus on their feelings, thoughts, and visions, and not let themselves be distracted by their surroundings or their smartphones.

One patient I treated with MDMA, Marco, lived alone for more than a decade after he moved out of his parents' house. As a self-employed computer scientist who worked from home, he scarcely left his apartment. He only spoke to people while on holiday, mostly in Asia or Africa. Repeated attempts to become "normal" through psychotherapy failed. He felt misunderstood by the therapists he saw. His problem wasn't an inability to strike up contact, but confusion about why he should do so in the first place. He didn't understand people who were happy in relationships, because he was so alienated from his own social needs and feelings. Before taking MDMA he had voiced the desire to be left alone in the treatment room, as he felt overly observed. Later, as the MDMA took effect, he was happy I had stayed. "I've never felt so good, as relaxed and social as I do today." Outside the clinic he heard people speaking French, a language he had hated in school. Yet now the language sounded much more positive, even erotic. He grew happier and happier that I had spent the entire day with him. "This is the first time I can see why people live with each other, why friends take each other out, why you say happy birthday to someone, talk about your holidays, and ultimately get married and have children. You probably don't believe me, but until now it was a mystery to me." He began to sob upon realizing this, overcome by the wonderful strangeness of this new form of intimacy that included others.

The most common reason women give for leaving men is their lack of emotional availability. British psychologist Katie Anderson examined the effects of MDMA on couples through interviews. As one man reported, "I wasn't emotionally available enough I don't think maybe ever for the woman and it really just kind of kicks your ass down that road [of low intimacy]...I don't think...I could've gone down that road maybe ever...I didn't have the vulnerable life. I didn't go through major break-ups. I didn't, you know. I've never really taken major risks in relationships. One way or the other, I was just a serial dater my whole life and, although compassionate towards people I'd dated, it kind of stayed more on the surface and you just, that's all removed during a heavy MDMA experience...one of the things I was afraid of that it wasn't going to stay or was just, am I developing a chemical romance? But it wasn't...it stayed."[215]

Another of the couples Anderson interviewed, Emily and Dan, used MDMA's intimacy effects to process a conflict in their relationship after Emily had cheated, which hurt Dan deeply. Both had a desire to save the relationship. While on MDMA Dan reported feeling "like you're floating in a warm tub of warm goo and you're just totally protected and you can say anything...it's overpowering...It's like, no matter what she said, it was like everything made me love her more and more...you come back down off of that but now you have two associations with that information. You got the typical response where you're angry and pissed off...and you also have this, this connection and association to it where it's like the deepest connection you've ever had with a person at the same time."

For her part, Emily said the treatment "certainly gives you a point to reflect back on and works as a reminder to be like that [feelings of high intimacy]...both of us could be more affectionate...I certainly think it's had

215 Katie Anderson, host, "The experiences of couples who take MDMA together," webinar, Middlesex University London, *Drugs and Alcohol Research Centre Webinar Series*, 2021, https://www.youtube.com/watch?v=XIGoIwm4IVE.

a lasting effect...knowing now that it's like absolute truth is out, I would't want to bring a line back into our relationship, you know, even little things. And just having this nice, clean slate and not wanting to ruin it."[216]

As these examples show, the forms of intimacy psychedelics open up are a lesson in human vulnerability. The hope is that psychedelics may lead to more humane forms of psychiatry and psychotherapy.

Summary

Human beings complain in greater and greater numbers of feeling disconnected from their bodies and other people. In ancient Indian and shamanic cultures, psychedelics were responsible for fostering group cohesion and integrating young people into the community through initiation rites. This same approach can strengthen the efficacy of modern individual and couples' psychotherapy. Psychedelics shift our perspectives and help us walk in another's shoes. This can play a decisive role in allowing for forgiveness and improving interpersonal relationships. Psychedelic intimacy effects, meanwhile, offer patients an experience of profound connection with themselves, which becomes important for successfully establishing intimacy with others later on.

216 Ibid.

Chapter 6
Right Self: The Path to Transcendence

"I'm not myself anymore" is one of the most common reasons people who take their own lives write in their farewell notes. Psychologically, the subtext is that they can no longer live up to the expectations they place on themselves. The causes of suicide are of course varied. Perhaps the individual hasn't lived up to professional expectations or in their love lives, or maybe their emotional and psychological state has changed so drastically they no longer recognize themselves. Aging or illness can also frustrate the expectations one has about one's body.

Self-inflicted suffering is much older and more ingrained is us than the modern world's fixation on self-reliance. Nietzsche wrote that "during the longest period of the human past nothing was more terrible than to feel that one stood by oneself. To be alone, to experience things by oneself, neither to obey nor to rule, to be an individual—that was not a pleasure but a punishment; one was sentenced 'to individuality.'"[217] The Buddha considered the self to be a central source of suffering, concluding that exposing the self as an illusion was an important step on the path to enlightenment.

The self is made up of various parts; the expectations we place on ourselves are an expression of the "narrative self," or whatever we know to be true about ourselves. Psychological research also speaks to the "narrative gravity of the self,"[218] since our minds naturally organize incoming information to fit into our personal narratives. The narrative self is both an effective and necessary structure that helps us navigate the world, as self-knowledge is not primarily a store of factual knowledge but rather guides how we think, feel, behave, and relate to other people. But while stories are

217 Friedrich Nietzsche, *The Gay Science* (Vintage, 1974).

218 Daniel Dennett, "The Self as a Center of Narrative Gravity," in *Self and Consciousness: Multiple Perspectives*, eds. F. Kessel, P. Cole and D. Johnson (Erlbaum, 1992).

fundamentally open-ended, allowing them to be spun on and on, a disproportionate gravitation toward self limits this openness in fundamental ways. In this context we might say that people who kill themselves no longer have any idea how their life story might continue to develop in a meaningful way. The perceived lack of options is short-lived for the most part, and nearly everyone who survives a suicide attempt wants to keep living. In principal, this indicates that we are capable of adjusting our self-expectations to our living circumstances.

In Western culture, the narrative self is given greater emphasis than in the East, especially with the cultural value attached to work ethic since the Protestant Reformation. Freud conceived of the superego as a judge and censor, as well as one of the demands of the ego ideal. He placed it at the center of his theory of neurosis in psychoanalysis, assuming that the superego came about by individuals internalizing parental, cultural, and societal taboos and norms. This "critical function" of the superego plays an analogous role in the conscious and unconscious parts of self-narratives that are overly critical.

In the wake of World War II, the US saw an upturn in psychological self-help books for fighting off the critical, prohibitive superego with heroic narratives to raise readers' self-esteem; titles like *How to Become a Superstar* or *You're the Best Woman* dominated the bestseller lists for more than two decades. While the books were an attempt to bolster the self and counter psychological maladies through positive self-talk, invoking phrases such as "I'm the best" or "What doesn't kill me makes me stronger," clinical research now shows that these strategies are accompanied by many side effects. People with overly high self-esteem are especially vulnerable to egotism and tend to respond to criticism or disregard with resentment, aggression, or violence. People with an inflated sense of self-esteem also show an increased need for admiration and can lack empathy. All this means that a grandiose self-narrative makes it more difficult to integrate our weaknesses, all the slings and arrows of fortune, and to admit our own dependence on other people and our environment. In our contemporary world individualization, the increased focus on productivity, digitalization, and decreased physical activity have further heightened the prominence of the narrative self, and the degree to which we live in our heads.

Neuroscientific research has also given us signs that inflating and strengthening our narrative sense of self isn't an effective way of dealing with stress. Among the multiple networks within the brain, the "default mode network" connects a variety of conscious and potentially conscious regions that engage whenever our narrative self raises its voice. This occurs most often when things are quiet, and we aren't pursuing any particular kind of activity—thus "default mode," the brain's standard operating procedure when there isn't any specific, outwardly oriented task to complete. In experiments, researchers have been able to activate the network by asking test subjects to judge their own accomplishments or personalities. People who regularly think about or criticize themselves, or object to their fate in life—those who are preoccupied with their self-narrative in other words—tend to exhibit a default mode network that is overly active. Hyperactivity of this sort raises the risk of burnout or depression. Default mode activity decreases in states where we forget ourselves, when we lose ourselves in the smell of a flower for instance, disappear into a game or a song, or enter a flow state while baking a cake. Experienced meditators are capable of consciously lowering the activity of their default mode network, which has a calming effect on the stress system. Stimulating the narrative self by invoking mantras of our own heroism, by contrast, runs the risk of sending the default mode network into overdrive, raising our stress levels in the process.

The counterpart to the narrative self is the "minimal self" that we experience in flow state, or moments in which we merge with our own sensory perception and activity. The minimal self contains the intuitive "I" quality of consciousness, all the things that I experience as "my own," and corresponds to direct physical and sensory experience in the present moment. It also raises a seemingly odd paradox: On the one hand our body is a given object—we can observe and describe it and the movements it makes—yet at the same time it is this living, breathing body with which we perceive and experience the world—including our bodies themselves—as subjects. This means that our self-consciousness cannot be understood in abstract or philosophical terms alone, or as a zero point in a system of coordinates. It is a physical phenomenon. The Buddha said that the cosmos begins and ends in the body; by this logic, alienation from our own bodies is tantamount to a restriction of consciousness. What is more, our everyday consciousness always has a certain stance toward the world, a perspective, so is never fully transparent or open.

Since the minimal self only deals in very short spans of time (about a third of a second), it does not know any narrative form. It pieces impressions gathered from different sense organs into a whole that we experience as belonging to ourselves. Synesthesia, described above in chapter 1, plays an important role in constructing the minimal self as an experience that ties different sensory perceptions into each other—experiencing red in terms of warmth, for instance. Aligning perception with action is another key way we create the minimal self.

Within the brain, the salience network is responsible for creating the minimal self. Salience acts as a precursor to attention, assessing a given stimulus's prominence and importance. The network contains the insular cortex and the front cingulate cortex, regions of the brain that are responsible for consciously perceiving internal states like one's breathing, heartbeat, and physical movements, but also sensations such as pain and emotions. In an interesting turn, the same structure is used in perceiving others' physical and emotional states, forming the basis for our ability to feel empathy.

One neuroscientific study conducted of 15,892 people with illnesses like schizophrenia, bipolar disorder, depression, and addictive and compulsive disorders showed a reduced salience network in nearly every case, a fact that expresses itself clinically in a lack of empathy for oneself and others.[219] Weakened consciousness of the minimal self, i.e., direct experience of the self, lead further to excessive activity on the part of the narrative self in the form of mental absence, difficulty concentrating, an inability to feel pleasure, and brooding.

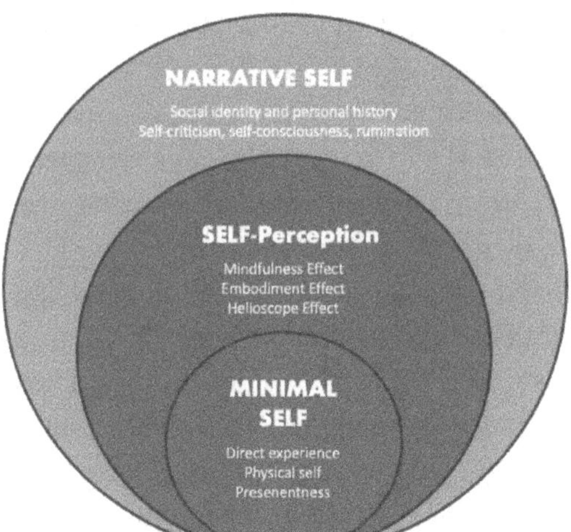

Fig. 6–1: Model of the self with the narrative and minimal selves.

219 Madeleine Goodkind, Simon B. Eickhoff, Desmond J. Oathes, Ying Jiang, Andrew Chang, Laura B. Jones-Hagata et al., "Identification of a Common Neurobiological Substrate for Mental Illness," *JAMA Psychiatry* 72, no. 4 (April 1, 2015): 305.

What role might psychedelics have to play in this context? Put simply, one could say that they strengthen the minimal self at the expense of the narrative self. This process has been referred to, somewhat misleadingly, as "ego dissolution" or even "ego death," since the experience of the minimal self takes on a diffuse, impersonal quality. It is through the narrative self alone that we are able to regard and judge ourselves as objects; the minimal self possesses no such capacity. Research literature also describes the "narrative gravity of the self" lessening under the influence of psychedelics; weakening the magnet that under normal circumstances draws all thought, feeling, and experience toward the self. In its place there arises a new, more relaxed order of things, where the "I" isn't continually dominating as the boss and other types of information gain prominence.

This dissolution of self can be explained in terms of the REBUS theory; psychedelics loosen the brain's expectations on experience. The first chapter explored what this means in terms of perception: Now, instead of demanding "Nothing new please!" the brain says to the sense organs, "Send me the whole gamut of impressions, I want to bathe in them!" As we saw, this can make the folds in one's own trousers so thrilling that they are able to entertain for hours on end. In chapter 3 we saw the way in which loosening our expectations of reward can transform the world into a land of milk and honey—a place of unexpected desire and pleasure, where an act as simple as drinking water becomes an event that one attends with a profound sense of satisfaction, astonishment, and gratitude. In this chapter I look to address the dissolution of the most fundamental expectation of all: that of the self. A dissolution of this nature allows us to experience ourselves in entirely new ways or, in extreme cases, to immerse ourselves in selfless awareness.

Dissolution of self does not just concern the psyche; it involves the entire body. The difference experienced between one's one hand and the hand of another grows smaller. Under the influence of psychedelics the immune system, tasked with distinguishing between endogenous and exogenous, is dampened; this is significant because autoimmune diseases—which could be interpreted as a form of alienation from one's own body—have risen dramatically in recent decades. Recurring individual reports of psychedelics curing allergies or preventing the incidence of autoimmune diseases like ulcerative colitis give good cause to investigate such effects systematically.

The healing potential of self-dissolution is not found in psychedelic therapy alone; it can also occur spontaneously, without the help of substances. Even a rationalist as hard-boiled as British mathematician and philosopher Bertrand Russell advised making "your interests gradually wider and more impersonal, until bit by bit the walls of the ego recede, and your life becomes increasingly merged in the universal life. An individual human existence should be like a river—small at first, narrowly contained within its banks, and rushing passionately past rocks and over waterfalls. Gradually the river grows wider, the banks recede, the waters flow more quietly, and in the end, without any visible break, they become merged in the sea, and painlessly lose their individual being."[220]

Hungarian author Arthur Koestler described the relaxing effects of his own experience of self-dissolution: "The 'I' ceases to exist because it has, by a kind of mental osmosis, established communication with, and been dissolved in, the universal pool. It is the process of dissolution and limitless expansion which is sensed as the 'oceanic feeling,' as the draining of all tension, the absolute catharsis, the peace that passeth all understanding."[221]

Aldous Huxley emphasized further the potentially long-term effects of ego dissolution through psychedelics: "But the man who comes back through the Door in the Wall will never be quite the same as the man who went out. He will be wiser but less cocksure, happier but less self-satisfied, humbler in acknowledging his ignorance yet better equipped to understand the relationship of words to things, of systematic reasoning to the unfathomable Mystery which it tries, forever vainly, to comprehend."[222]

In psychedelic therapy, the dosage is chosen so that ego dissolution occurs only in part, allowing the patient to consciously direct and perceive his or her experiences. Complete loss of control should be avoided, since it will lead to insecurity and holds no therapeutic potential. One patient of the German psychiatrist Thorsten Passie described the experience as "having a feeling that I could guide and help shape my experiences...I could help shape them with full awareness. I also never felt like I was being helplessly swept along in a maelstrom. Far from it, I could set break points, could say 'Now I'm going to try and put that in words,' even though it was all happening without words. 'Stop, go back again,' really like a video recorder,

220 Bertrand Russell, *Portraits From Memory: And Other Essays* (Touchstone, 1956).

221 Arthur Koestler, *The Invisible Writing* (Random House, 2011).

222 Huxley, *The Doors of Perception*.

'stop, go on, go back again,' like a still image that you blow-up, just in this case for feelings."[223]

Psychedelic dissolution of self is typically described in phrases like:

> I am experiencing my "self" or "me" dissolving.
>
> I feel unity with others.
>
> I feel my sense of self-importance decreasing.
>
> I feel far less absorbed with my own problems and concerns.

The experience is quite different from the self-reinforcement that many resilience and mental fitness programs set as their goal. Studies show that the following experiences do *not* grow stronger under the influence of psychedelics:[224]

> I feel especially unique.
>
> I feel especially sharp and able to compete.
>
> I feel especially self-aware and confident of myself.

Disorders of the Self

Since the self is involved with every aspect of our experiences and actions, nearly all psychological disorders can be seen as disorders of the self. Psychological health and well-being and personal growth all come with a sense of self that is at once centered while remaining transparent, open, and unrestricted. It doesn't rely on a fixed center because it can rest safe and sound in free-floating perception. It is well acquainted with the boundaries

---

223 Torsten Passie and Thomas Dürst, *Heilungsprozesse im veränderten Bewusstsein: Elemente psycholytischer Therapieerfahrung aus der Sicht von Patienten*, (Verlag für Wissenschaft und Bildung, 2009).

224 Matthew M. Nour, Lisa Evans, David Nutt, and Robin Carhart-Harris, "Ego-Dissolution and Psychedelics: Validation of the Ego-Dissolution Inventory (EDI)," *Frontiers in Human Neuroscience* 10 (June 14, 2016): 1-13.

of normality and rationality and is extremely adept at working with them without forgetting its own boundless nature.

The "neurotic self," meanwhile, elevates the risk of stress-related illness like anxiety disorders or depression and is characterized by an excessive concern with drawing boundaries. Unable to effectively integrate unconscious fears and wishes or traumatic experiences, it is continually taken up with fending them off. It takes a great deal of energy to do so, manifesting in exhaustion, listlessness, or rigid, inflexible behavior. Nor does this self know what it truly needs, or does so only vaguely, leading to a "false self," an inauthentic, alienated way of life. In 2011, German neuroscientist and philosopher Georg Northoff and I proposed examining excessive focus on the self as a central cause of depression, basing the suggestion on findings in neuroscience.[225] The article garnered a great deal of attention in the scientific community at the time and is finding renewed relevance today amid the growth of psychedelic therapy. Clinically, excessive focus on the self expresses itself in chronic depression and patients who speak more frequently in the "I" form, reflecting on and criticizing themselves disproportionately—all speaking to exaggerated expectations of oneself. One patient of mine deep in the throes of depression described the experience of her excessive self-focus dissolving as follows: "My 'I' is no longer in the middle. I'm no longer so important to myself. Nothing else has changed about my situation otherwise. It feels really good. Airy, relaxed. I'm not depressed at all anymore. That hasn't happened for years."

The patient I discussed in the introduction to the book experienced her own sort of dissolution or opening of self under the influence of esketamine. Her husband likened her improvement to a flower blooming, accompanied by her depressive symptoms vanishing. In her depression she had been much more egocentric, speaking only of herself. During her treatment with esketamine she behaved as she had before her illness—always willing to help, taking interest in life, and open to the world around her.

There is little research to date on the impact of psychedelics on more complex disorders of the self. In the case of borderline personality disorders the self is split into different pieces. This creates insecurity regarding one's true identity, rapidly shifting states of emotion, and unpredictable behavior. One extreme form of the split self is dissociative identity disorder, where

225 Gregor Hasler and Georg Northoff, "Discovering Imaging Endophenotypes for Major Depression," *Molecular Psychiatry* 16, no. 6 (May 23, 2011): 604–19.

different states of personality, or split identities, alternate in controlling the person's thoughts, feelings, or behavior. People with disorders like these have often suffered from severe trauma in the past; time will tell whether MDMA is suitable for helping patients process their traumatic experiences.

Cases involving the "psychotic self," as arises with schizophrenia, have a severe impact on the minimal self, depriving the person of physical awareness and self-experience or self-feeling. People will suffer from a lack of boundaries and a center point. They also suffer from their fundamental differences to other people, a situation that brings a terrible sense of loneliness. Since psychedelics can strengthen the frightful experience of losing one's borders and self, treating psychotic patients with them is currently discouraged.

Psychedelics and Spirituality

The dissolution of the self offers an important access point to spirituality. While it is always a matter of interpretation whether a given experience is spiritual or is only experienced as such, we can say that people most frequently experience this sort of ego dissolution in a spiritual context.

One possible reaction to ego dissolution is a feeling of awe or experience of eternity, or connection to something greater than ourselves. Many people will even feel themselves merging or melting into a greater whole. Awe, wonder, and sense of astonishment all call our notions of ourselves and the world into question and urge us on to update them in light of what we've just experienced. This helps to explain why encounters with mysteries or transcendence can be so transformative—they alter the ways we understand the universe and our place in it. This holds important implications for psychotherapy, with dozens of studies showing that spiritual experiences under the influence of psychedelics assist in the therapeutic process—the more pronounced the spiritual experience is, the greater the progress shown with psychiatric issues.[226] The link is especially evident with addictive disorders but has also shows up when treating depression and anxiety disorders.

I will now distinguish between psychedelic and spiritual experiences in the two most prominent religious traditions, the Abrahamic and the Vedic.

226 David B. Yaden and Roland R. Griffiths, "The Subjective Effects of Psychedelics Are Necessary for Their Enduring Therapeutic Effects," *ACS Pharmacology & Translational Science* 4, no. 2 (December 10, 2020): 568–72.

In the Abrahamic tradition as it has developed in Judaism, Christianity, and Islam, the experience of self-dissolution creates an awareness of ourselves as creatures who are overcome by their dependence and insignificance in relation to that which stands above all beings. Abraham gives straightforward expression to this sense of awe when he says: "Now that I have been so bold as to speak to the Lord, though I am nothing but dust and ashes."[227] The experience diminishes and elevates at the same time—it can make us both more humble and more grateful, two core elements in resilience.

US documentary filmmaker Michael Wiese described a similar of sense of awe he felt during a shamanic ayahuasca ceremony. While under the influence of ayahuasca he underwent a dissolution of self that he experienced as his "brain opening." After this came a vision in which Mother Ayahuasca guided him into a room resembling a nursery, where "everywhere...[was] the support and love of all the child's previous ancestors going back to pre-history."[228] It was evident to Wiese that the ancestors had gone to immeasurable lengths to meet any possible desires or wishes the child who would soon arrive might have; the carvings and decorations were more refined and elaborate than the Taj Mahal. When Wiese asked who the child was, somebody answered "This room is for you. You are the Child." Wiese was overcome by the response; he was flooded by a sense of awe as he realized, "I am worthy of the love of the Great Mother Ayahuasca! She has poured her most magnificent creativity into preparing and creating this room for me!" This was followed by "a second, deeper wave of realization.... All humans are Divine Children. She provides for us all. We are already living in a Paradise!"[229] As Wiese's experience shows, the self in the Abrahamic tradition never dissolves entirely since the relationship to God is so central. The same holds for shamanic traditions, where the experience of relationship is front and center.

Experiences of self-dissolution are an essential part of spirituality in the Vedic tradition out of which Hinduism and Buddhism emerged, something that doubtless has to do with the fact that the psychedelic soma has inspired the tradition for millennia. The *Rig Veda*, for example, describes

227 Genesis 18:27.

228 Michael Wiese, quoted in *The Psychedelic Explorer's Guide: Safe, Therapeutic, and Sacred Journeys* by James Fadiman (Simon and Schuster, 2011).

229 Ibid.

the experience as "self-purifying, o Soma, you will enter the sea."[230] The notion of dissolving in an ocean became an important model of spiritual experience in the East, and currently exerts a strong influence on spiritual development in the West. In modern psychedelic research, the expression "oceanic boundlessness" is officially used as a term to measure and describe the dissolution of the self and the positive feelings associated with it. (In the next chapter I will describe my own experience of a negative, fear-ridden self-dissolution.) The oceanic theme was taken up and further developed in the late Vedic scripture of Upanishads, culminating in the formula "Atman = Brahman," which equates the living, breathing sense with the breathing, living cosmos. The self dissolving into the ocean provides a vivid, striking image for this insight. The authors of the Upanishads added other elements to this image, such as one mentioned in a key passage of the *Chandogya Upanishad*. In the course of instructing his son Svetaketu, Uddalaka tells him:

> As bees, dear boy, produce honey by gathering together the nectars from the flowering trees in every direction, those nectars become one single honey. And just as those nectars do not get the idea "I am the nectar of this tree, I am the nectar of that tree," indeed in the very same way, dear boy, all these beings, having sprung from Being, do not know "We have sprung from Being." Whatever they are in this world—tiger, lion, wolf, bear, worm, flying insect, biting insect, or mosquito—that they become. That which is the finest essence, the whole universe has That as its soul. That is Reality, That is the Self, and That is you, Svetaketu![231]

The great spiritual importance of such experiences is emphasized throughout the Upanishads, for example, "He who has insight in this becomes the one ocean, the sole seer. This is the highest goal, the highest attainment. This is highest world. This is his highest bliss! On just a fraction of this bliss do other creatures live."[232] Yet the creators of Indian philosophy were also pragmatists, returning time and time again to the practical uses of their teachings, as with the way they release fear in the student: "When a

230 Jamison and Brereton, *The Rigveda: The Earliest Religious Poetry of India*.

231 Olivelle, *The Early Upanishads*.

232 Ibid.

man sees all beings within his very self, and his self within all beings, what bewilderment, what sorrow can there be, regarding the self of him who sees this oneness?"[233]

The oceanic dissolution of self isn't unique to the Indian tradition, however, but appears elsewhere. Jesus may have had an "Atman = Brahman" moment, for example when he said, "I and the Father are one" or "the kingdom of God is within you."[234] Even so, the Abrahamic religions have generally suppressed spirituality that rests on self-dissolution, discouraging individual pathways to God as opposed to official revelation or teachings. Individual spirituality that relies on direct experience was designated as pejoratively "mystical," so as to section it off as part of a secret teaching or cult. Mystic traditions nevertheless took root in Judaism, Christianity, and Islam as in the "mystical" Gospel of Thomas, where Jesus explains that self-dissolution indicates one possible path into the Kingdom of God: "When you make the two into one, and make the inner like the outer and the outer like the inner, and the upper like the lower...then you'll enter [the kingdom]."[235] This is mirrored quite closely by the peyote experience as James Slotkin describes it: "When I concentrated on anything, all my immediate experience fused with it harmoniously, with no distinction between internal and external aspects of experience. I found it very easy to become absorbed in any idea which I contemplated.... The Peyote permits one to have a sustained series of mystical experiences lasting for hours, rather than a brief one as is true under ordinary conditions."[236]

Indian yoga instruction adds a layer to the notion of self-dissolution, with implications for psychedelic therapy. It maintains that the experience of "Atman = Brahman" is not the ultimate reality but can itself be transcended, leading to an impersonal state that is compared to a loving but wholly inactive observer. In this state, consciousness is fully autonomous and impassive and neither pain nor fear exist, as phenomena that are always linked to a personal destiny. Instead, the narrative self fully withdraws so that consciousness is left regarding itself. On the outside, the fully realized yogi who achieves this impersonal state continues to live in the physical,

---

233 Ibid.

234 John 10:30.

235 Mark M. Mattison, trans., *The Gospel of Thomas*.

236 James Slotkin in David Ebin, *The Drug Experience: First-person Accounts of Addicts, Writers, Scientists and Others* (Grove Press, 1965).

material world as before, due to karmic remains that he or she still must live out. Yoga instructions compare the fully realized yogi to a potter's wheel that continues to spin from the speed it has achieved, though the vessel is already complete. The accomplished yogi is fully at ease and balanced, and impervious to stress. Even the fear of death is a foreign concept. They are fully present as a person at any given moment. They continue to cook her food, lift stones, and move about, but all of it simply happens—there is no one cooking, lifting stones, or moving about—it happens all by itself. The state constitutes a form of "awakening" that isn't a religious experience but an insight, a revelation that has nothing to do with God. As soon as we learn that the self is free, everything that befalls us—pain, emotion, unsettling thoughts—no longer belongs to us, the teaching goes.[237]

Many patients experience similar states during psychedelic-assisted therapy, regarding themselves and their lives from the perspective of a loving but uninvolved observer. One of my patients described it as "everything turning, but I am entirely at ease within this turning and observe without moving." Over the long term this can strengthen self-transcendence, a capacity I describe in what follows.

Meditation in Buddhism has the goal of directing our attention to the present moment, and adopting a nonjudgmental, accepting stance toward experience as it unfolds. The practice strengthens the minimal self at the expense of the narrative self, in a process that is comparable to psychedelic experiences of self-dissolution. Profound experiences of self-dissolution are rare in meditation however, and then often only in the case of long-time meditators. One important study by the Swiss psychiatrist Franz Vollenweider on the impact of psilocybin on long-time meditators showed the experience of oceanic boundlessness to be quite similar whether it comes about through meditation or through psychedelics.[238] The study demonstrated further that experienced meditators were able to continue with their normal meditation practice during the acute phase of the psilocybin, with the substance deepening their meditative state. States of self-dissolution and oceanic feelings were much more frequent and intense among long-time meditators in comparison to people who had no experience with meditation.

237 Eliade, *Yoga: Immortality and Freedom*.

238 Lukasz Smigielski, Michael Kometer, Milan Scheidegger, Rainer Krahenmann, Theo Huber, and Franz X. Vollenweider, "Characterization and Prediction of Acute and Sustained Response to Psychedelic Psilocybin in a Mindfulness Group Retreat," *Scientific Reports* 9, no. 1 (October 24, 2019)

Experience with meditation also meant that the potential side effects of high dosages of psilocybin, like fear or confusion, did not appear. Magnetic resonance imaging conducted on the study participants showed that the dissolution of self they experienced in meditative states, deepened by psilocybin, was accompanied by a weakened default mode network, i.e., a less dominant narrative self.

A follow-up to the Vollenweider study showed that the impact of the psilocybin continued after the fact, with meditators who had taken the substance showing greater mindfulness in everyday activities than those who had received a placebo. Four months after their experiences on psilocybin, reverberations from the loosened borders of the self were still measurable in patients through magnetic resonance imagery.[239]

Psychedelic research has also provided dramatic proof that many people can have spiritual experiences without believing in supernatural forces or divinities.[240] This form of spirituality goes by "natural" or "naturalistic," since it makes do without "unnatural" assumptions such as the existence of God. US philosopher Jerome Stone describes naturalistic spirituality as follows: "We are spiritual, first, when our sense of connection is enlarged. Second, we are spiritual when we aspire to greater things, when we attempt to realize our ideals. Finally, we are spiritual when we ask the big questions. Note that these three—connection, aspiration, and reflection on profound questions—are all forms of enlarging our selves, of breaking through the narrow walls of the ego."[241]

Psychedelic spirituality is less concerned with achieving a different spiritual plane than with opening to our "natural" world by means of self-transcendence. Psychedelic-assisted therapy fosters the following characteristics one might term spiritual:

> Posing questions to oneself about a higher meaning in life that transcend the personal self

---

239 Lukasz Smigielski, Milan Scheidegger, Michael Kometer, and Franz X. Vollenweider, "Psilocybin-assisted Mindfulness Training Modulates Self-Consciousness and Brain Default Mode Network Connectivity with Lasting Effects," *NeuroImage* 196 (August 1, 2019): 207–15.

240 Chris Letheby, *Philosophy of Psychedelics* (Oxford University Press, 2021).

241 Jerome A. Stone, "Spirituality for Naturalists," *Zygon* 47, no. 3 (August 23, 2012): 481–500.

Taking responsibility and having higher ideals in life that transcend the personal self

Feeling compassion for other living beings and nature, and experiencing oneself as part of a living world

Experiencing life affirming moments. These moments come rarely but are powerful enough to be unforgettable, occasioning descriptions like "mystical," "abundant," "eternal," "calm," and "acceptance."

In what follows I would like to discuss several aspects of self-change that are especially relevant to psychedelic therapy and respond to what I call psychedelics' "self-transcendence effects."

Fig. 6–2: "A missionary from the Middle Ages claims to have found the place where heaven and earth touch." (Camille Flammarion, *L'atmosphère*, Paris 1888).

Self-Transcendence

While self-transcendence can be seen in a spiritual light, it is also a term in modern psychology related to the higher self. An article in the journal *Science* reported on how self-transcendence in the use of language can reduce stress. People who processed stress using the "I" form—"Getting fired really hurt me" or "I regret this decision bitterly"—were less resilient than people who generalized their problems in phrases like "Getting fired can really hurt" or "You can really regret some decisions." The latter is a subtle form of self-transcendence that we practice almost daily, by not immediately relating circumstances or situations to the self but initially seeing them as independent.[242]

In fact, "self-transcendent" or "objectivizing" coping strategies are among the most effective at our disposal—much more so than those looking to raise our self-esteem.[243] Research shows further that techniques of self-transcendence are easily applied and available to everyone. In one study, students were purposely excluded from a group to provoke a stress response. Afterward they were asked to write an essay about an assigned topic. In doing so, the group of students asked to write about self-transcendent topics—"Perhaps being excluded had a higher purpose" or "I feel connected with everyone else who was excluded"—showed far less stress than those who were asked to write about self-amplifying topics like "I'm still the best" or "I'm probably too intelligent to belong to this group."[244]

The results reveal self-transcendence not as a passive experience or form of self-absence, even self-alienation, but an active process of opening and overcoming oneself. In what follows, I look to show through the lens of generally agreed upon factors in resilience that psychedelics do not just dissolve the ego but strengthen the self while also relativizing it.

---

242 Ariana Orvell, Ethan Kross, and Susan A. Gelman, "How 'You' Makes Meaning," *Science* 355, no. 6331 (March 24, 2017): 1299–1302.

243 Thomas L Webb, Eleanor Miles, and Paschal Sheeran, "Dealing with Feeling: A Meta-Analysis of the Effectiveness of Strategies Derived From the Process Model of Emotion Regulation," *Psychological Bulletin* 138, no. 4 (July 1, 2012): 775–808.

244 Aleah Burson, Jennifer Crocker, and Dominik Mischkowski, "Two Types of Value-Affirmation," *Social Psychological & Personality Science* 3, no. 4 (February 1, 2012): 510–16.

Self-Efficacy

"Self-efficacy" refers to a conscious or unconscious conviction that we are capable of handling difficult situations and challenges and influencing our environment. The thought "I can do it!" speaks to a high expectation of self-efficacy. It enables us to take up challenges and be creative. Thoughts like "I can't accomplish anything, my situation is hopeless!" or "I'll never do that!" by contrast, attest to low expectations for one's self-efficacy, a state that raises the chances of fear and burnout. Experiences of self-efficacy do the most to raise our expectations of a positive outcome. Most often this is conceived of in terms of external success; when I accepted my current position as professor in Fribourg, for instance, I began reading French newspapers and books to improve my French. Noticing that my colleagues could gradually understand me better and began to speak French with me without any prompting, it increased my motivation to further perfect my French.

Psychedelics, meanwhile, can reinforce our sense of self-efficacy through a sense of inner achievement. Typical psychedelic experiences that increase self-efficacy are:

> Experiencing that I can be different than expected.
>
> Seeing firsthand that there is potential within me that I hadn't recognized yet.
>
> I know now that my self-understanding relies on narratives that I can change.[245]

Psychedelics also give us an experience of self-efficacy at the general level, since a psychedelic experience always represents an adventure and psychological challenge if faced without distraction. One online survey of people who had experienced a challenging psilocybin trip found that the greater the challenge, the more meaningful the trip was rated as being. Respondents' sense of well-being also increased with challenging trips, though only if the challenge was short lasting, i.e., if it lasted less than the effects

245 Letheby, *Philosophy of Psychedelics*.

of the psilocybin. When the entire trip was distressing or challenging, the sense of well-being diminished.[246]

This is a striking example of one way that self-efficacy functions: A challenge that can be overcome strengthens our self-confidence, while a challenge to which we are passively exposed tends to do the opposite. This phenomenon could indicate the use of lower dosages of psychedelics in treatment, as these doses might support patients in having a positive experience of self-efficacy. "I intentionally immersed myself in my feelings and swam in the direction of my deepest fear," a patient of mine said, describing a similar experience. "Behind the fear there was grief, and behind that, pain. When I reached my pain, my negative feelings dissolved and just the pain was left, which I was able to bear without any fear. I'm proud that I was so courageous, and that I reached my pain on my trip. I sense that even without LSD I have the power to face my mental pain."

One experience of self-efficacy specific to psychedelics is that of a unified consciousness despite all the changes in perception, as opposed to the sort of division or fragmentation that occur in psychotic states. The experience shows the self at work, strengthening our trust in it, an original and basic form of self-trust. Psychosis is often accompanied by intense loneliness, with the disruptions in the self prompting a fundamental and painful sense of otherness and separation from the world. The comforting sense of solidarity or connection that psychedelics can elicit, meanwhile, is a sign that the self's ability to integrate experiences remains intact, itself a basic form of self-efficacy.

Beyond psychological experiences of self-efficacy, psychedelics can also give us transcendental experiences of self-efficacy. The notion that I both can and must control everything by myself is an illusion. Active, willful self-control quickly leads to exhaustion, termed *ego depletion* in psychology. "Go with the flow" isn't just a hippie saying about floating down a river, but a scientifically proven strategy for resilience. The river in this case doesn't simply refer to the external circumstances of our lives but the current that flows through us exerting a mysterious force. The feeling is one of

246 Theresa M. Carbonaro, Matthew P. Bradstreet, Frederick S. Barrett, Katherine A. MacLean, Robert Jesse, Matthew W. Johnson et al., "Survey Study of Challenging Experiences After Ingesting Psilocybin Mushrooms: Acute and Enduring Positive and Negative Consequences," *Journal of Psychopharmacology* 30, no. 12 (September 27, 2016): 1268–78.

unconsciously being led, resulting in spontaneous action that we understand as our own, though we did not consciously initiate or control it.

The Indian concept of *karma*, the Sanskrit word for "deed," ties into the various levels of self-efficacy. In a moral sense karma speaks to the long-term impact of our actions—on our success or happiness in life for instance—and thus to the importance of maintaining correct moral behavior. Yet karma also has a mystical meaning as an evolutionary force flowing through us, which describes the causal chain that binds us to the world. It is this notion of karma to which the Buddha refers in his statement that the self is an illusion.

Experiences of the self dissolving while on psychedelics allow us to perceive this karmic, causal, and transpersonal current, since it allows the minimal self to experience action and perception as completely aligned, the dissolution of the I within the flow of experience. It is akin to a flow state where a person dives into an activity purely for its own sake. The self becomes physical. Time flies by. Each thought, each action, each moment follows inevitably from the last, as when playing a piece of music. The flow of karma is the true subject of the *Tibetan Book of the Dead*, containing the promise that by patiently and steadily perceiving the current a person will be able to exert a beneficial influence over it, increasing the harmony and happiness of all.

Jungian psychotherapy lies very close to this concept of karmic flow. For Jung, healing proceeds from the collective unconscious, led by an inner intelligence whose wisdom vastly exceeds that of any individual therapist or school. This is the "higher self," which lies at the heart of what Jung termed the "individuation process."

Transcendental self-efficacy can be a particularly important experience for patients with compulsive disorders who often live under the exaggerated notion that they are deliberately and consciously responsible for everything and must continually intervene in life's current. One patient of mine suffered from a compulsion to wash his hands. He had to clean them at least once every hour in order to keep bacteria and possible diseases at bay. The compulsion was so time consuming that he had to halve his workload. Fifteen milligrams of psilocybin strengthened his fears of dirtiness without improving the compulsion; it was only at 25 milligrams that he experienced a breakthrough, recognizing that his fears had vanished without his having to act.

"Now I see," he said, excited. "I don't have to do anything at all!" Psilocybin gave him a lesson about "going with the flow." The world may be a dirty place, but our bodies have developed strategies for dealing with it over millions of years. "You don't always have to wash your hands. They'll wash themselves." The lesson recalls that of Carlos Castaneda's shamanic teacher Don Juan: The power of the fully realized warrior is the power of inaction. In other words, the absolute passivity of the minimal self is necessary for spontaneous activity.

Self-Acceptance

For the founder of cognitive behavioral therapy, US psychiatrist Aaron Beck, a lack of self-acceptance plays a key role in depression, revealing itself through excessive self-criticism, denigration or humiliation, even self-loathing and rejection. This understanding of depression has taken on greater and greater significance in light of the rise in depressive disorders over the past decades, brought on in part by lowered self-acceptance. One study of forty thousand college students arrived at the conclusion that self-aimed perfectionism in Western countries had grown by 32 percent from 1989 to 2016.[247] The more defined a country was by ideals of accomplishment or work ethic, the greater the rise. Yet perfectionism is also one form of lacking self-acceptance, which greatly increases the risk for depression, eating and anxiety disorders, body dysmorphia, and suicide. Conversely, a well-developed acceptance of oneself, as captured in the following statements, is recognized as a factor in resilience:

> I am generally self-aware and see myself in a positive light.
> I like most aspects of my personality.
> In many regards I take joy in what I've accomplished in life.
> When I look back on my life I'm satisfied with the course it's taken.[248]

---

247 Thomas Curran and Andrew P. Hill, "Perfectionism Is Increasing Over Time: A Meta-Analysis of Birth Cohort Differences From 1989 to 2016," *Psychological Bulletin* 145, no. 4 (April 1, 2019): 410–29.

248 Carol D. Ryff, "Psychological Well-Being Revisited: Advances in the Science and Practice of Eudaimonia," *Psychotherapy and Psychosomatics* 83, no. 1 (November 19, 2013): 10–28.

Clinical psychology views self-acceptance as a prerequisite for change, a state that can be achieved by accepting one's mistakes instead of criticizing or hoping to make up for them. Self-love, in other words, means allowing ourselves to be less than perfect in some aspects of our lives. Unconditional self-acceptance makes us particularly resilient. Often we only love ourselves when we are doing well, or have reached a goal; unconditional self-acceptance, meanwhile, teaches us to love ourselves no matter what happens. We are still valuable, even if we do fail or make a mistake. Granted, that doesn't mean that we shouldn't improve ourselves. On the contrary—a healthy sense of self-acceptance is a good point of departure for change and self-betterment.

Psychedelics are considered "disruptive" substances because they have the potential to interrupt self-critical narratives—Freud's superego. With their inner critic silenced for once, many patients report being overcome by a wave of self-love they hadn't known before. I myself don't love the term "disruptive" for the aggressive overtones it carries, though it does point to the potentially long-lasting effects of the superego's dissolution. Around half of the patients who undergo treatment with LSD report a long-term increase in self-acceptance.[249] In one study I conducted with colleagues Samir Suker and Yoan Mihov at the University Hospital in Bern, we were able to show that ketamine relieved symptoms like feeling worthless or self-denigration in severely depressed patients who weren't responding to classic antidepressants.[250]

In his book *Philosophy of Psychedelics*, Chris Letheby suggests that the central working mechanism for psychedelic therapy is first disrupting and then reworking the narrative self.[251] The studies he draws on to do so count experiences of self-transcendence as central to psychedelics' antidepressive effects and hold changes in the default mode network—the neural groundwork for the narrative self—to be the most important traces that remain of psychedelic treatment in the brain.

---

249 D. B. Blewett and N. Chwelos, *Handbook for the Therapeutic Use of Lysergic Acid Diethylamide-25 Individual and Group Procedures* (The Multidisciplinary Association for Psychedelic Studies,).

250 Gregor Hasler, Samir Suker, Georgios Schoretsanitis, and Yoan Mihov, "Sustained Improvement of Negative Self-Schema After a Single Ketamine Infusion: An Open-Label Study," *Frontiers in Neuroscience* 14 (July 1, 2020)

251 Letheby, *Philosophy of Psychedelics*.

US author Robert A. Durr describes the sort of self-acceptance that may arise through ego dissolution through the lens of one patient's experience: "Although I lost all sense of 'me-ness,' the sense of 'I-ness' was intensified unbelievably.... It was simply a sense of 'is-ness' or 'am-ness.' I wasn't anything—I simply was. And at these moments of really ecstatic clarity there was such a peace and rest and at the same time such exuberance and wildest joy."[252] As soon as the self is no longer an object to be judged by the superego, self-acceptance automatically emerges. Over the long term the experience attenuates the influence of the superego, which is no longer taken to be an objective reality but revealed as a construct.

The pioneering psychedelics researcher Robin Carhart-Harris draws an informal comparison between this retrofitting of the self and shaking a snow globe. The image captures well the dynamic of dissolution and a new, playful order arising, as it does the growth in flexibility and neuroplasticity. In this regard, we might also call the self-transcendence effect the "snow globe effect."

Initial findings that ketamine and psilocybin may lower the risk of suicide hold great promise, especially because classic antidepressants do not lower the risk of suicide and may even raise it in the first weeks.[253] It is safe to assume that this astonishing capacity is due to the self-transcendence effect. That isn't to say that psychedelics can't also heighten the risk of suicide, if for example a patient expects too much from a treatment and clings to it as the proverbial last straw, only to come away disappointed and with a diminished will to keep living if the impact is not all they hoped for. This makes it essential to set detailed expectations for treatment and clarify the risk of suicide during preparatory sessions.

---

252 R. A. Durr, *Poetic Vision and the Psychedelic Experience* (Syracuse University Press, 1970).

253 Stephen Ross, Gabrielle Agin-Liebes, Sharon Lo, Richard J. Zeifman, Leila Ghazal, Julia Benville et al., "Acute and Sustained Reductions in Loss of Meaning and Suicidal Ideation Following Psilocybin-Assisted Psychotherapy for Psychiatric and Existential Distress in Life-Threatening Cancer," *ACS Pharmacology & Translational Science* 4, no. 2 (March 18, 2021): 553–62.

Self-Responsibility

By far the most important psychotherapeutic office in the world of classical antiquity was the Oracle of Delphi, who listed the era's most powerful and influential people among her clientele, from the King of Thebes to Alexander the Great. The entire Mediterranean world's conviction in the absolute reliability of the oracle made it a regional center point for a long time.

Originally the oracle had belonged to the earth goddess Gaea, visible from the fact that only women were entitled to assume the role of Pythia—the priestess who served as oracle. The shamanic roots of the oracle, meanwhile, are revealed in the trance state that the priestess entered into to deliver the oracle. Those seeking answers were also ushered into an altered state of consciousness by priests in preparatory sessions that included rituals and meditation exercises.

The temple at Delphi differed from all the others in ancient Greece. The adyton, a small chamber below the main floor of the temple set off to the side, hosted the encounter between the seeker and the Pythia. The intimate space kept the psychedelic vapors emerging from a fissure in the earth at a high enough concentration to alter participants' consciousness; geologists suspect ethylene, as the gas has a sweet smell that ancient sources also comment on. Breathing in even small quantities of ethylene can provoke benign trance states and psychedelic experiences.

Even the inscription above the entrance to Apollo's temple at Delphi, "Know thyself," indicates one method of psychotherapy, namely that of unravelling individual problems, doubts, and concerns by confronting the self. In this regard, exploring the "inner world" would help solve problems in the "outer world."

The preparatory sessions, the shamanic roots, the psychedelic gas, the intimate therapeutic space, the aspects of self-transcendence—all attest to the many parallels that exist between the Oracle of Delphi and modern psychedelic therapy.

Nietzsche, who had a profound knowledge of ancient Greek culture, summarized the oracle's function as follows: "The Greeks learned gradually to organize the chaos because, in accordance with the Delphic teaching, they directed their thoughts back to themselves, that is, to their real needs, and let the apparent needs die off. So they seized possession of themselves again."[254]

The term I give for this psychological process is *self-responsibility*. By it I do not mean taking full responsibility for everything at all times. It can be entirely appropriate to get drawn into something, for instance, to let oneself go, or merge into a family or group. Yet from time to time we should "take possession of ourselves again" to consider our priorities. This is the task of the healthy narrative self. The Greeks didn't seek out the oracle day after day, but every couple of years at most.

Studies confirm that people who undergo modern psychedelic treatment experience "Delphi-like" phenomena. One of the most common effects in a survey of experiences with psilocybin was patients recovering "a sense of what is most important and vital in their lives, such as being present in the moment or being kind to other people."[255] Patients wrestling with addiction showed especially striking evidence for Delphi-like phenomena. In one study on nicotine cessation, the insights brought on through psilocybin often revolved around self-knowledge and self-responsibility, enabling patients to reconnect with core values that had faded over the years for one reason or another. Those included things like recognizing the importance of health, of breath, pausing, and the beauty in life. One smoker discovered her true self to be a non-smoker, for instance. As she put it, "It felt like I'd died as a smoker and been resurrected as a non-smoker. It was how I perceived myself, and it's how I felt. So I jumped up and I said, 'I'm not a smoker anymore, it's all done.'"[256] Framed in Heideggerian terms, if I "dissolve," or open my consciousness anew, the better and more effectively I am able "resolve" myself, or act.

As with self-efficacy, self-responsibility also has a transcendental aspect; Chris Letheby writes about it as one aspect of ego dissolution on psychedelics. "Attention is no longer guided exclusively by adaptive and egocentric goals and agendas; salience attribution is no longer bound to personal

---

254 Friedrich Nietzsche, *On the Use and Abuse of History for Life* (Richer Resources Publications, 2010).

255 Belser et al., "Patient Experiences of Psilocybin-Assisted Psychotherapy: An Interpretative Phenomenological Analysis," 354–88.

256 Tehseen Noorani, Albert Garcia-Romeu, Thomas C. Swift, Roland R. Griffths, and Matthew W. Johnson, "Psychedelic Therapy for Smoking Cessation: Qualitative Analysis of Participant Accounts," *Journal of Psychopharmacology* 32, no. 7 (June 25, 2018): 756–69.

concern.... Rather it seems as if the experiences, although intense and fascinating, are no longer automatically attributed to an entity."[257]

This idea is largely in line with the wisdom teachings of the Hopi, whose highest spiritual aim is to become like a "hollow bone." The hollow bone is an image for self-responsibility, with the self conceived in broad, transcendent terms. The aim proceeds from the experience that freeing oneself from egocentric beliefs, fears, unhealed wounds, doubts, and worries allows a person to better serve others. The image of the hollow bone (or reed) appears in many Native and shamanic traditions. Carlos Castaneda's shamanic teacher-figure Don Juan advised his student to surrender his self-importance in order to see the world and make contact with the plant world. This closely echoes the experiences of one forty-four-year-old patient faced with a life-threatening case of esophageal cancer who was tormented by fears about dying. After being treated by Swiss psychiatrist Peter Gasser with LSD, the patient reported that "your inner self dies away, I think, and you are left looking at the whole...you begin to build relationships with plants and the entire living world around you. You think less about yourself, you think—beyond borders."[258]

Right Self

The Buddha's statement about the illusory nature of self has provoked no end of philosophical debate from ancient times to the present day. Yet the Buddha did not mean to say that the self holds no practical value. Most children do not like brushing their teeth. First the parents brush their kids' teeth, in time explaining to them why it is important. The child only learns to brush their teeth independently once he or she is able to picture themself in the future and identify with people who haven't brushed their teeth, and are thus forced to deal with toothaches, problems chewing, and high dental fees. I wouldn't write this book if I wasn't able to imagine myself in the future taking pleasure in the interest of readers. The Buddha never questioned

257 Chris Letheby and Philip Gerrans, "Self Unbound: Ego Dissolution in Psychedelic Experience," *Neuroscience of Consciousness* 2017, no. 1 (January 1, 2017)

258 Peter Gasser, Katharina Kirchner, and Torsten Passie, "LSD-assisted Psychotherapy for Anxiety Associated With a Life-threatening Disease: A Qualitative Study of Acute and Sustained Subjective Effects," *Journal of Psychopharmacology* 29, no. 1 (November 11, 2014): 57–68.

this type of self. What he did grasp was that the self often turns into a great existential problem because we expect too much of it—that it will always remain the same and be coherent, for instance. It was this abstract, philosophical concept of the self that he deemed an illusion and pointed out as one of the principal causes of human unhappiness. This is in line with what many people who have sought to take their own lives report: they do so because they could no longer fulfill their self-expectations.

The Buddha favored what he called the "Middle Way." Total selflessness leads to suffering (cavities, to stick with the previous example), but the notion of an eternal, immutable self will also inevitably lead to frustration for being unrealistic. The Buddha's compromise was to develop a true, realistic self through meditation that would awaken the transcendent self while tending to the worldly self as well.

As I explained in the introduction, this same concept provided inspiration for the book. Each chapter contains the word *right* in allusion to the Eightfold Path, a central and practical teaching of Buddhism that leads to the cessation of suffering, and finally to enlightenment. "Right" in this case isn't intended in a moralizing sense, but in terms of the Middle Way as "realistic" and "holistic." When we relinquish our expectations and prejudgments, we will experience both ourselves and the world in a more realistic and holistic way. Psychedelic therapy has a great deal to contribute along the way.

Summary

The self relates to every aspect of our experience and action. Psychological disorders can thus be described as disorders of the self. An inflated or excessively limited notion of self can lead to arrogance, envy, isolation, and depression. Disorders in our sense of self are also a leading cause of suicide. Psychedelics are uniquely equipped to loosen the expectations we put on ourselves, bringing profound relaxation. Psychedelic ego dissolution is also an important source of spirituality, although the experience of self-transcendence on psychedelics is not necessarily spiritual. The experience of opening and overcoming oneself is generally recognized as a more effective factor in resilience than inflating our sense of self-worth. Experiences of self-efficacy on psychedelics present patients with a sense of being guided unconsciously, and access to hidden stores of wisdom, helping them overcome existential challenges.

Chapter 7
Right Identity: The Path to Unity

When we think of identity, we often picture something fixed or stable. People talk about "stable" personalities or a person "finding themselves" as though it were something final. When things stay "identical" to themselves, it means that they demonstrate the same characteristics now as they did in the past. To stay connected with our past, we also define ourselves via previous experience. Resilience, by contrast, requires flexibility and change. The result is a possible tension between identity and resilience. Sometimes changes in our identities are necessary, which presents a challenge. And even if the need to identify with the past is justified, we should avoid becoming its victim. Nietzsche considered this problem in some depth in his pivotal work *On the Use and Abuse of History for Life*:

> There is a degree of insomnia, of rumination, of the historical sense, through which the living comes to harm and finally is destroyed, whether it is a person or a people or a culture.
>
> In order to determine this degree of history and, through that, the borderline at which the past must be forgotten if it is not to become the gravedigger of the present, we have to know precisely how great the *plastic force* of a person, a people, or a culture is. I mean that force of growing in a different way out of oneself, of reshaping and incorporating the past and the foreign, of healing wounds, compensating for what has been lost, rebuilding shattered forms out of one's self. There are people who possess so little of this force that they bleed to death incurably from a single experience, a single pain, often even from a single tender injustice, as from a really small bloody scratch.[259]

259 Nietzsche, *On the Use and Abuse of History for Life*.

As Nietzsche would have it, living a healthy and active life requires us to develop a force that will allow us to appropriate and absorb—you could say "digest"—the past with all its traumatic moments so as to fashion a new unity out of them. If this force should fail, however, we must be able to forget what we have been unable to integrate. Nietzsche thus pinpoints two functions of neuroplasticity that are a key research topic in contemporary psychiatry and psychotherapy.

Forgetting and Psychotherapy

Let's begin with forgetting. The brain forgets the better part of all the information that flows through its nerve cells; every night the new memory traces, or synaptic connections that formed during the day, are examined for whether they are necessary for survival. Most aren't and are erased. The problem is that the process does not include traumatic experiences—losing a partner or falling off a bridge—because the brain holds them to be important for survival. This means that traumatic experiences collect in the brain, giving them greater potential to define our identity than others. This often turns them into Nietzsche's "gravedigger of the present," or post-traumatic stress disorders in the language of modern psychiatry, though it doesn't just include symptoms of post-traumatic stress but depression, burnout, anxiety disorders, psychosomatic symptoms, and sensitivities of all kinds.

Clinical psychology has concerned itself with forgetting for decades now, developing methods of treatment aimed specifically at helping patients forget traumatic memories. One important finding in this context has been that for a patient to forget a traumatic experience, they must learn to accept it. For the traumatic memory to be stored as a new and more positive version that doesn't elicit fear, this acceptance also must occur in a constructive, safe, and supportive environment. The problem is that for nearly half of all patients, this form of therapy is ineffective. Emotional avoidance, fragmented memory, or the simple inability to complete a round of therapy because the burden of active remembering is too great are all reasons that limit the effectiveness of therapy, and often lead patients to discontinue treatment. Chapter 1 previously introduced psychedelics' ability to facilitate acceptance of traumatic experience in patients through their mindfulness effects and protect against retraumatization through the helioscope effect.

Animal research is now showing psychedelics to possess still other properties that explain their effectiveness in treating PTSD. Take for example the challenges of generalizing unlearning. If a test mouse learns that a light blinking means its feet receive an electric shock, it will freeze in fear anytime a light blinks, even if an electric shock does not follow. If the mouse is subsequently placed in a green cage and learns that a light blinking isn't something to be feared and there will be food instead, over time the blinking light will provoke less and less fear. That doesn't mean, however, that the brain has forgotten the connection between the blinking light and the electric shock. If the mouse is set back in a red cage and sees a blinking light, it will freeze all over again. In other words, unlearning the danger hasn't been generalized—the light still signals the same danger as before, it has just been assigned a positive connotation in the green cage. This is a fundamental issue in dealing with the consequences of trauma in psychotherapy, as patients may learn within a therapeutic environment that people, bridges, or spiders aren't dangerous, only to have the fear return in everyday life.

Other animal studies show, however, that MDMA can help generalize unlearning by improving neuroplasticity in the amygdala, which is the center of fear learning.[260] That is to say, if the mouse learns that a blinking light in a green cage does not pose a threat while on MDMA, it is much more likely not to feel fear in the red cage either. In scientific terms, MDMA generalizes a learned sense of safety, which will manifest in diverse environments. The discovery holds tremendous implications for psychotherapy, even if we don't fully understand the mechanisms behind the astonishing effect. Unlearning fear likely involves covering over the fear-inducing memory with a positive experience, meaning the old traces of memory remain beneath and may resurface depending on the environment or stress. There are initial signs now however that the disruptive effects of MDMA and other psychedelics allows them to erase even these traumatic traces.[261]

It is worth adding that the erasure doesn't affect the entire memory, just the traumatic part. One patient I treated with MDMA for a trauma disorder

---

260 M. B. Young, R. Andero, K. J. Ressler, and L. L. Howell, "3,4-Methylenedioxymethamphetamine Facilitates Fear Extinction Learning," *Translational Psychiatry* 5, no. 9 (September 15, 2015)

261 Holly S. Hake, Jazmyne K. P. Davis, River R. Wood, Margaret K. Tanner, Esteban C. Loetz, Anais Sanchez et al., "3,4-methylenedioxymethamphetamine (MDMA) Impairs the Extinction and Reconsolidation of Fear Memory in Rats," *Physiology & Behavior* 199 (February 1, 2019): 343–50.

described it as "seeming like these [traumatic] memories were set back in place in the brain in a different constellation—one that doesn't cause so many issues like bad dreams, intrusive thoughts, or fear-filled nights. The effect has lasted up to this day, one and a half years after my last MDMA session."[262] The patient had lost the fear he associated with his story without forgetting the story.

Nietzsche's Plastic Force

We come now to what Nietzsche termed the "*plastic force*...of growing in a different way out of oneself, of reshaping and incorporating the past and the foreign, of healing wounds, compensating for what has been lost, rebuilding shattered forms out of one's self." Nietzsche proposes this plastic force as an alternative to forgetting; it finds its parallel in psychedelic therapy in the period of integration that follows a psychedelic experience. This work can be aided either by individual or group sessions. Individual sessions are conducted one-one-one with a psychotherapist; neo-shamanic ceremonies have proven effective for group sessions, where a speaking stick is passed around in a circle. The person holding the stick is called on to speak about their psychedelic experience while the other participants and the therapist listen attentively and without judgement. The sessions can help patients integrate contradictory, stressful, or embarrassing experiences and insights while also encouraging a feeling of belonging and connection to a group.

Integration will often stretch over a long period of time, sometimes years. I personally never administer psychedelics to patients more often than four times a year. The integration sessions that occur in the interim teach the patient to incorporate the extraordinary, multifaceted, multilayered, personal, and suprapersonal experiences of the psychedelic state into their daily awareness. As a therapist, I take care to attend to different levels of the psyche like feelings, thoughts, sense impressions, fantasies, and behavior. The word *integration* comes from the Latin verb *integrare*, which

262 Allison A. Feduccia and Michael C. Mithoefer, "MDMA-assisted Psychotherapy for PTSD: Are Memory Reconsolidation and Fear Extinction Underlying Mechanisms?," *Progress in Neuro-Psychopharmacology & Biological Psychiatry* 84 (June 1, 2018): 221–28.

means to "make whole," "refresh," and "start again." The point, in other words, is to fashion a new unity out of many different parts.

Integrating traumatic experience can be stressful. Following a phase of denial or rationalization, strong feelings of rage, but also embarrassment or shame may surface, often followed by depressive moods, which signal the beginning of acceptance. This is explained by the fact that traumatic experience is often entirely or partially unconscious, and becoming aware of and integrating such experiences presents a special challenge for the psyche.

Identity and Integrity

Identity-related issues and disorders are increasingly common. People feel unmoored from any sense of cultural identity, or must fight for their identities as part of minority groups that does not receive full recognition. At the same time, personal identity has never been more important. In her book *Grit*, US psychologist Angela Duckworth shows that in societies based on achievement, a well-integrated identity is necessary for continuing to pursue goals over an extended period of time. The long days and nights of work, the setbacks and disappointments, the struggle and the sacrifice are all worth it for those with stamina, because the effort is consistent with and strengthens their identity. In this case identity operates like a compass, giving everything subordinate to it a direction, aim, and purpose.

A vague and contradictory identity, by contrast, will prompt the feeling that one doesn't fit, and that one's psychological, social, and physical experiences don't form a greater whole. This often leads to a negative self-image, a depressed sense of self-worth, and low motivation. Discovering unity within oneself thus represents a decisive step on the path to maturity and resilience.

Psychedelic pioneer Ram Dass suffered from a contradictory identity throughout his life, with his outspoken liberal views in contrast with his conservative upbringing. His family was wealthy enough that as a young man he could afford his own airplane, yet this didn't bring him happiness and he longed to be a "normal person." As a psychology professor at Harvard he found it difficult to identify with the rational distance of the cooly observing researcher; he was a highly emotive, empathetic person who would have much preferred to give everyone a hug. Moreover, as a bisexual man he felt equally at sea among the heterosexual majority as in the growing gay rights movement. He felt so uncomfortable with the veneration he received for his influential spiritual self-help book that he was forever claiming to be an uninspired everyman.

In part due to the struggle with his own identity, Ram Dass began to investigate the heart and mind-opening effects of psychedelics, working alongside Timothy Leary in conducting self-experiments both alone and in groups. US journalist Don Lattin describes one of Ram Dass's psilocybin trips (Dass was still going by Richard Alpert at the time) in his book *The Harvard Psychedelic Club*:

> Alpert started really coming onto the psilocybin. There was too much talking in the kitchen, so he walked into the living room, a darker and more peaceful setting. He sat down on the sofa and tried to collect himself. Looking up, he saw some people over the in the corner. *Who were they? Were they real?* Then he started to see them as images of himself in his various roles. They were hallucinations, but they seemed so real. There was the professor with a cap and gown. There was a pilot with a pilot's hat. There was the lover. At first, he was a bit amused by the vision. *Those are just my roles. That role can go. That role can go. I've had it with that role.* Then he saw himself as his father's son.... That was terrifying. He started to call out for Tim [Leary]. *Wait a minute. How can I call out to Tim? Who was going to call for Tim? The minder of the store, me, would be calling for Tim. But who is me?* It was terrifying at first, but all of a sudden Alpert started watching the whole show with a kind of calm compassion.[263]

In Alpert's experience, the protective, helioscopic quality of the psilocybin put the full range of his struggles with identity on display with great clarity, allowing him to accept them calmly and compassionately. In a workshop decades later, Dass commented: "I used to be so ashamed of all my sexual wierdities. Boy, did I go out of my way to practice duplicity.

263 Don Lattin, *The Harvard Psychedelic Club: How Timothy Leary, Ram Dass, Huston Smith, and Andrew Weil Killed the Fifties and Ushered in a New Age for America* (Harper Collins, 2009).

And do you know now I couldn't care less. It is what it is.... You don't stop neurosis, you stop identifying with it."[264]

I have treated Yasmin over the past fourteen years for severe depression. While she has since gone on to become a professor of biochemistry at a prominent university, the only way she managed to finish her studies and start her academic career was on a combination of antidepressants, lithium, and thyroid hormones. I treated Yasmin with LSD to deal with the side effects of the other drugs. After the third and most dramatic session, she commented that "another interesting aspect was a very strong sense of what was important and what wasn't. My entire world became vastly simplified, and many things—a lot of things really—clearly didn't matter. That's definitely a simplification based on the trip, and I think it's what lets people think they have seen some great truth. The simplification isn't at all realistic, but it helps tremendously in ordering your feelings and redefining your 'basic knowledge.' That's very useful."

Yasmin improved a great deal after her third session, writing in one email: "I think the changes...are an astounding result, it's incredible how alive I feel. If this lasts, I might say it feels like true healing. We'll see what the following months bring." Step-by-step she was able to set aside the other medications she was taking, and to date hasn't relapsed into depression. I don't want to stir hopes of psychedelics as a miracle cure with Yasmin's story. The majority of my patients with severe psychiatric illnesses still depend on classical psychotropic drugs despite psychedelic options. At the same time, it would feel dishonest not to tell her story.

I have experienced the integrative power of psychedelics firsthand. After taking LSD myself, my teacher and guide Peter Oehen asked what the most important aspect of my experience had been. While I was somewhat taken aback by the directness of his question, I had no trouble answering: "I feel more whole, more like a person." It was a powerful experience for me to recognize that everything in my life, which I often experience as a muddle of contradictions, with all the excessive fears and a curiosity that ranges from the individual human being in all their uniqueness and vulnerability to the natural sciences and rationalism to the Indian Vedas and Western mysticism—that it should all coexist in perfect harmony.

---

264 Ram Dass, *Becoming Nobody: The Essential Ram Dass Collection* (Sounds True, 2019).

Psychedelic experience opens the door to change, but the lasting benefits only come with integration, where psychological energy is released and transformed. Integration applies the insights gained during the patient's psychedelic journey to everyday life, fusing old aspects of psychological experience with new to fashion a new self. Old, deeply rooted habits and convictions gradually give way to more realistic and holistic ones, making for deeper, more authentic relationships. In this regard psychedelics invite us on a journey of growth and healing that can develop over the course of months, years, and possibly a lifetime.

Part of the process can involve calling one's identity into question, sometimes in humorous ways. US comedian and author Lewis Black, for instance, forgot his name under the influence of LSD. *One of the things that is a linchpin between you and those around you is your fucking name,* he thought to himself at the time, but didn't want to ask his friends who probably would have worried about him, making the situation worse. He tried to find out his name instead by consulting a dictionary for over an hour that felt like twenty-six years. When he realized his wallet was in his pocket he went for it, only to get scared just before opening it: *What if there is nothing in there but Monopoly cards?*[265] The thought terrified him at first, but then he couldn't stop laughing. Finally, he opened the wallet and found his name on his ID.

Mystical and Buddhist Traditions of Integration

There is little psychedelic research or present knowledge as to how dramatic experiences like these bring lasting changes and improvement to personality and psychological health. Yet the broader question of how expanded states of consciousness affect personality is anything but new. The German concept of *Bildung* traces back to the mystical traditions of the Middle Ages, a term with a wide range of meanings including "education," "training," "development," and "formation."[266] *Bildung* is the lifelong process of holistic becoming, the evolution of body, mind, and spirit. According to Meister Eckhart, *Bildung* comes through mystical experiences that

265 *Have a Good Trip*, Donick Cary, 2020.

266 Michael Egerding, *Bild und Modell. Zur Frage der Bildung in der deutschen Mystik.*

present a person with an image of his or her existence.[267] Eckhart draws attention to the link between mindfulness and *Bildung*, advising that we do not grow attached to things but remain free of them. He argues further that *Bildung* is connected to ego dissolution: "A person must learn to create himself out of all his gifts" in order to remain empty and receptive to things "that know neither time nor space."[268] In Eckhart's view, love, concentration, and openness provide the foundational pillars of *Bildung*, which gives a person the opportunity to encounter the diversity of reality within himself. And since the variety we encounter within ourselves and our world is never ending, *Bildung* can be seen as a lifelong process, where one understanding opens the door to the next.

German mystic Johannes Tauler also emphasized the effects of *Bildung* on our identities. For Tauler, mystical experiences catalyze us towards play with alternative forms of our identity, arriving at new approaches toward life as our conceptual understanding evolves.[269]

The Buddha, too, stressed that meditation wasn't an end in itself, but a means toward cultivating compassion, sympathetic joy, and loving kindness, alongside realistic self-perception and mental clarity. Clarity helps us better understand how our minds work, especially mental paths that lead to discomfort, unhappiness, stress, and pain. A crucial step in this process lies in recognizing the impermanence of all mental phenomena, the way we cling to them or reject them, and our stress-provoking tendency to identify with them. Psychedelics can help foster this understanding. One way they do so is by temporarily suspending the ego and its patterns of clinging and aversion while fostering a sense of well-being and joy. Buddhist instructors are constantly reminding students that these kinds of insights are quickly forgotten in everyday life, which is why they must be steadily cultivated and developed. Twelfth-century Korean Zen master Chinul placed continuous development at the center of his teachings, a method he called "sudden awakening, gradual cultivation."[270] Though recognizing early on that he possessed a "Buddha nature" (i.e., was capable of enlightenment), he still made a sincere effort to root out deeply conditioned negative

267 In German there is a slight double entendre here, with the word for "image," *Bild*, contained in the term *Bildung*.

268 Meister Eckhart, *Deutsche Predigten und Traktate* (Nikol, 2007).

269 Egerding, *Bild und Modell. Zur Frage der Bildung in der deutschen Mystik.*

270 Joseph Goldstein, *Mindfulness: A Practical Guide to Awakening* (Sounds True, 2016).

habits in his everyday life. Having learned firsthand that sudden awakening couldn't serve as a substitute for gradually cultivating one's practice, he warned: "After awakening you must be constantly on your guard. If deluded thoughts suddenly appear, do not follow after them.... Then and only then will your practice reach completion."[271]

Over the long term, and enriched by psychedelic experience, the notion of *Bildung* in German mysticism and cultivation in Buddhism can help patients understand and deepen their therapeutic process. Through repeat sessions and gradual psychotherapeutic integration, the psychedelic effects of mindfulness, positivity, meaning, perspective shifts, and self-transcendence can be cultivated to provide a source of inner strength and refuge.

In what follows, I highlight psychedelics' alchemical effects and their singularity effects, both of which come as a result of increased neuroplasticity. These qualities can prove particularly supportive in fostering both Buddhist cultivation and *Bildung*.

Alchemy

Jung's school of analytic psychotherapy, which involves a patient coming to terms with their unconscious to achieve psychological integration, relates to psychedelic therapy in several ways. Jung's term for the process of integration was the "transcendent function," which he compared to the art of alchemy: "This remarkable capacity of the human psyche for change, expressed in the transcendent function, is the principal object of late medieval alchemical philosophy...the secret of alchemy was in fact the transcendent function, the transformation of personality through the blending and fusion of the noble with the base components, of the differentiated with the inferior functions, of the conscious with the unconscious."[272]

The predecessor to modern chemistry, alchemy was an effort to transform both literal matter and psychological "materials" with the goal of transmuting pre-existing matter into a higher and more resilient unity. It concurs exactly with Nietzsche's "plastic force."

---

271 Ibid.

272 Carl Jung, *Collected Works of Carl Jung*, Vol. 7 (Princeton University Press, 1966).

Alchemy originated from efforts to derive medical remedies from gold as part of Ayurveda (*ayus* meaning "life," *veda* meaning "knowledge"), an Indian healing practice that focuses not only on curing illness but also on enhancing overall health.[273] The forerunners to this original form of alchemy can be found in the *Rig Veda*, which contains hundreds of hymns describing the ritual-alchemical processes necessary for producing the psychedelic soma. Every implement and process used had a spiritual significance; breaking up the stems of the soma plant with a mortar and pestle were compared to an act of ritualized intercourse, while crushing up the pieces of stalk with stones on a board was seen as ritual dismemberment, and a precondition for transformation. The sap was then clarified by sieve over a fire of sheep hair, which was equated to ablutions and purification rites. The filtered drops of soma stood for the pure rays of the morning sun and rebirth. After the second pressing, the orange-colored liquid was mixed with milk, which the authors of the *Rig Veda* compared to a white garment enshrouding the soma. The result was a mild, sweet drink with a golden-yellow color. The vessel that contained the potion of the gods was called "ocean." In Sanskrit the word *soma* means "distillation" or "extraction," and soma is likened to the process gilding, all indicating that the effects of the psychedelic were seen in an alchemical light.

In the West, *spagyrics* is the equivalent term for Ayurveda's concept of alchemical healing. The word consists of the Greek words for "extracting" or "separating," *spao*; and *egeiro*, which means "uniting" or "joining together." Swiss physician Paracelsus posited spagyrics as the essential principal underlying alchemical medicine. The term also offers an image of the healing process, of separation or dissolving, followed by integration at a higher level. Significant transitions in the natural world also rely on the model of spagyrics—in the pupa stage, a caterpillar dissolves into a slimy liquid before emerging anew as a butterfly. Another term for psychedelic therapy is *psycholyse*, or psychic dissolution, which in many ways continues the tradition of alchemical healing found in Ayurveda and spagyrics.

In the transition from the Middle Ages to the modern era, alchemy formed an important undercurrent within the rational worldview that had begun to dominate our shallower layers of consciousness. In the context of sweeping Enlightenment-era "rationality" that looked to divide and order,

273 Srinivasan Kalyanaraman, *Indian Alchemy: Soma in the Veda* (Munshirm Manoharlal Pub Pvt Ltd, 2004).

alchemy served as the feminine-holistic shadow, akin to the relationship between the psychedelic state and our rational everyday consciousness. Alchemy isn't some esoteric escape from reason, however, but a practice that sets rationality and intuition in dialogue. In the process it has created an entire series of symbols of enduring value for wholeness and integration which, according to Jung, are filled with implications for psychotherapy. Alchemy's lasting powers of attraction are visible in the perennial inspiration it provides, including for some of our own era's most popular books, from Paulo Coelho's *The Alchemist* to J. K. Rowling's *Harry Potter and the Sorcerer's Stone*.

One of the foundational texts of Western alchemy is *The Emerald Tablet*, also known as the *Smaragdine Table*, which describes the unity of the cosmos and the individual as "that which is above [being] like to that which is below, and that which is below [being] like to that which is above, to accomplish the miracles of one thing."[274] The experience of unity and oneness are both common and important to psychedelic experiences. In a seeming paradox, studies show that experiencing a dissolution of the boundaries of the self goes hand-in-hand with the experience of unity.[275] Patients who have experienced the boundaries dissolving between themselves and their environments have reported other changes in their consciousness as well, such as:

> Everything joins together to form a whole.
>
> It seems as though my surroundings and I are one.
>
> Conflicts and contradicts come undone.
>
> I experience the past, present, and future as a single thing.

---

274 Robert Steele and Dorothea Waley Singer, "The Emerald Table," *Proceedings of the Royal Society of Medicine* 21, no. 3 (January 1928): 485-501.

275 Erich Studerus, Alex Gamma, and Franz X. Vollenweider, "Psychometric Evaluation of the Altered States of Consciousness Rating Scale (OAV)," *Plos One* 5, no. 8 (August 31, 2010)

Alchemists went to great lengths to discover unity within themselves and in nature.[276] Before the Scientific Revolution of the sixteenth century, chemical experimentation and ambitions—such as the transmutation of base metals into gold—were inseparably intertwined with theoretical and metaphorical ideas about nature and the self. From the seventeenth century onward, earlier alchemical experiences and experiments increasingly came to be interpreted as symbolic explorations of the self and spiritual development. Many pictured life as a process full of transformations in which each person must try to find "our gold," i.e., our deepest and most innate unity. Signs of the emergence of material gold in alchemical experiments included sudden sparks, changing colors, or unexpected reactions, prompting fits of enthusiasm in the alchemists. While the reactions often proved disappointing—the chemical experiment failed, and everything turned black as coal—the alchemist's passion drove them on to further experiments. Anyone who had caught glimpse of the golden sparks couldn't forget it. Each alchemist had to find their own way, and each had their own personal tricks, preferences, and equipment. Most were mavericks, dreamers, seekers. Disputes over the right methods were rare; asking an alchemist how to bring about a certain transformation would elicit the reply: "You'll have to find out for yourself."

Everybody did agree on the existence of the philosopher's stone, which allowed for and catalyzed transmutation, though its nature remained a secret. Paracelsus suspected a mercury-like solvent capable of dissolving hardened substances including iron, tin, and sheet metal without altering or destroying the basic elements. The stone was thus also seen as a rejuvenating, purifying, and vital elixir that could bring a fresh start to the halting alchemical process and lead to new sparks, changes in color, or unexpected reactions, instilling a new sense of enthusiasm and vigor in the experimenter. The stone drove the alchemists on to continue their search for treasure and their form of resilience—rust-resistant gold.

Seen in the light of modern chemistry, suppositions of leading alchemical pioneers and reformers such as the Swiss physician Theophrastus von Hohenheim, commonly known as Paracelsus, weren't entirely off the mark; today, state-of-the-art methods allow us to transform mercury into gold in reactors through irradiation. What enabled the alchemists' psychological

276 Lawrence M. Principe, *The Secrets of Alchemy*, narrated by Gary Tiedemann (Function, 2023), 5, Kindle.

inspiration, however, remains a mystery today. One of the founders of Western alchemy, Zosimos of Panopolis, left behind the following cryptic message: "Receive this Stone which is not a stone, a precious thing that has no value, a thing of many shapes that has no shape, this unknown which is known by all."[277] It is my hypothesis that the philosopher's stone is a state, induced by psychedelic substances, that acts like a solvent for the psyche, loosening it and allowing for psychological change and reconstitution. The thought is based on the following considerations:

Jung viewed alchemy as a projection of our unconscious onto the discipline of chemistry and compared alchemical texts and depictions to dreams. Yet alchemy's frequent mentions of brilliant colors and iridescent light, clouds, fantastic animals, shape-shifting, and spiritual or mystical experiences all sooner recall the psychedelic state. Dreams are usually colorless and sketchy, while alchemists emphasize how the philosopher's stone unites all colors within it, that or how the dazzling colors of the peacock's tale light up within the transformations. It seems plausible that through exposure to fire, their close proximity to chemical reactions, and breathing in gasses, a number of alchemists would have entered a psychedelic state, which they later described in their work. The illustration below shows two alchemical depictions that Jung selected for his own work on alchemy; the originals would have been in full color. The similarities to psychedelic experience immediately suggest themselves.

In the Chinese Tao, the philosopher's stone is also called "the golden pill," indicating a pharmacological element in alchemical transformations.[278]

Alchemy ascribes different phases to the process of transformation, eventually leading to a higher unity. This in turn recalls the cycle of preparation, ingestion, and integration sessions one finds in psychedelic therapy.

As discussed, Paracelsus compares the philosopher's stone to a mercury-like solvent. This is a good image for the psychedelic state, where complex problems are broken down into clearly delineated constitutive parts, aiding in their resolution. Psychedelic therapy is thus "solution-oriented"— it isn't just patients, in fact, who have reported psychedelics helping them to solve specific problems, but engineers, artists, and scientists as well.

---

277 Dennis W. Hauck, "The Roots of a Science of Consciousness in Hermetic Alchemy," 2016, p. 47

278 Kalyanaraman, *Indian Alchemy*.

Alchemists viewed every transformation as a gift, recognizing a divine power at work even in the surface disintegration of a stone or a coin rusting. Adopting a stance of gratitude in this way relates to a psychedelic form of openness I discuss in the final chapter. For alchemists, the entire cosmos was embedded in a complex, intertwined, and interdependent whole; from this perspective, pharmacological and therapeutic work is always linked to a higher unity.

Alchemists invented a universal language that was understood around the world. Alchemy exists across cultures, and books about alchemy are popular wherever they are published. Psychedelics likewise foster understanding amongst all people, and generate experiences that link people the world over, not least by dissolving our cultural expectations and biases.

Alchemists often likened their transformations to a journey. The Greek myth of Jason's journey to the Golden Fleece was especially popular. This recalls psychedelic "trips" to a higher unity.

Alchemy is about connections both in the chemical and figurative sense, forging new connections with oneself and all the elements one encounters in the world. This is comparable to the feeling of connectedness that arises under the influence of psychedelics.

Alchemists repeatedly stressed the importance of the container in transformation; the philosopher's stone would only work in the right environment and with the right starting materials. This echoes the importance of set and setting in psychedelic therapy.

The philosopher's stone was said to be born out of a matrix, an alembic, a womb, or an egg, all of which are symbols for cyclical time, a typical experience in the psychedelic state. The moon for alchemists stood for a new unity arising out of transformation, recalling the moon as a symbol for soma in the *Rig Veda*.

The alchemists' notions regarding the "matter" with which they were working were just as ill-defined and indeterminate as our notions about the consciousness we are treating with psychedelics. We don't even know why consciousness exists. Neither science considers facts alone but interprets signs as well, meaning that both retain an edge of mystery. The unity that alchemy and psychedelics transmit is not unequivocal or without contradictions. On the contrary, it imparts the fullness of life with all its paradoxes, and the experience of opposites as a greater whole.

Alchemy has numerous spiritual and symbolic aspects, but cannot be reduced to them. Alchemists made important contributions to modern chemistry, inventing porcelain and printer's ink among other things. In discovering the astounding malleability of matter alchemy resembles the modern neurosciences' discovery of the astounding malleability of the human brain, a capacity called neuroplasticity that can grow through the use of psychedelics.

Alchemists were forever underscoring the importance of concentrating and meditating on one's work, and warning against running away from it. This is akin to modern psychedelic therapy, which gives patients eye shades and meditation instructions in encouraging them to concentrate on their experience (or "work"), and not allow themselves to get distracted.

Fig. 7–1: Psychedelic consciousness as depicted in alchemical art. Left: *Anima Mercurii* or "Mercury Soul" (from Leonhardt Thurneysser zum Thurn, *Quinta Essentia*, 1574). At right: The marriage of water and fire as depicted by Indian alchemy (from Jung, *Psychologie und Alchemie*, 2021).

Alchemists were the first people in the West not to experience spirituality outside of themselves—in nature, the sky, or at an altar—but inside, as an inner transformation. This makes them the direct predecessors next to the Eastern tradition to psychedelic spirituality.

Herman Hesse describes an alchemical transformation in *Journey to the East*, an influential book within US hippie circles. The following passage features Leo, a close friend and muse of the narrator. The narrator notices

> a candle in a metal candlestick fixed to the wall of the niche. A matchbox lay there. I lit the candle and the strange double figure was now brightly illuminated.
>
> Only slowly did it dawn upon me...I begin to suspect and then perceive what it was intended to represent. It represented a figure which was myself, and this likeness of myself was unpleasantly weak and half-real; it had blurred features, and in its whole expression there was something unstable, weak, dying or wishing to die...the other figure which was joined to mine to make one, was strong in colour and form...I now saw the double figure representing Leo and myself, not only becoming clearer and each image more alike, but I also saw that the surface of the figures was transparent.... Inside the figures I saw something moving, slowly, extremely slowly, in the same way that a snake moves which has fallen asleep. Something was taking place there, something like a very slow, smooth but continuous flowing or melting; indeed, something melted or poured across from my image to that of Leo's. I perceived that my image was in the process of adding to and flowing into Leo's, nourishing and strengthening it.[279]

One patient of Claudio Naranjo's describes a similar experience with MDMA: "It was as if I was being myself for the first time, but I also remembered what it was like to be myself. I was alive for the first time, truly alive. There was a sentence that stayed with me during the entire work that night and in the days that followed and that still resonates with me today: 'Oh! What longing I felt for myself!'...like Pinocchio, who turned into a real child. It is going from being a tormented soul to having a true self."[280]

One patient I treated with LSD for severe depression saw a shimmering light as a sort of golden thread that led her through the experience. "The shimmering light is tying everything together," she said. "It represents the overall meaning, the reason anything exists to begin with. The colors contain all the nuances that make up life itself, they are like all the living beings in existence." Following her session, she felt certain that the colors were always in her subconsciously, though at times she lost access to them.

Alan Watts described the alchemical aspects of the psychedelic experience as allowing for the

---

279 Hermann Hesse, *The Journey to the East* (Vision Press, 1933).

280 Naranjo, *My Psychedelic Explorations*.

> awareness of polarity. This is the vivid realization that states, things, and events that we ordinarily call opposite are interdependent, like back and front, or the poles of a magnet. By polar awareness one sees that things which are explicitly different are implicitly one: self and other, subject and object, left and right, male and female—and then, a little more surprisingly, solid and space, figure and background, pulse and interval, saints and sinners, police and criminals, in-groups and out-groups.... The "I" feeling, to be felt at all, must always be a sensation relative to the "other"—to something beyond its control and experience. To be at all, "I" must begin and end. But the intellectual jump that mystical and psychedelic experiences make here is in enabling us to see that all these myriad I-centers are us—not, indeed, a personal and superficially conscious ego, but what Hindus call the *paramatman*, the Self of all selves.[281]

Jung also describes the mystical aspects of experiencing unity: "The special sense of unity is common to all forms of mysticism, and likely arises out of the general contamination of the contents [i.e., from the alchemical process of dissolution].... If we attempt to picture a state in which nothing is distinct, we would doubtless perceive everything as being one. This makes it likely that the unique experience of unity springs from subliminal knowledge of the universal connection in the unconscious. " The neuroscientific equivalent of this state is an enhanced connection between brain regions and neural networks that usually operate separately during normal rational consciousness.

A further sort of "alchemical" transformation, this one into a power animal, is also oft reported in shamanistic traditions. The transformation speaks to a wish for unity with the force and spontaneity of the animal. The shaman dances as his animal as a way of welcoming its spirit. It is noteworthy that the power animal is never a domesticated animal or livestock but always wild creature: a hawk, a puma, a tiger, a snake, or a fish. Patients also identify with animals during psychedelic treatment. Under the influence of psilocybin, one patient previously convinced that her power animal was a dove transformed into an eagle. For a while she danced the eagle in the office, fluttering her wings. In our subsequent integration sessions, she

281 Alan Watts, "Psychedelics and Religious Experience," *California Law Review* 56, no. 1 (January 1968): 74–85.

wore a necklace with an eagle feather. She also developed from a dove into an eagle in her professional work, assuming leadership of a school in an appropriate and timely developmental step.

The alchemists were convinced that charring things and making them black was a necessary precursor to great transformations. One patient of mine, who had overcome alcohol dependency and entered therapy because he was afraid of a relapse, described his own experience of charring while on psilocybin in the following way: "Something is dying...my identity as a dependent and addictive person was still there and is dying now, the empty vessel that I am. But a new person is emerging, freer, happier, like a dancer in a field of flowers...there's a fog, and I feel that something very powerful is developing in it. It reminds me of being eighteen. My body dissolves, the entire fabric, and I lose control of my bowels, it's like crashing down, everything is falling, but beneath there is a crystal that cannot be destroyed."

When Is Enough, Enough?

After my last LSD session with Peter Oehen I considered my firsthand experiences with psychedelics finished, something external circumstance seemed to confirm when Peter sold his beautiful treatment center and entered retirement. I was ready for the phase to be over; what I had experienced under Oehen's guidance was powerful and lasting enough that I didn't expect any added benefit from further experiments. Oehen assured me that it wasn't necessary to try out every psychedelic available, and that the experiences were broadly similar. Alan Watts shared the opinion, urging "if you get the message, hang up the phone." If psychedelics communicated something important to you, in other words, you were better off leaving well enough alone.

Peoples' first experiences with psychedelics are often the most riveting, creating a very strong mindfulness effect. After enough experiences more and more patterns of avoidance will creep in, so that the therapist must remind the patient to maintain a mindful attitude. Patients typically move through various phases of different lengths, which can stretch out over multiple sessions:[282]

282 Robert Masters and Jean Houston, *The Varieties of Psychedelic Experience: The Classic Guide to the Effects of LSD on the Human Psyche* (Park Street Press, 2000).

The sensory level: Sensory perception occupies the center of attention, slight movement in a picture or sounds growing louder, for example. This encourages mindfulness toward the body and the senses.

The recollective-analytic level: In this phase experiences are personalized, the barriers to the unconscious grow permeable, personal conflicts arise, traumatic experiences are recalled, and new solutions and perspectives emerge at the level of personality.

The symbolic level: This phase is marked by experiences of symbolic dramas with archetypal content. The sense of time shifts and symbols of cyclical time (like birth and death) arise. Transpersonal feelings, or feelings that do not only concern one's person but incorporate a feeling of a greater whole, will often come up.

The integral level: A phase in which true spiritual experience is possible, a sense of unity for example, emptiness or spiritual openness.

In the experience of Jean Houston and Robert Masters, the US psychedelic pioneers and spiritual teachers responsible for developing this schematic of different phases, only 5 percent of people who took psychedelics reached the final phase of deep integration.[283] Most of those who did were people of mature age with a long-term spiritual practice, making it unrealistic to set the spiritual state, or integral level, as a therapeutic goal.

Ayahuasca and Alchemy

A year after what I supposed was my last personal psychedelic experience, an unexpected discovery threw my decision into doubt. In an intricate linguistic study, my colleague Adrian Hase analyzed thousands of psychedelic trip reports on the Internet. The initial findings revealed that the psychedelic quality of ayahuasca significantly differed from other psychedelic substances such as LSD, psilocybin, MDMA, and ketamine.[284]

283 Ibid.

284 Hase et al., "Analysis of Recreational Psychedelic Substance Use Experiences Classified by Substance," .

The results came as a surprise to me, and I began to read through the Internet accounts. Ayahuasca did in fact seem to have a much stronger effect on the body than other substances. The experience of dissolution seemed less psychological or spiritual than physical, recalling Naranjo's assertion that ayahuasca was capable of activating root and sacral chakras.

Somehow the study results left me feeling obligated to expand my experience with psychedelics by participating in an ayahuasca ceremony. It was anything but easy to find the right context, however. Everything I found smacked of commercialism and gave little impression of earnestness or authenticity. I came across a host of sobering comments online: one woman recounted a fight breaking out between her and the organizers—while the ceremony was still in session—over the cleaning costs for a blanket she had vomited on. Another participant had discovered that the shaman alleged to have flown in especially from South America was actually working in Germany as a waiter, and wasn't even aware that a difference between the ayahuasca plant and an ayahuasca brew existed. All of this strongly cautioned against participating in such experiences.

Months passed, and I had nearly forgotten about the matter when I made an unexpected acquaintance at an event about psychedelic philosophy in the Netherlands, a Buddhist with relatives in Switzerland who immediately struck me as reliable and trustworthy. He led a meditation center in Amsterdam and occasionally took part in ayahuasca ceremonies. We agreed to keep in touch to deepen our conversations about Buddhism and psychedelics. Over the course of our conversations online, he mentioned that a shaman of whom he thought very highly was going to lead a ceremony in Switzerland, which he planned on attending. The shaman was Portuguese and had studied anthropology in Brazil. His ceremonies didn't attempt to imitate the traditional forms, taking a more neo-shamanistic approach. The ayahuasca brew, however, was prepared according to the exact instructions of Amazonian shamans. Though the ceremony wasn't open to the public and intended only for a small group, my acquaintance was open to asking the shaman whether I might join. After a wait filled with anticipation, several weeks later an invitation arrived to a "mountain retreat" at a farmhouse in the Swiss Jura.

A crowd of familiar faces was there to greet me as I came up to the farmhouse, backpack and air mattress in tow. Switzerland is small, and most were doctors and psychotherapists I already knew from my work in hospitals or professional training as a psychotherapist. Others I didn't know possessed a great deal of experience in psychotherapy and meditation, with most working as life counselors or coaches. There were also two younger students in search of answers in their professional and personal lives.

The shaman introduced the ceremony, revealing some of the first pearls from his vast treasure trove of practical experience and knowledge concerning anthropology, plant biology, pharmacology, and religion. We sat in a circle. Everyone introduced themselves and described what had motivated them to take part in the ceremony. I was struck that nobody had come just for the fun of it; the recurring motif was rather smaller or larger life crises. I found out, for instance, that an ER doctor I knew was considering switching his line of work to becoming a psychotherapist.

It was pitch black by now; a candle burned in the middle of the circle. At everyone's side was a small bucket, in case of nausea. One after another we approached the shaman, who poured some brown liquid into a glass. The shaman knew I was a beginner in ayahuasca, so when I came to sit in front of him we had a brief conversation. He encouraged me not to take a beginner's dose but proceed straight to a standard dose, since I had been fine during my other experiences with psychedelic substances. I agreed and took a couple of large sips of the dark concoction, which aside from a nauseating bitterness also had the pleasant flavor of licorice.

After everyone had ingested the ayahuasca brew, my Buddhist acquaintance led us in a meditation. Meditation, to my mind, is the golden path into the psychedelic state, and in just a few words he managed to bring about a state of peace and relaxation in the group. Meditating, I slipped into an alternate, highly physical, and deeply unsettling world that I described the day after in a journal entry:

> After about forty minutes I feel a force climbing up from my abdomen toward my head, like somebody was taking hold of my entire body. My head is tightly connected to my body, which is pleasant. But the connection becomes so strong that it somehow disintegrates, like when kids in a sandbox pile too much sand on a sandcastle and it collapses. After collapsing physically from all the pressure, other parts begin to fall apart too. All my senses come undone. Strands of light fall disintegrate into individual beams, the music disintegrates into individual tones. In the end, I disintegrate. I hear myself saying

things like: "You have to finish that by the end of the week," "Unfortunately you aren't eligible for therapy," or "No, I'll take the train instead." *How unimaginable that I would say those things,* I think, as though the sentences weren't mine. *How could I ever be capable of making such clear statements and delivering them so clearly amidst the whirl of impressions and thoughts?*

Now I see a friend who recently died in a coffin in front of me. He looks completely different, almost completely decayed. Frighteningly close and touching and totally foreign at the same time. A host of incompatible feelings creeps over me: grief, joy, boredom, fascination, fear, surprise, disgust, and all of them create an irrepressible feeling of nausea, an unbearable excess, a thousand pounds of emotional mayonnaise all splitting apart. I look at my hand. It doesn't belong to me. It is totally withered and foreign. I see the bones showing through, like on an X-ray. I make out smells of medicine, ether and ammonia, but it also smells like flowers and rotten cheese. Nothing makes sense. I look at myself in the bathroom mirror. What I see isn't me, but a poorly assembled photo collage. The penetrating eyes of a blankly staring reptile combined with the swollen red nose of a drinker. The lips are oddly oversized and misshapen, covered in festering herpes blisters. The cheeks and forehead are dented and pocked like car doors. The hair seems to be made up of different, badly worn toupees. *You have to look at all of this as an intellectual adventure,* I think, *as an advanced mindfulness exercise*. But it's no use. My condition feels bad, really bad. I know that I won't last much longer. I want to go home. A disintegrative force comes from within, it's in the body, every fiber is being dissolved from within. It's a horrible feeling. Somehow I still exist, I'm able to reflect on the experience, but I'm lacking the imagination to see or experience myself as whole or coherent. This isn't an adventure, it's a total catastrophe. I'm afraid, and feel the sweat on my hands. I keep glancing back at the clock. Time seems to stand still. It's only 11:30. I remember the shaman's instructions to give oneself up to Mother Ayahuasca, and ask for her help.

"Mother Ayahuasca," I plead, "I know that Gregor Hasler is an illusion, that Gregor Hasler is a story I've invented. You don't have to show me, I know already! Please, please stop smashing me into

> pieces." But she doesn't stop. She doesn't ease her grip. My Buddhist friend begins to dance in the middle of the room. He looks as overpowering and strong as a dancing bear. *What a body image,* I think, *what self-consistency he must have to be able to dance like that.* I try focusing on my breath, but that too dissolves into individual, unrelated movements. The nausea increases. I have to vomit. I lie down. Hold on! Suddenly geometric figures appear on the distant horizon, like signs from another world. There are green triangles and blue squares, and they begin to form a pattern. I feel this is a good sign. I remember my first year in high school, where my interest in geometry helped me overcome my identity crisis. By now the entire room is full of geometric patterns, mandala fragments falling like manna from heaven. I feel a sense of relaxation, my hands and shoulders gradually release. My right leg starts to tremble, then shake. I feel that this is good, that I can shake out the disintegration this way, that shaking like this is the path to a new unity.

The following day we sat back down in a circle, and everyone spoke about their experience. Most had been mild, harmless. One participant said it had been very beautiful, a wonderful trip through fields and forests, but that they had expected more. Still, I wasn't the only one who had a "bad trip." One of the younger participants was crying with her hand pressed against her lower abdomen; she talked about bad experiences that had resurfaced, and which she would now to have to work through.

For the rest of the day we had time for ourselves, to go on walks or talk in the dining room. I appreciated others' sympathy; one other participant thought I had undergone a shamanic initiation, a sort of ritual death where the shaman intentionally allows his psyche to be split into pieces, giving him an ability to function in different realities. Another woman who was versed in mythology compared my trip to the dismemberment of the Egyptian god Osiris and spoke of the Greek god Dionysus, who drew his power to inspire from being dismembered then reassembled on multiple occasions. Another participant looked up a passage from the Gospel of Thomas on her smartphone, which she thought might help me assimilate my experience: "For this reason I say, if one is whole, one will be filled with light, but if one is divided, one will be filled with darkness."[285] Still others offered practical

285 Mattison, *The Gospel of Thomas*.

tips for the next time: Don't eat anything the day before; don't lie down but always try to stay seated; and more than anything—ask for help in a situation like that. The conversations helped me to experience myself as newly assembled, still somewhat unsteady to be sure, but full of compassion and energy.

That evening, before the second session, the shaman gave his own personal story. As a young man he had played guitar in quite a successful rock band, though not successful enough for him to base his life around it. A short while ago he had had reconnected with his former bandmates after a long time of not seeing each other. When they heard that he now led ayahuasca ceremonies using calm, relaxing music they had all burst out laughing. As he told us the story the shaman let out his own heartfelt laugh at himself, and we all joined in, laughing about the ceremony and ourselves. It was a wonderful moment, a divine laughter, and I was overcome by a deep sense of belonging among these dreamers and seekers, alchemists and journeyers, a group I had likely always belonged to.

Singularity

Coming to terms with difficult twists of fate present one of the greatest challenges in the process of integration. As Swiss psychotherapist Ose Hein characterized the sentiment of a patient she treated with LSD for severe anxiety due to an advancing cerebral disease, "Everything so far had had its place on his path, and it deeply inspired him that everything had a purpose, that nothing had been in vain."

Accepting one's own fate is the highest form of alchemy. In psychedelic therapy it feeds into what I call the "singularity effect," allowing patients to integrate fateful conditions, events, or life circumstances they might perceive as restrictive into a single, unbroken identity and story. The process is comparable to digestion, and how our intestines and digestive glands handle difficult-to-assimilate foods. As I wrote in *Die Darm-Hirn Connection* ("The Gut-Brain Connection"), "Digesting means enduring the world, taking it in, dissolving, transmuting, assimilating, getting over, recognizing, processing, and overcoming."[286] In this context, the singularity effect represents a sort of neural digestion.

Apart from this digestive capacity, long-term resilience also depends on the feeling of freedom. The feeling of freedom is as mysterious as the science of alchemy; as US philosopher Daniel Dennett phrased it, "Our tales are spun, but for the most part we don't spin them; they spin us."[287] In that case, how do we even feel free to begin with, and why is this feeling so important?

Let's say that one morning a man thinks to himself, *I want to be free like a rock star!* and leaves his family out of a spontaneous sense of adventure. The odds are that looking back he will judge his impulsive decision as immature and *un*free, because arbitrary, unjustified acts of will aren't actually free will. The freedom of a rock star is also like so many other cliches of freedom—an illusion. Rock stars must play the same songs every week, even if they are sick to death of them. Their calendars are planned out years in advance by their managers. Their movements are restricted by their fame. The list goes on.

Despite the constraints of our lives, we are probably much freer than we imagine ourselves to be. At one point in his life, the man who left his family so he could be "free" decided to start that family. His feeling that he is unfree as the father of a family is based on a misunderstanding of himself. It is much easier for us to feel free buying a plane ticket to California than helping our kids with the daily chores. That doesn't mean, however, that the flight to California is true freedom.

The first step toward feeling free means understanding free will, and seeing that it isn't arbitrary willpower or acting on impulse.[288] As one patient put it, "I actually most prefer being by myself. So why do I do so many things in public? Why did I say I was willing to house my mom and take care of her? Why do I let myself be led around by seemingly practical constraints? Why have I never learned to listen to myself and do what I want to do?" An LSD session helped her understand that the surface desire to be alone concealed a deeper need to experience human closeness and be there for others.

---

286 Gregor Hasler, *Die Darm-Hirn Connection: Revolutionäres Wissen für unsere psychische und körperliche Gesundheit* (Klett-Cotta, 2020).

287 Daniel Dennett, *Consciousness Explained* (Little, Brown and Company, 1991).

288 Peter Biere, *Das Handwerk der Freiheit: Über die Entdeckung des eigenen Willens* (Hanser, 2001).

Understanding where will originates and how it develops not only helps people feel more free, but also helps them live in greater alignment. Sometimes a shift in our identities is necessary if our experienced or practical sense of will is constantly coming into conflict with our self-image (a father vs. a rock star). The more we come to know and experience our desires directly, the larger the inner world with which we can identify becomes. Psychedelic therapy helps in this regard by bringing unconscious desires to our attention. At the same time, the alchemical effect loosens our identities, allowing new relationships to self and will to form.

Not infrequently, psychedelics lead to the insight that we had no other choice in whatever situation we're reflecting on. Even our neurotic sides, our anxieties, habits, and mental blockages are ultimately an expression of a will we call our own. The point, then, isn't by any means to reject all the forms of resistance that disrupt our sense of liveliness or spontaneity. The recipe for liberation isn't to stifle our will, as foreign and obstructive as it may appear. Rather, we must understand and integrate it, listen to it and make room for it, instead of allowing it to operate like a ghost in the machine. Somewhere, among all the injustice, every symptom, every resistance, every fate has its justification.

In his famous series of Gifford Lectures on religion, US psychologist William James said, "Whoever not only says, but feels, 'God's will be done,' is mailed against every weakness."[289] The singularity effect helps us recognize "God's will"—one's fate, or deepest and highest will, in other words—as our own. This understanding holds tremendous cultural importance, and has been expressed and modeled by all the great spiritual teachers.

When the Buddha ate the meat that would poison him to death, he knew very well that it was poisoned. He consciously let fate take its course, turning it into his own free decision. Socrates would have been able to flee from the death sentence the Athenian court passed on him, but he accepted his fate. His words before drinking the poison hemlock were: "I may and must pray to the gods to prosper on my journey from this to that other world."[290] He accepted the higher will of the court, in other words, in faith that it matched God's will and thus his own. Jesus knew from the very beginning that he was destined for the cross. He made no attempt to escape his fate,

289 William James, *The Varieties of Religious Experience* (Longmans, Green and Co., 1902).

290 Plato, *Euthyphro, Apology, Crito, Phaedo* (Prometheus Books, 1988).

declaring: "Not my will, but yours be done" in the garden of Gethsemane.[291] Shortly before his death he cried out, "My God, my God, why hast Thou forsaken me?" A very human question pointing to the vast challenge in accepting his lot.[292] The spiritual figures of our own times are also masters of singularity, capable of building new unity out of traumatic and disjointed life experiences. Nelson Mandela sat in jail for twenty-seven years in his struggle for the freedom of South Africa. Yet his time there didn't embitter him; he possessed a remarkable ability to "assimilate" the punishment, accepting it as his own fateful lot in life. As the country's first black president, the same ability later gave him the strength to mediate between black and white people and undo the apartheid system.

The singularity effect is related to the "mana personality" as it appears in Jung's work. For Jung, *mana*, a Polynesian and Melanesian term, is an archetypal power found in certain holy figures that resides within all of us. Integrating this force represented the decisive step in the process of individuation for Jung. He recognized that when we experience a dissolution of self, mana falls to "something which is the desired 'mid-point' of the personality, that ineffable something betwixt the opposites, or else that which unites them, or the result of conflict, or the product of energetic tension: the coming to birth of personality, a profoundly individual step forward, the next stage."[293] This "profoundly individual step" is consistent with the singularity effect, which psychedelics enable us to experience by initiating a dissolution of self. Within this "most individual" state, the archetypes we each carry within ourselves (animus and anima, the heroine, the child, the mother, or the sage, for instance) cease to be independent beings and become functions of how we relate to our unconscious minds. The state is akin to the "great power" of shamans and the extraordinary efficacy of figures like the Buddha, Socrates, Jesus, and Mandela. Mana's force is revealed in the businessman's power of persuasion, the teacher's charisma, and the creative inspiration of the artist. According to Jung, becoming aware of the mana personality is a crucial step in detaching oneself from one's parents and other authority figures and building a separate identity. In indigenous culture, initiation rites helped to make mana tangible; since psychedelic

291 Luke 22:42.

292 Matthew 27:46.

293 James Graham Johnston, *Jung's Indispensable Compass: A Guide to Navigating the Dynamics of Psychological Types* (MSE Press, 2016).

experiences are often linked to initiation rites, we might also call the singularity effect the "initiation effect." In Jung's work mana is a force that helps us reflect "not on 'what one should,' but on what one *can* and *must*."[294]

The singularity effect thus involves digesting the truly difficult experiences in life and twists of fate in a way that allows us to accept them and incorporate them into our identities. Alongside the alchemy effect, it makes it possible to develop one's identity under even the most difficult of circumstances. Both lead us toward "right identity," the middle path between consistency and change. That which is seemingly solid grows flexible and ephemeral, while the cryptic or clandestine becomes an integral part of who we are and may become in the future.

Summary

Resilience contains within it the power to both integrate the past and be free of it. The narrative effects of psychedelics help support this process by improving our memories, while the helioscope effect allows us to accept traumatic memories. Psychotherapy sessions that occur in between sessions where psychedelics are ingested encourage patients to integrate challenging experiences in the interests of developing a practically minded and resilient identity. The psychedelic alchemy effect helps reconcile and link varied and contradictory parts of our personality for a higher unity to emerge. The singularity effect in turn helps us transform the vagaries of fate and severe impositions on our living circumstances into a singular, profoundly individual identity.

294 Carl Jung, *Die Beziehung zwischen dem Ich und dem Unbewussten* (dtv, 1991).

Chapter 8
Right Openness: The Boundless Path

In 2004, an earthquake in the Indian Ocean unleashed a series of devastating tsunamis along the coastlines of Thailand and Indonesia. The death toll reached 230,000 people, many of them fishermen. The nomadic fisherman of the region, however, survived—their shamanic culture kept them open to the signs of the sea, and they had quickly recognized that bottom-dwelling fish were at the water's surface, while dolphins were swimming farther below. For the fishermen it was a signal that something wasn't right, and they were better off on land. Other fishermen focused only on turning as large a profit as they could, missing the warning signs and dying in the floods. Openness to ecological phenomena can be a life saver.

Psychological research measures personality according to five criteria: openness, extroversion, agreeableness, conscientiousness, and neuroticism. Compared to conventional antidepressants, psychedelics lower our neuroticism and increase extroversion, or the interest we take in social contact. Psychedelics are also unique in their ability to increase mental openness.[295] Patients who undergo intense mystical experiences during their psychedelic sessions stand an especially good chance of growing more open in the coming months and years. By "mystical," I mean experiencing bouts of profound meaning that are difficult to encapsulate in words, since our notions

---

295 Katherine A. MacLean, Matthew W. Johnson, and Roland R. Griffiths, "Mystical Experiences Occasioned by the Hallucinogen Psilocybin Lead to Increases in the Personality Domain of Openness," *Journal of Psychopharmacology* 25, no. 11 (September 28, 2011): 1453–61; D. Erritzoe, L. Roseman, M. Nour, K. MacLean, M. Kaelen, D. Nutt et al., "Effects of Psilocybin Therapy on Personality Structure," *Acta Psychiatrica Scandinavica* 138, no. 5 (June 19, 2018): 368–78; José Carlos Bouso, Rafael G. Dos Santos, Miguel Angel Alcazar-Corocles, and Jaime E. C. Hallak, "Serotonergic Psychedelics and Personality: A Systematic Review of Contemporary Research," *Neuroscience & Biobehavioral Reviews/Neuroscience and Biobehavioral Reviews* 87 (April 1, 2018): 118–32.

of self and place in time are temporarily suspended and we are enveloped in a deep sense of happiness that leaves us speechless. Psychedelics have the potential to stop or even reverse the trend of decreased openness with aging.

Openness encompasses a broad range of characteristics that include fantasy, imagination, flexibility, creativity, an interest in art, perceiving feelings in oneself and others, and intellectual engagement. People with a greater degree of openness are receptive to new ideas and motivated to explore new realms of experience. An openness to act means not being stuck in one's ways, and ready to try out something new. Psilocybin especially increases openness to act among depressive patients.[296]

Psychological disorders, meanwhile, are often characterized by a lack of openness. Patients might complain they "don't see a way out," or say things like "If I don't get this promotion, my life won't have any meaning," or "I can't live without her love." All these are signs the patient has no Plan B, and no idea how to exit their mental cul-de-sac. A lack of openness can also manifest as false hope; the wife who hopes her abusive husband will become someone else; the black sheep of a company who hopes to soon become boss; the man who hopes that investing in corrupt coal mines will make him a billionaire—each are at risk of depression.

Mental dead ends and false hopes resemble infinite loops, a common problem in computer science. Despite software developers' best efforts to avoid it, programming errors still lead to sequences of instructions that will run indefinitely if left alone, forcing us to reboot our computers. The mystical experiences that can occur during psychedelic therapy— and also in meditation, while experiencing art or nature, listening to music, or even spontaneously—seem to act much like a reboot for our brains. Conventional psychotropic drugs likely don't have this effect because they don't significantly increase neuroplasticity, which is an important mechanism for expanding openness.[297] Psychedelics increase openness at different levels:

Action: Trying out something new, finding new ways, detours, or loopholes, expanding the stage we act on, leaving our comfort zone

296 Erritzoe et al., "Effects of Psilocybin Therapy on Personality Structure," .

297 Lameese Eldesouky, "Openness to Experience and Health: A Review of the Literature," *Yale Review of Undergraduate Research in Psychology* (2013): 24–42.

> *Experience*: Accepting the fact that we do not control the future, which is the precondition for having experiences, or becoming experienced.
>
> *Intellect*: Greater mental interest, creativity, and flexibility, an openness to unconventional solutions, broad-minded thinking
>
> *Values*: Openness to diversity, accepting other opinions and cultures
>
> Openness of this variety not only offers protection against psychological disorders, but physical symptoms of stress as well, like heart attacks and certain forms of dementia.[298]

Openness also reveals itself in the form of willingness, a key term in acceptance and commitment therapy. These forms of therapy have a great deal in common with psychedelic therapy, including a focus on mindfulness and openness. In psychotherapy, willingness signals a capacity to take the world as it is and accept what it has to offer. It does not involve desire, will, or emotion, nor is it passive endurance. Rather, it is a decision to take a step forward, to choose a new path. This step does not have to be a large one—it might mean calling up a friend who you angered or hurt, or addressing a conflict with a partner even when it's uncomfortable to do so.[299]

Aside from its practical and psychological manifestations, openness can also take existential form. One term for openness in existential philosophy is "world disclosure," a process that occurs at two levels. First is the world that has already been disclosed, and in which we find ourselves: the one captured by language, interpreted, and given a symbolic structure. At the second level lies a disclosure of new horizons of meaning, the revelation of previously concealed, unspoken, or not-yet symbolized dimensions.

Existential openness is an important capacity in Robert Musil's novel *The Man Without Qualities*, described by the author as a "sense of possibility":

> If one wants to pass through open doors easily, one must bear mind that they have a solid frame: this principle...is simply a requirement

298 Ibid.

299 Steven C. Hayes, Kirk D. Strosahl, and Kelly G. Wilson, *Acceptance and Commitment Therapy: The Process and Practice of Mindful Change* (Guilford Press, 2011).

> of the sense of reality. But if there is such a thing as a sense of reality—and no one will doubt that it has its raison d'être—then there must also be something that one can call a sense of possibility.
>
> Anyone possessing it does not say, for instance: Here this or that has happened, will happen, must happen. He uses his imagination and says: Here such and such might, should or ought to happen. And if he is told that something is the way it is, then he thinks: Well, it could probably just as easily be some other way. So the sense of possibility might be defined outright as the capacity to think how everything could "just as easily" be, and to attach no more importance to what is than to what is not.[300]

Musil's "man without qualities" is a figure who abstains from defining things in any way in his own life so as to remain open to new options and constellations. He experiences the resulting freedom in moments of "day-bright mysticism" that Musil describes as "spring and fall, speech and nature's silence, and the magic of life and death too, mingled in this picture... time stood still, a thousand years weighed as lightly as the opening and closing of an eye...although space did not seem to exist any longer either: despite these contradictions, the world seemed filled with transfiguration in all its parts."[301] The experience of this sense of possibility holds a clear affinity with psychedelic consciousness.

Nietzsche in turn describes existential openness as "waiting for nothing" or a "goal without a goal," comparing it to a game or joy itself.[302] When I take delight in something, I neither merge entirely with it nor remain entirely apart. I must remain attentive to it without falling completely under its spell. There are things in the world that can only be obtained with this kind of openness; falling in love is one example.

Related to this is Meister Eckhart's notion of *Gelassenheit*: "releasing" or "letting go." The term denotes a state of mental availability that allows a person to receive things as they come and let them be in their uncertainty and mystery. German philosopher Geog Wilhelm Friedrich Hegel compared this sort of intellectual openness to a ripped sock, writing that "a mended

---

300 Robert Musil, *The Man Without Qualities*, vol. 2 (Vintage, 1996).

301 Ibid.

302 Nietzsche, *The Gay Science*.

sock is better than a torn sock; not so with self-consciousness."[303] Holes and rips, in other words, keep our consciousness open to unanticipated possibilities, wonder, the absolute, mercy, and everything else that wouldn't pass through a sock with all the tears mended.

Mental openness is also of central concern in Indian philosophy. Multiple passages in the *Rig Veda* celebrate the consciousness-opening effects of soma, stating that it brings the "feeling of being set free and released into boundless open space" and the "feeling of infinite expansion"; that it possesses "a thousand channels and a hundred streams," that "our heart becomes an ocean" and the "golden Divine Doors open up," as it "opens the doors of poetic thoughts."

The authors of the Upanishads developed a fascinating philosophy of openness based on the experience of psychedelic opening. The word *upanishad* means "hidden connection" or "hidden identity" in Sanskrit, and connotes the link or total identification between something finite and concrete (the eye) and something eternal (the divine sun). The concrete, tangible parts of life already contain the eternal and incomprehensible, while the hidden connections that psychedelics allow us to experience open our limited, tangible world to boundlessness. As I explored earlier, the formula "Atman = Brahman" already posits that our inner life, when it opens, is identical to the eternal cosmos. Thus, one finds passages such as these in the Upanishads: "When a man knows 'I am Brahman' in this way, he becomes the whole world. A man who thinks 'He is one, and I am another,' does not understand anything."[304] The Sanskrit word *om*, an undying sound free of fear, as the Upanishads explain, doesn't carry any specific meaning. Rather, it expresses a kind of openness that transcends any concept and isn't reliant on facts or particular insights. Om is more akin to an open realm, a fundamental declaration of acceptance that precedes any insights that this openness might foster.

The Upanishads refer to many experiences of self-openness without explicitly describing them, since they could only be described in the negative: "One can only say: Not—, not—. This universal, supreme self is ungraspable, for it cannot be grasped, it is undecaying, because it is not subject to

303 Karen Ng, *Hegel's Concept of Life: Self-Consciousness, Freedom, Logic* (Oxford University Press, 2020).

304 Olivelle, *The Early Upanishads*.

decay. It does not tremble in fear and does not suffer injury, it is freedom from fear."[305]

Austrian philosopher Edmund Husserl stressed that all the perceptions we have about a given thing or idea represent only a minuscule portion of all the possible perceptions that could be had about it, writing that "everything objective that stands before me in experience and primarily in perception has an apperceptive horizon of possible experience, own and foreign. Ontologically speaking, every appearance that I have is from the very beginning a part of an open, endless, but not explicitly realized totality of possible appearances of the same, and the subjectivity belonging to this appearance is open intersubjectivity."[306] By expanding and changing the realm of perception and questioning the self's exclusive claim to subjectivity, psychedelics allow us to experience the perennially open, intersubjective nature of the world, and thus of the higher self.

Patients will often declare themselves unable to describe their experiences of existential openness. in fact, language for such states does not exist. Such a language would be one in which we do not take possession of the things and people around us but let them be, or protect them as they really are. Since no such language exists, the authors of the Vedas turned to poetry. We find the same in the West; Aldous Huxley compared his own psychedelic experiences to the poetry of William Blake, whose writing on hidden connections seems to evoke the Upanishads: "To see a World in a Grain of Sand / And a Heaven in a Wild Flower / Hold Infinity in the palm of your hand / And Eternity in an hour."[307]

The consciousness-opening effects of psychedelics go hand-in-hand with significant growth in neuroplasticity, which doubles the possibilities of synapses making contact. That means that half of the synapses of a given nerve cell already exist and are connected with other nerve cells, while the new synaptic ends created by psychedelics are free and open to establish new connections. This same combination of determinate and indeterminate makes up human existence, *dasein* in German. *Da* or "there," refers to our current, specific situation in the here and now, much like the preexisting synapses. *Sein*, or "being," on the other hand is the indeterminate, open, transcendental portion of our existence, comparable with the new synapses

305 Ibid.

306 Shaun Gallagher and Dan Zahavi, *The Phenomenological Mind* (Routledge, 2012).

307 William Blake, *Auguries of Innocence and other Lyric Poems* (CreateSpace, 2014).

that are able to forge new connections, resulting in new meanings and possibilities. Psychedelics shift the relative weight of the term, bringing us from the givenness and restrictions of *da* to the openness of *sein*. The resulting freedom is more than a negative "freedom from" (symptoms, for example)—it is also a "freedom to," which is openness, the birth of joy, originality, fantasy, vibrancy, creativity, and inspiration. Openness is a form of love.

Opening can also bring lightness and ease to our experience, in some cases enough lightness to soar. This quality of the psychedelic experience is typical of both ketamine and esketamine. One extremely shy patient of mine lived a "small life" tucked away in her parent's house. During regular esketamine sessions, she experienced her body growing powerful wings. She started flying, fascinated by the feeling of freely changing her altitude and direction. There was a steady breeze blowing; sometimes she flew with it, sometimes against. The experience helped her put aside her shyness and become more open toward life.

Potential Problems with Psychedelic Openness

Before discussing openness in its highest form of transformative openness, I'd like to raise a couple of issues. The unique ways in which psychedelics promote openness, however, can bring undesired consequences: Pessimists may grow more open to pessimistic thoughts, people who tend to believe in conspiracies may become more open to them. This makes it important to foster the "right" kind of openness—the kind that encourages personal resilience and living among the full diversity of human community.

The helioscope effect relates dialectically to psychedelic openness, its protective capacity enabling patients to open to their psychedelic experiences without harm by filtering out the potentially harmful "light" of insight in targeted fashion. In the field of astronomy, the helioscope was a necessary invention for researching the surface of the sun, and thus of existential importance for better understanding life on earth. Yet even with the helioscope effect, there are patients for whom the experience of psychedelic opening is too much. They include those who entertain magical thinking, conspiracy theories, or megalomaniac impulses; people who suffer from these and other impairments to their sense of reality should not be treated with psychedelics. Studies show that under certain psychosocial conditions—a stressful or hostile environments for example, with psychotic crises or the heightened risk of suicide—limiting openness with classical psychotropic drugs (antipsychotics, for instance) may even be necessary.[308]

Transformative Openness

"Transformative openness" is a radical form of openness that describes a readiness to become a different person. We go through many such experiences when we are young; our first steps, first words, the first time we earn money by ourselves, our first relationship, first sexual experience—any and all of these can be profound transformations. The adult the child becomes sees the world differently, sets different values, priorities, and goals. Some of these transformations may develop almost naturally over years, while sometimes we need a readiness with an "all or nothing" quality. One Zen saying says that you can't jump over a river in two steps. Nobody is "a little bit" pregnant.

We do not consent to most of our early transformative experiences; they simply happen to us. At some point we must recognize that our parents won't do our laundry for the rest of our lives. Later in life, by contrast, we must actively decide: Do I want to turn to a new profession? Start a family? Have a kid? Move to the country and build a house? The difficulty in doing so is that we cannot imagine what our values and desires will be after the transformation. We may observe the satisfaction or difficulties other people have encountered following their own transformations, but we can hardly predict the ways we ourselves will change. Would the mindfulness, community, and peace of a Buddhist monastery really be preferable to digital communication, film evenings, and travel? Or would we find ourselves longing for smartphones, Scarlett Johansson, and the beaches of Abu Dhabi? Only the transformation itself, i.e., the experience of being a monk, could truly answer such questions.[309]

A central question in modern philosophy asks whether it is impossible to imagine the experience of another consciousness without directly experiencing it oneself. In looking to address the problem, US philosopher

308 Igor Branchi, "The Double Edged Sword of Neural Plasticity: Increasing Serotonin Levels Leads to Both Greater Vulnerability to Depression and Improved Capacity to Recover," *Psychoneuroendocrinology* 36, no. 3 (April 1, 2011): 339–51.

309 Laurie Ann Paul, *Transformative Experience* (Oxford University Press, 2014).

Thomas Nagel made one of the most influential contributions to the philosophy of consciousness hands down in "What Is It Like to Be a Bat?" Bats hear the world through sound waves they send out into the darkness. This in turn produces a sound, an echo, or a sort of music that tells them what the darkness is like. As humans, we cannot conceive of the quality of this experience. The octopus is another example, a highly intelligent mollusk whose arms are capable of thinking and acting independently of the rest of its body. What is it like to have arms that act and think on their own? Is it even remotely comparable to Princess Leia's experience in *Star Wars*, receiving far-off messages from Luke Skywalker, Han Solo, or Obi-Wan Kenobi as they go about their solo missions in the vastness of space?

Another way of understanding this phenomenon is to picture a girl who has spent her entire life in a room filled with clothing and objects that are all black and white. Would it do her any good to be told about meadow green or turquoise blue? Wouldn't she have to first experience the colors for herself to gain an understanding of them? Alternatively, picture a boy who has eaten nothing but porridge and potatoes since birth. How could you explain the pleasures of a bar of Swiss chocolate to him? The problem takes on existential importance in the case of people who never experienced love from their parents who were absent or otherwise overburdened. What is it like to be loved? What is love? Is love worth the risk?

Nagel goes as far as to posit the experience of "what is it like" as the defining characteristic of consciousness: "But fundamentally an organism has conscious mental states if and only if there is something that it is like to be that organism—something it is like for the organism."[310]

Transformations that turn us into new people pose immense challenges to our stress systems, which are highly sensitive to environmental uncertainties and are constantly trying to avoid them whether through fight, flight, or by freezing—stamping out a dangerous insect, running from a snake, or going rigid when the doctor tells us that foreign cells were found in our blood. But how is our stress system supposed to react when absolutely everything grows uncertain, even the preferences, values, or goals that are supposed to protect us from danger? My hypothesis is that our bodies respond by producing their own psychedelics—DMT, for instance—that are

310 Thomas Nagel, "What Is It Like to Be a Bat?" *The Philosophical Review* 83, no. 4 (October 1974): 435–450.

intended to preserve us in the face of the stress of transformation. The following arguments speak in favor of the idea:

- Research on psychotropic drugs has led again and again to the discovery of similar messenger substances that are produced within the body itself. They include the stimulant dopamine; the calming substance serotonin; endorphins, which build trust and block the perception of pain; GABA, which triggers fear; and acetylcholine, which boosts concentration.[311] Given findings to date, we can expect that psychedelic research will lead to the discovery of new messenger substances.
- Stimulating a specific serotonin receptor will trigger a psychedelic state. The extreme specificity of the neurobiology argues for the fact that our brain has a specialized, endogenous "psychedelic" system. This is further supported by many patients reporting on the psychedelic state as "somehow familiar," an intrinsic experience.
- Psychedelic states can arise even without psychedelics—with near-death experiences, for example. These states carry tremendous importance within cultures and religions the world over, supporting the notion that they are more than a chance reaction within the brain to an unknown chemical substance.
- A psychedelic brain system makes sense from the perspective of evolutionary biology, as fight-flight-freeze is not an option when it comes to enduring the transformative stress involved in situations like birth or death. Only one possibly strategy exists, and that is openness. Psychedelic experience adopts the same strategy.

The best and most common example of transformative stress is motherhood, a state that cannot be mastered by the classic stress responses of fight, flight, or freeze. Pregnancy alone involves significant psychological and physical change. This is followed by birth, with all its unimaginable pain and joy, then breastfeeding, caring for the newborn around the clock, and the intimate lifelong connection that strikes such a strong contrast to our autonomous, consumer-oriented, transactional, and disposable culture. How

---

311 Josef Zehentbauer, *Körpereigene Drogen: Garantiert ohne Nebenwirkungen* (Patmos, 2020).

would the motherhood transformation feel? How would I personally react to this transformation, with my needs for autonomy and life goals? Would my needs change? Would I long for my previous autonomy, or be taken up into a shared consciousness with my child without a second thought? There is also the fact that the transformation isn't dictated by the mother alone, but in large part by the child. Will the child be healthy? Or will they suffer from a rare disease? US philosopher Laurie Ann Paul asks all these questions in her book *Transformative Experience*, where she shows that the most important things in life are only understood through direct experience.[312]

Birthing and birth, as it turns out, played a critical role in the discovery of LSD. In 1935, Albert Hofmann proposed a chemical study of ergot to his bosses at the company Sandoz in Basel, Switzerland. Ergot is a fungus that lives off cereal grains; while poisonous to humans in large quantities, in smaller amounts it holds medicinal properties. As early as 1582 the city doctor of Frankfurt, Germany, Adam Lonitzer, had used ergot as a birthing aid. He did so with good cause; ergot contracts the uterus, is hemostatic, and relaxes the vegetative nervous system by inhibiting the effects of the stress hormone adrenaline. All three effects help with birth, and the lysergic acid found in ergot is the fundamental building block for everyone. In his research, Hoffman discovered that lysergic acid broke down quickly, making it unsuitable as a medication on its own. Instead, he tried to make the delicate substance more lasting by bonding it to other chemicals. One of those bonds resulted in lysergic acid diethylamide, or LSD, which had a strong effect on the uterus in animal experiments. Yet the LSD also made the test animals restless, leading Sandoz to discontinue research into the substance as a birthing agent.

Other of Hofmann's compounds did prove effective in clinical research. One component of ergot he discovered became a bestseller under the name Hydergine, as the first medication to promote blood flow to the brain and support brain function in general. It became apparent from this success that the benefits of ergot were not limited to the uterus in birth but extended to the brain. Hofmann's suspicions about how strongly LSD affected the brain led him to produce it again five years later. In an unintentional self-experiment, he finally discovered LSD's effects on the brain—the state that today we call "psychedelic."

312 Paul, *Transformative Experience*.

The story supports my hypothesis that psychedelic substances are produced within the body to support the brain during the birthing process, especially with the transformative openness that plays such a central role to the psychological, social, and spiritual process of becoming a mother. The hypothesis is further supported by the observation that people with an interest in ayahuasca ceremonies and psychedelic treatment often find themselves in transformations of their own; they are looking to bring something new into the world. All of this indicates that psychedelics can be meaningfully used outside of psychotherapy as well, assisting people who are confronting important life changes.

Birthing

Becoming a mother is an excellent example of a transformative experience because almost all women undergo deep transformation in the process. Their perceptions change, allowing them to recognize the voice of their child even from a deep sleep and wake up instantly. A mother's sense of time adjusts to the rhythms of the child. Her reward system begins to change during pregnancy, preferring certain beneficial foods. Following birth her interests refocus toward the child while other rewards grow less important. The new mother's sense of meaning in her own life changes, as do her relationships. Simply put, everything that I have described in the previous seven chapters of this book changes, from perception to identity.

The birthing effect that I propose here is not stand-alone like the other psychedelic effects I've described, but a sort of interplay between effects that allows for transformation. To achieve such transformations the brain will doubtless rely on specific mechanisms, among them endorphins, oxytocin, and DMT, which have evolved for the purpose, with some of these substances that—like the psychedelic DMT—raise neuroplasticity, most likely playing an important role.

It isn't motherhood alone that bears similarities to the psychedelic state, but childbirth itself (by my assumption as a result of "psychedelics" produced within the body itself). As a medical student I had the chance to work as a maternity nurse in England, an experience that gave me a lasting impression of the birthing process. Looking back, I see any number of aspects that birthing shares with psychedelic effects:

Right perception: For many women, birth represents a significant challenge that can rekindle old experiences and fears. Soon-to-be mothers must be prepared to explore their sense of vulnerability. Mindfulness and the helioscope effect can help them better understand their experiences. It is ultimately in nature's interest for women to want to give birth again. Humans also have tremendous physical resources especially for birth at their disposal. The body of the mother softens and grows adaptable. The embodiment effect, moreover, set in motion by "psychedelics" produced within the body, activates the brain stem and improves bodily intelligence.

Right time: In looking to find the rhythm of the birth and labor contractions, a woman necessarily enters cyclical time. Birth is an organic process that works in cycles (contractions), not centimeters. This notion of time is further bolstered by the archetype effect. Focusing on rational, linear time, in terms of progress as measured by how many centimeters out the child is, disrupts resilience.

Right reward: The expecting mother must come to see that nature has a plan for her, that she is built to give birth, and that creation is originally linked to life. Positivity and peak experiences strengthen this perspective.

Right meaning: Rational understanding is checked during birth, giving way to intuitive, feeling, and vivid thinking, with revelatory and visionary effects contributing. Birth confers a tremendous amount of meaning, which helps mothers endure the pain.

Right relationship: Relationships are experienced on a highly physical, intimate level. The mother must also alter her perspective to incorporate the child's into her own; the same perspective shifts and intimacy effects we see with psychedelics can help in doing so.

> *Right self*: The psychedelic effect of self-transcendence can help mothers to move past habitual responses to stress (fight, flight, or freeze) and develop new openness to life.
>
> *Right identity*: Becoming a mother is accompanied by significant changes in a woman's identity and social role, a process supported by the psychedelic alchemy effect. Birth is unfortunately also associated with humanity's most severe psychological difficulties, in the case of a miscarriage for instance, severe handicaps, or infant mortality. The singularity effect can help mothers "digest" and integrate these sorts of experiences.

Feminist theologian Elisabeth Moltmann-Wendel writes about birth as "an act of insight, of realization. The birth of a female insight of trusting the body, the belly, one's own life experiences. This isn't to espouse some ideology of motherhood, but to make it clear that knowledge can no longer bypass the human body. Instead of reason, which did not do justice to life, it is now wisdom, *Sophia* [in Greek], that is called for."[313] The exact same thing might be said for psychedelic therapy.

In focusing on birth and motherhood, my intention isn't to cast it in a religious light or banish women to the traditional role of being a mother. The transformation of fatherhood has become more and more important, and expecting to become a father isn't all that uncommon of a reason for taking psychedelics. The male experience of birth forms part of Michael Pollan's dramatic experience with 5-MeO-DMT, also called the "toad" since it appears in the poison of the Colorado River toad. The substance ranks as the Everest of psychedelics for its strong ego-dissolving effects. Pollan describes his own complete dissolution: "Terror seized me—and then, like one of those flimsy wooden houses erected on Bikini Atoll to be blown up in the nuclear tests, 'I' was no more, blasted to a confetti cloud by an explosive force I could no longer locate in my head, because it had exploded that too, expanding to become all that there was."[314] Pollan quickly returns to normal reality following this explosion of self, like an astronaut after a brief visit to space:

---

313 Moltmann-Wendel, *Wenn Gott und Körper sich begegnen*.

314 Pollan, *How to Change Your Mind*.

> With the rediscovery of my body, I felt an inexplicable urge to lift my knees, and as soon as I raised them, I felt something squeeze out from between my legs, but easily and without struggle or pain. It was a boy: the infant me. That seemed exactly right: having died, I was now being reborn. Yet as soon as I looked closely at this new being, it morphed smoothly into Isaac, my son. And I thought, how fortunate—how astounding!—for a father to experience the perfect physical intimacy that heretofore only mothers have ever had with their babies. Whatever space had ever intervened between my son and me now closed, and I could feel the warm tears sliding down my cheeks.[315]

In other words, Pollan's total disintegration was in fact preparation for giving birth. This gets at my notion of the birthing effect, which transforms the entire person in order to open them, or prepare them for something new. Pollan's motivation in writing a book about psychedelics was in turn based on Roland Griffith's study, in which test subjects rated their psilocybin experiences as some of the most meaningful in their entire lives, comparable to "the birth of their first child or the death of a parent."[316]

Pollan also indicates that many of the cancer patients he interviewed for his book described birthing effects during psychedelic therapy. One patient with cancer of the bile duct reported the following experience on psilocybin: "This period of my journey seemed to be about the feminine.... The considerable feminine energy all around me made clear the idea that a mother, any mother, regardless of her shortcomings...could never NOT love her offspring. This was very powerful. I knew I was crying...it was here that I felt as if I was coming out of the womb...being birthed again. My rebirth was smooth...comforting."[317]

Rebirth plays an important role across cultures and religions. Both the Buddha and Socrates compared themselves to midwives, helping people to be reborn as a higher self. Different forms of rebirth can be distinguished from one another:[318]

---

315 Ibid.

316 Griffiths et al., "Psilocybin Can Occasion Mystical-type Experiences Having Substantial and Sustained Personal Meaning and Spiritual Significance," 268–83.

317 Ibid.

318 Carl Jung, *Schriften zu Spiritualität und Transzendenz* (Patmos, 2013).

Archaic initiation and rites of passage: Rites reflecting the view that upon birth humans are not yet complete but must be born again in a spiritual sense.

Rebirth as rejuvenation: A form of rebirth that occurs within the span of an individual life. Often it is only one part of us that is rejuvenated, an illness lessens or is cured, for example, or we experience greater energy, ambition, or sense of purpose.

Reincarnation: Literal rebirth into another life, but with the same personal characteristics as before.

The transmigration of souls: An important concept in Indian philosophy; the Buddha, for example, experienced a long journey in between births. The Buddha never deliberately explained whether it is just karma that continues on, or also specific individual aspects. *The Tibetan Book of the Dead* discusses the topic.

Resurrection: The recovery or reconstitution of human existence after death as a transformed being, as a subtle body, or spiritual being.

In psychedelic therapy, rebirth typically takes the form of initiation or rejuvenation. Recollections of being born are not uncommon. Jung warned against interpreting these phenomena in overly literal or spiritual fashion, which for him were all psychological transformations. "Rebirth is not a process that we can in any way observe," he wrote. "We can neither measure nor weigh nor photograph it.... We have to do here with a purely *psychic* reality, which is transmitted to us only indirectly through personal statements.... The mere fact that people talk about rebirth, and that there is such a concept at all, means that a store of psychic experiences designated by that term must actually exist."[319] This is in line with my hypothesis that psychedelics, whether produced by the body or taken during therapy, promote neural transformations that can be experienced psychologically as rebirth.

The second, higher life that emerges after rebirth is characterized by a single quality: openness. Openness is the basis for physical healing, but also

---

319 Carl Jung, "Concerning Rebirth," *The Collected Works of Carl Jung, Volume 9, Part 1* (Princeton University Press, 1969).

for cultural and spiritual life. In archaic cultures, healing means the rebirth of the ill person. While modern life may not recognize rebirth per se anymore, longing for the experience of initiation hasn't vanished entirely; quite the contrary, as the growing interest in psychedelic therapy demonstrates.

I would like to conclude this section on psychedelic birthing effects with an exercise from Italian midwife Verena Schmid, that can help give a direct experience of openness and accepting it:

Close your eyes, take a moment for yourself. Direct your attention to your breath, noticing the slow, even movement, the rise and fall of the in-breath and out-breath as they come and go like waves, coming and going, coming and going.

Gradually let your breath come more and more slowly, let it flow slowly, gently letting yourself be rocked back and forth by your breath, back and forth, back and forth.

Notice your body as it slowly expands, expanding and opening.

Notice the breath flowing down the spinal column, an endless river flowing through your core like a gold ribbon, head to toe, heaven to earth.

Notice how the breath opens the body, your body is opening, expanding, expanding still more, stretching out into space, your body is open, the golden ribbon grows broader, broader still, broader still.

Explore your openness, this vast space, letting it grow as wide as you're able.

Notice how that openness and expanse feels, immerse yourself in the feeling.

You can choose now whether you'd like to stay with this feeling or keep going.

If you feel ready, you can call to your child now:

Soul of heaven, I'm ready to receive you.

I'm ready to receive you and give you refuge and body in me.

I'm ready to be your channel, so that you can enter this world.

I'm ready to receive you and bring you into life, into my life and yours.

I'm ready to love you, and to take joy in your love.

I'm ready to accompany you on your path, to sustain and support you.

I'm ready, I'm ready.

Stay with your sensations, your feelings, the images that arise, take your time.

When you feel ready, slowly come back into your body and sense it, its solidity and concrete quality. Breathe in deeply and slowly open your eyes.[320]

Lighting Effects

In closing this chapter, I would like to return to psychedelics' startling capacity for generating openness in the form of mystical states, and the importance of those states in making therapy succeed.

While many different kinds of mystical states exist, in those brought on by psychedelics light is especially common as a sign of opening or openness. Rebirth out of darkness is a typical experience under soma in the *Rig Veda*, signifying the rebirth of the moon, the symbol for soma. The text describes the moon as a cosmic force that gives a higher meaning to the rising and falling away of life and reconciles us with death by offering us a perspective on rebirth. In this context, rebirth is experienced as light, with

320 Verena Schmid, *Schwangerschaft, Geburt, Mutter werden* (Elwin Staude, 2015).

many hymns in the Rig Veda revolving around the light that soma grants us:[321]

> Soma beams forth, is radiant, it is all light, to see the splendor.
>
> Soma brings us wisdom and light.
>
> Primordial soma, make the lights shine for us.
>
> Soma transports us in inexhaustible light.
>
> Soma, enter us as a light-finder.
>
> The purifying soma has created radiant light, destroying the black darkness
>
> Soma, your worlds of light reveal the cosmic truth to us.

In the *Rig Veda*, reaching the light is connected with freedom from fear; in later Indian philosophy as well—in the Upanishads for example, as well as teachings in yoga and Buddhism—experiencing a pure light is an important goal in spiritual development. In Buddhism the color of the light one experiences indicates the relative success of the meditation. In *The Tibetan Book of the Dead*, the consciousness of the dying person is bathed in light, and the resolve with which he or she determines to pursue the undefiled light determines their fate after death. Zen Buddhism calls the highest form of consciousness *satori*—"super consciousness" or "the consciousness of consciousness"—which is akin to emptiness. As one patient described this luminous emptiness, "All thoughts had vanished, so that in the end I was only perceiving emptiness and light. It was a wonderful, liberating feeling." In the *Chandogya Upanishad*, we read: "Now, far above here the light that shines from heaven on the backs of everything, on the backs of all things, in the very highest of the high worlds—it is clearly this very same light

321 Rainer Stuhrmann, "Capturing Light in the Rigveda: Soma Seen Botanically, Pharmacologically, and in the Eyes of the Kavis," *Electronic Journal of Vedic Studies* 13, no. 1 (2006): 1–93.

here within a man.... Anyone who knows this will become handsome and famous."[322]

Light and illumination are central themes in Christian and Islamic mysticism as well. Saint Augustine believed that God made up the innermost part of every person, writing: "You were more inward to me than my most inward part and higher than my highest."[323] He further referred to the innermost and highest parts of himself as the "light of my heart."

Light is associated with healing in cultures the world over. Shamans report on dramatic experiences with light while under the influence of psychedelic plants. One Mazatec shaman is quoted in a ceremony with the words: "I am the dry lightning, says. I am the lightning of the comet, says. I am the dangerous lightning, says. I am the big lightning, says. I am the lightning of rocky places, says. I am the light of the dawn, the light of day, says."[324] Romanian anthropologist Mircea Eliade describes shamanic initiation rites among the Eskimo, in which the apprentice suddenly experiences a mysterious light throughout his body, head, and brain—an inexplicable searchlight beam, a burning fire. This enables him to see in the dark, both in the literal sense but also metaphorically, as he can see even with his eyes closed, and perceive things and events that remain hidden to others.[325]

Alan Watts also described mystical experiences he had while on LSD and mescaline in terms of light energy:

> The awareness of eternal energy, often in the form of intense white light, which seems to be both the current in your nerves and that mysterious *e* which equals *mc2*. This may sound like megalomania or delusion of grandeur—but one sees quite clearly that all existence is a single energy, and that this energy is one's own being. Of course there is death as well as life, because energy is a pulsation, and just as waves must have both crests and troughs, the experience of existing must go on and off. Basically, therefore, there is simply nothing to worry about, because you yourself are the eternal energy of the universe playing hide-and-seek (off-and-on) with itself.[326]

322 Olivelle, *The Early Upanishads*.

323 Saint Augustine, *Confessions* (Oxford University Press, 2009).

324 Munn, "The Mushrooms of Language," .

325 Eliade, *Shamanism: Archaic Techniques of Ecstasy*.

326 Watts, *The Joyous Cosmology*.

German author Ernst Jünger described light effects of his own while on LSD, as "colors [getting] brighter, as if the Nubian sun had begun to shine or as if matter was radiating more intensely. It seemed to me as if, up until that moment, I had only perceived shadows of the light; now everything became essential. Even when I closed my eyes the colors did not cease to shine."[327]

Rick Strassman, a professor of psychiatry in the US, also reports on test patients experiencing an inner light in his DMT studies: One described: "I immediately saw a bright yellow-white light directly in front of me...I was consumed by it and became part of it. There were no distinctions—no figures or lines, shadows or outlines. There was no body or anything inside or outside. I was devoid of self, of thought, of time, of space, of a sense of separateness or ego, or of anything but the white light. There are no symbols in my language that can begin to describe that sense of pure being, oneness, and ecstasy. There was a great sense of stillness and ecstasy."[328]

One patient I treated with psilocybin for depression on a sunny day noted with amazement how "beautiful it is that today has so much light. I love the sun. It's odd, when I close my eyes, it gets even brighter." Another patient I treated with LSD over the course of a severe alcohol dependency no longer saw a path out of what his life had become, and had set his last hopes on psychedelic therapy. Over three agonizing hours all he saw were dark colors and he had the feeling of vomiting his entire life into a black mass. Suddenly however, he saw light, and called out, "LSD pushes me into an opening." This experience of opening didn't entail any concrete goals or projects, but rather the feeling that new goals and projects were possible. He subsequently abandoned his plan to take his own life.

Near-Death Experiences: The Light at the End of the Tunnel

As I've discussed above, throughout the course of a human life some forms of stress will occur that cannot be overcome through fight, flight, or freezing. Aside from birth, the prospect of death presents another such challenge. I hypothesize that the psychedelics our own bodies produce help us

327 Ernst Jünger, *Approaches: Drugs and Ecstatic Intoxication* (Telos Press, 2022).

328 Strassman, *DMT: The Spirit Molecule*.

overcome stress by encouraging greater neuroplasticity. Should that be the case, these endogenous substances should play an important role at death as well as birth. As it turns out, near-death experiences show many similarities to psychedelic experience.

A "near-death experience" refers to a state where a person perceives they are near to death—taking a life-threatening fall, for instance. Such proximity to death can elicit any number of changes in consciousness. A typical one might be journeying through a tunnel into a light-filled expanse, recalling the lighting effect just discussed. Other experiences include a feeling of peace and bliss, akin to the positivity effects I described under psychedelics. Feelings of love and empathy with loved ones may also arise, echoing the perspective shifts psychedelics bring, while changes in the experience of time, or a sense of timelessness, show great similarities to their archetype effects. Retrospective flashbacks were events from the person's past play out internally show a similarity to psychedelics' narrative effect, which activates our autobiographical memory. The experience of lightness and leaving one's body is close to what Kurt Stocker, Matthias Hartmann, and I identified as a typical effect of ketamine.[329]

Near-death experiences are also comparable across cultures, suggesting that a neurobiological mechanism is at work. Among other things, it might function to counteract simply being overcome by fear of death, and confer peace, mental clarity, improved perception, or slow-motion experiences. Any of these would help a person near death to make the best use of any lifesaving opportunities present—grabbing hold of a branch or a vine, for example. Gauging the right response to falling out of a tree has been essential from an evolutionary perspective, since our ancestors regularly climbed tall trees in search of honey, fruit, or game.[330] In this context, psychedelic narrative effects might work to mentally classify the potentially fatal event. This is especially pronounced among Westerners who lack the notion of a transpersonal consciousness. The brain attempts to find a biographical slot for an event that cannot be understood at the individual level. Often this

329 Kurt Stocker, Gregor Hasler, and Matthias Hartmann, "The Altered-State-of-Consciousness Aspect of a Feeling of Lightness Is Reported to Be Associated with Antidepressant Benefits by Depressed Individuals Receiving Ketamine Infusions: A Systematic Analysis of Internet Video Testimonials," *Psychotherapy and Psychosomatics* 88, no. 3 (January 1, 2019): 182–83.

330 Vivek V. Venkataraman, Thomas S. Kraft, and Nathaniel J. Dominy, "Tree Climbing and Human Evolution," *Proceedings of the National Academy of Sciences of the United States of America* 110, no. 4 (December 31, 2012): 1237–42.

attempt assumes the form of an accelerated retrospective, where one's entire life story plays out within seconds.[331]

The discovery that near-death experiences and psychedelic experience hold much in common is not new. The Quechua word *ayahuasca* translates to "vine of death," or "vine of souls," because the substance will often bring up deathlike experiences, and "may foster contact with the dead."[332] Shamanic ecstasy has always included experiences of people's fate beyond the grave. In his research on shamanism, Mircea Eliade spoke of the archetype of "gaining existential consciousness," as it appears in states of shamanic ecstasy, primitive mysticism, and Plato's theory of the eternal soul.[333]

Phenomenologically speaking, near-death experiences are identical to psychedelic experience for psychiatrist and near-death researcher Bruce Greyson, a startling conclusion confirmed by Swiss religious studies scholar Jens Schlieter in a meticulous study.[334] Both are rated as highly meaningful and clearly recalled, even years later. Both foster resilience and have a transformative effect. Both lessen the fear of death and increase acceptance, and bring about a feeling of oneness with the universe. Both also lower the risk of suicide.

Near-death and psychedelic experience do not always work out for the best, however. Albert Hofmann had a terrifying near-death experience the first time he experimented with LSD: "I was seized by the dreadful fear of going insane. I was taken to another world, another place, another time. My body seemed to be without sensation, lifeless, strange. Was I dying? Was this the transition? At times I believed myself to be outside my body, and then perceived clearly, as an outside observer, the complete tragedy of my situation."[335] As with my own agonizing experience on ayahuasca, however, these sort of negative psychedelic states nearly always transition into a positive, light-filled expansion of consciousness.

---

331 Jens Schlieter, *What Is It Like to Be Dead?: Near-Death Experiences, Christianity, and the Occult* (Oxford University Press, 2018).

332 Ralph Metzner and Jace C. Callaway, *Ayahuasca: Hallucinogens, Consciousness, and the Spirit of Nature* (Thunder's Mouth Press, 1999).

333 Eliade, *Shamanism: Archaic Techniques of Ecstasy*.

334 Bruce Greyson, *After: A Doctor Explores What Near-Death Experiences Reveal About Life and Beyond* (Random House, 2021); Schlieter, *What Is It Like to Be Dead?*.

335 Hofmann, *LSD: My Problem Child*.

Orgasm can also bring on a near-death experience, with many cultures even referring to it as a "little death." It is fascinating in this regard that the effects of MDMA should bear so many similarities to the relaxed state after orgasm.[336] Both MDMA and orgasm trigger a strong release of the hormone prolactin, which is chiefly responsible for the growth of the mammary glands during pregnancy, and for milk secretion during breastfeeding. This in turn points to the evolutionary roots of the psychedelic experience, and the resilience of openness in the mammalian reproductive system.

Entering the Clearing

Many patients return from their psychedelic journeys recounting a field or forest clearing. One patient I treated for depression with esketamine reported being "in a dark forest climbing up a rocky path. Then I stood still because I was afraid to go any farther and trip over rocks. Suddenly a voice called out: 'Come up, you're free!' The path up was hard, demanding, but I kept going because I saw a light at the top. Up top I came to an open, very bright field. That's when I realized that the voice that had called was my own. I never realized that I could say something with such conviction and force. I met an entirely new side of myself."

Existentialist philosophy uses the clearing as an image for human existence. In a seminar for psychotherapists, Heiddegger argued:

> "Clearing" means "to be open." There is also clearing in darkness. Clearing has nothing to do with light but is derived from "lighten" [unburden]. Light involves perception. One can still bump into something in the dark. This does not require light, but a clearing. "Light" comes from "lighten," "to make free." A clearing in the forest is still there, even when it's dark. Light presupposes clearing. There can only be brightness where something has been cleared or where something is free for the light. Darkening, taking away the light, does not

336 Torsten Passie, Uwe Hartmann, Udo Schneider, Hinderk M. Emrich, and Tillman H. C. Kruger, "Ecstasy (MDMA) Mimics the Post-orgasmic State: Impairment of Sexual Drive and Function During Acute MDMA-effects May Be Due to Increased Prolactin Secretion," *Medical Hypotheses* 64, no. 5 (January 1, 2005): 899–903.

> encroach upon the clearing. The clearing is the presupposition for getting light and dark. It is the free, the open.[337]

The clearing isn't a likeness or copy, the dream of a past reality, or an unconscious desire. In this regard the "clearing" effect of psychedelics runs counter to psychoanalysis's aims that patients clarify and work through their life stories to date. The clearing effect is much more concerned with realities that have not yet existed or been desired, the potential realities that may arise in consciousness at any moment. It is consciousness driven on by neuroplasticity. Amidst the new, freely available synapses, an openness emerges through which light can fall. One Indian image for a clearing is the lotus, which liberates itself from the ocean of inner and outer necessities to rise above the tide and open itself toward the sky.

For Heidegger, *dasein*, or existence, does not have to be illuminated to begin with; it "clears" itself. *Dasein* is the clearing that the psychedelic lighting effect makes apparent. In its ultimate form, neuroplasticity is the realization of emptiness, the unformed, unbecome, unborn, unmade. This emptiness is not nothing, it comprehends the beginning and the end. It is total enlightenment, nirvana in the Buddhist sense—the unconditional, undefined, non-expectant experience of emptiness.[338]

The psychedelic experience of being light itself is not simply the experience of being illuminated, as though by a spotlight. It means more than that, seeing something in a new light for instance, as though on an X-ray image or under a microscope. To be light is to be in the realm of pure possibility, existing as something undetermined or imminent, or in the sense of a layout, a sketch. It is the light of creation and design.

In describing the "cleared" consciousness, British mystic Douglas Harding wrote that

> the first characteristic is that it has no boundaries, no fence round it, no edges; it's absolutely unlimited in all directions. The second

337 Martin Heidegger, *Zollikon Seminars: Protocols, Conversations, Letters*, trans. Franz Mayr (Northwestern University Press, 2001). The German word for clearing, *Lichtung*, includes the word for "light," *Licht*. As the translators of the *Zollikon Seminars* note, "with the term 'lighten,' Heidegger is referring to lightening a load in the sense of clearing away the forest's. The later Heidegger uses this metaphor to describe Da-sein's 'clearing.'"

338 Rupert Gethin, *The Foundations of Buddhism* (Oxford University Press, 1998).

> characteristic is that it is absolutely clear, clean, empty of contamination. It is utterly simple, totally transparent, empty of everything but itself, empty even of itself, clearer than glass, cloudless, an infinite sky. The third characteristic is that it is also full of the world. Because it's empty, it's full—full of the scene, whatever the scene is, absolutely united with it. The fourth characteristic is that it is awake, it's aware, it's conscious. And the fifth characteristic is that it is right where you are.[339]

British philosopher Walter Stace wondered rightly how such a consciousness might even be experienced, since

> there would be no mental content whatever but rather a complete emptiness, vacuum, void. One would suppose a priori that consciousness would then entirely lapse and one would fall asleep or become unconscious. But the introvertive mystics—thousands of them all over the world—unanimously assert that they have attained to this complete vacuum of particular mental contents, but that what then happens is quite different from a lapse into unconsciousness. On the contrary, what emerges is a state of pure consciousness—"pure" in the sense that it is not the consciousness of any empirical content. It has no content except itself.[340]

The clearing of pure consciousness is also talked about as a "non-dual state," since no distinctions exist; subject and object dissolve into pure oneness. It is for the same reason that it is only possible to say what pure consciousness is not. This non-dual emptiness has a tremendous calming effect. Individuals who have found their light also beam it outward, potentially with a strong impact on their surroundings. As Jesus says in one verse in the Gospel of Thomas, "Light exists within a person of light, and they light up the whole world."[341]

The clearing effect also instills a great sense of connection, since the transparency of the "cleared" self allows it to see things as they truly are,

339 Douglas Harding, *Face to No-Face: Rediscovering our Original Nature* (Inner Directions, 2000).

340 Thomas Metzinger, "Minimal Phenomenal Experience.", Philosophy and the Mind Sciences, 2020, p. 8

341 Mattison, *The Gospel of Thomas*.

which in turn allows the self to be with them. Normally our consciousness is clouded by expectations or preconceived ideas that narrow the clearing. The lighting and lightening that allows us to be in touch with everything is the essential skill of the shaman the world over.[342]

The effect does more than the standard psychotherapeutic effects of illuminating, clarifying, or uncovering. It is rather a natal, neuroplastic, existential process out of which receptivity to a new center grows, a setting free that brings freedom, movement toward new possibilities. It is the experience of one's consciousness as a place for play, within which the disclosedness of existence becomes possible. The clearing in the forest grants us passage to the being that we are *not*, at the same time that it shows us the way to the being that we *are*.

However once in the clearing, clarity of thought, the goal of clarification-oriented psychotherapy, can sometimes be an obstacle. When we find ourselves in ambiguous, diffuse, or inscrutable situations, the clarifying power of the mind can be liberating. Yet once we've spent long enough in clarity, we come to the sense that it is not ultimate liberation. The broad path leads us to speechlessness. There are no incisive terms for the openness of the clearing, only allusions or pregnant images. We must let go in order to be transformed.

Many people are on the search for something. Most look externally, supposing to find the light in money, success, or prestige. The goal of psychedelic therapy, by contrast, is for patients to discover the light within. The clearing effect allows for that inner light to develop and become visible. This is essential—searching outside oneself will nearly always fail so long as we don't know what we are searching for on the inside, with our consciousness enshrouded in darkness. In India, the concept of a third eye emerged, believed to possess the ability to perceive inner light. The light isn't harsh but subtle, empathetic, soothing. It is the light of the soma moon and points the way to the clearing.

Entering the clearing means stepping into openness, involving oneself with openness, moving from closed to disclosed. Openness means freedom, though it is more than simply the freedom to act. It is a receptivity to an openness of being, to transformative openness, a willingness to transform.

Contemporary philosophy on consciousness talks about its "self-luminosity," comparing it to a fire or flame that illuminates itself and its

342 Eliade, *Shamanism: Archaic Techniques of Ecstasy*.

surroundings. The image points to the fact that the recognizer, the act of recognition, and the recognized all coincide within the consciousness as cleared by the self. Another way of expressing this is "witness consciousness," that we as humans are witness to consciousness and also one with it.[343] The *Svetasvatara Upanishad* writes: "The non-dual and resplendent Lord is hidden in all beings. All-pervading, the inmost Self of all creatures, the impeller to actions, abiding in all things, He is the Witness, the Animator and the Absolute...eternal happiness belongs to the wise, who perceive Him within themselves-and not to others."[344] Psychedelics can help us to discover this "inmost Self of all creatures" within ourselves.

Related to modern philosophy's notion of "self-luminosity" is Plato's comparison between visibility brought from the sunlight and the light of truth that comes from mental insight. The philosopher gives the inner light the final say in discovering the ultimate truth. The Greek term for truth, *aletheia*, play a central role in the comparison, which translated literally means "unconcealment." *Aletheia*, the truth, is also a clearing.

Beyond Language

William James similarly saw mystical states as characterized by possessing aspects that one couldn't encapsulate in speech. His definition matters in the present context since modern psychedelic research draws on his concept of mysticism. This means the positive states of consciousness that leave us speechless are largely what determine whether treatment will succeed or not. It is for the same reason that I ask the following questions of patients after a psychedelic sitting:

> Do you have a feeling that the experience you just had cannot be adequately described in words?
>
> Do you have a feeling that it will be difficult to talk about your experience with another person who hasn't had a similar sort of experience?

---

343 Miri Albahari, *Analytical Buddhism: The Two-Tiered Illusion of Self* (Palgrave Macmillan, 2006).

344 Swami Nikilananda, *The Upanishads—A New Translation* (Harper and Brothers, 1949).

It is striking to see how frequently the patients who benefit the most from psychedelic therapy answer in the affirmative. That doesn't mean that they can't describe other aspects of their experience quite precisely—changes in sight or sound, for example. Yet for the parts of the psychedelic experience that have to do with openness, words fail.

I myself experienced brief moments of a speechless mystical state while guided by Peter Oehen on LSD. Time was moving so slowly that I was able to actually observe language dissolving, and see the direct connection between its dissolving and the lights I was seeing with my eyes closed. It wasn't that I had lost all capacity for language; rather, it didn't make any sense in terms of what I was experiencing. It felt like a walk through a forest toward a clearing, with the words as the trees and plants shading out the light. The more the different elements of speech lost their meaning, the brighter the clearing grew.

First to go were verbs like *go*, *fall*, or *have to*. In the forest of language, they were the broad-leafed trees, and when they went they took with them the undergrowth and moss hanging about them—all the adverbs that qualified their action. This state of being without verbs and adverbs brought the Buddha to mind, sitting with peace and calm. The only verb that might capture the meaning of such an activity was *to be*. Everything was a tranquil, timeless being. The world rested in its being-ness. This rendered pronouns like *yours*, *mine*, *something*, or *one* meaningless, since relationships of possession and references to them no longer fit in with my experience. Everything came to me as a given, directly and simply from the self. As everything came to exist simultaneously and with the same value, conjunctions like *or*, *but*, and *although* were the next to lose their meaning, which had bordered the clearing like stinging nettles. Then the meaning of adjectives started to lose ground—there was no *big* or *small* chair anymore, but only the "chair" in its indescribable there-ness. Finally, even nouns lost their meaning, the chair or the blanket, those mighty evergreens that cast so much shade. Without them the clearing grew extremely bright, and it seemed as though all unities were dissolving into a still higher unity. The last words that still made sense within the clearing were the prepositions *in* and *with*. These seemed to be the lightest words, the words that blocked the least light and threw the slightest shadows. They grew like baby's breath around the clearing, allowing something to be perceived without necessarily determining it. So my mystical experience had something to do with "in," as in being "in" the world, with association and givenness. And it also had something to do with "with," as in being "with" things, with Peter, or with the light. An indescribable energy coursed through me.

This state didn't last long, and when I left it, I was standing in an enormous room. The room had doors, with each opening into new, even larger rooms. I felt lost. Then two figures came up to me one on either side and gave me their hands, which was very pleasant and calming. They were Wendy Doniger, the translator of the *Rig Veda*, and Patrick Olivelle, the translator of the Upanishads, both texts that had accompanied me for years. "This room is impossibly large, and it opens out into even larger rooms!" I said.

Wendy answered gently: "It is as it's written in the *Rig Veda*: 'released into boundless open space.' There is also a verse in the Bible, from Psalms: 'Thou hast set my feet in a large room.'"

Now it was Patrick's turn to explain: "The nerve cells in the human brain, which form so many new buds, branches, and trees from a single drop of soma, so that an almost infinite number of new connections can be created—they are an image of the law of abundance that you have experienced. But this plasticity is in everything, in the fern, the ocean, the Milky Way, throughout the entire universe. That means that an innumerable number of endlessly large rooms and worlds can arise, most of which remain invisible and unconscious."

Unnerved, I struck an unnecessary pedantic tone: "'Fear' comes from the Latin *angere* and means 'drown' or 'choke,' and the German word for fear, *Angst*, is related to the word for 'narrow.' Is this room the treatment for my fear?"

Patrick nodded. "Yes, we also call this room, which is accessible to all, 'free of fear,' 'Brahman,' or 'immense self.' There are two sentences that never pass through here: 'That's why I did something good,' and 'That's why I did something bad.' A person who knows this grows peaceful, calm, patient, and collected."

Wendy then opened the door to a room that resembled the interior of the Hagia Sophia in Istanbul, only one hundred times larger. Off in the distance we glimpsed the mosaic of the Virgin Mary in a dark blue robe, holding the Christ child, who raised his right hand in blessing. "Is this the room of mercy?" I asked Wendy.

"It is," she replied, "and it is endlessly large, though sadly, hardly anybody knows about it."

Summary

On average, patients who enter mystical states during psychedelic sessions stand to benefit especially from therapy, reporting greater mental openness in the following months and years. One radical form of openness is a readiness to become somebody else, also called "transformative openness." Motherhood and experiences of rebirth are two classic examples. Psychedelics promote these sorts of transformations by increasing neuroplasticity. The birthing effect of psychedelics incorporates all the effects described previously in the book, in the way that birth changes a mother's perception, sense of time, sense of meaning in life, relationships, self, and identity. In a metaphorical sense, the birthing effect can help patients enter a new phase in life. The clearing effect describes a situation in which an extraordinary state of openness (and increased neuroplasticity) is experienced as a luminous emptiness. The psychedelic lighting effect grants us access to the beings we truly are.

Conclusion

There is no doubt that psychedelic therapy represents a paradigm shift in psychiatric treatment, as supported by the following reflections:

> Psychedelics are psychoactive drugs that are administered either a single time, or infrequently. This lies in contrast to conventional treatment by medication, where the medication must be taken daily over a long period of time.
>
> The acute effects of psychedelic therapy—especially patients' mystical experiences—suggest long-term effectiveness.
>
> The substances do not arouse inhibitions, the chief mechanism for standard psychotropic medication, but increase sensitivity and openness.

In this book, based on my practical experience as a psychiatrist and psychedelic therapist, I have tried to chart the course of this new path of treatment for patients, family members, professional colleagues, and the interested public. In doing so the project has become fairly wide ranging in addressing the breadth of neurological, psychological, and social effects. More than anything, it was important to me to communicate the importance of direct experience in psychotherapy, to allow patients to speak in their own words, and to point out that psychedelic therapy is not a new invention but has existed for millennia, in shamanic, indigenous, and Indian traditions among others.

Neither the opportunities nor the risks of psychedelic therapy can be determined conclusively at present. Still, that doesn't rule out a conscientious, step-by-step approach toward allowing such therapies, as is currently being taken in Switzerland. Quality and secondary research will help to determine benefits and risks within larger patient groups. In doing so, the following questions strike me as especially important:

> Who does psychedelic therapy work for? Does mental openness, cultural values and attitudes, or higher education determine effectiveness? How effective would psychedelic therapy be for children, adolescents, and the very elderly?
>
> Which psychotherapeutic model is best suited to making full use of psychedelic effects? Do tried-and-true methods have to be modified, or new methods developed?
>
> What are the long-term effects of psychedelic therapy? How often should psychedelics be administered?
>
> To what extent do psychedelics promote resilience? Are they effective in preventing relapses in mental illness? Are they effective in improving resilience for healthy people?
>
> What should be done about the "side effects" of psychedelics, like fearful states or increased depression? Should these unpleasant effects be taken into account when gauging the success of treatment? If not, how might they be avoided?
>
> What form should psychedelic therapy take legally? What kind of training do psychedelic therapists have to undergo? How can quality be assured?
>
> How expensive will the therapy be? Who will bear the costs?

For all the unanswered questions and the complex nature of psychedelic research, I would still like to stress that it is quite simple to understand how psychedelic therapy works. In truth, it is the simplest and most natural thing in the world, and what many patients who have lost access to this simplicity need. It is a lesson in being without doing anything. It lets us examine and take pleasure in the world without expectation or judgment. It is a lesson in perception, in seeing, hearing, smelling, tasting, and feeling. It is an openness to what is rewarding and positive in life.

Psychedelic states are not unique to psychedelic therapy; presumably they show up regularly in meditation or contemplation, or in our transformative, mystical, and near-death experiences. Through these states we learn about ourselves as feeling beings. We learn to perceive and value ourselves and others. We learn how to get along with ourselves and others. We learn that we are social beings. We learn that at heart, we are loving beings, and we learn how to enrich our relationships and our solitude with this love. We learn how to be simple, to be ordinary, to be empty, to be nothing. We learn to reflect on our values and set new ones. We learn how to feel free by coming to terms with our past and developing a visionary power to actively shape our futures, and discovering clearings of freedom. We learn that within the limited scope of our lives, something unlimited exists. Psychedelic states reveal what was there all along.

It's paradoxical: Psychedelic therapy—presently the most unconventional form of psychotherapy in existence—is a lesson in the simplest and most basic things in life.

Thanks

I would like to thank Peter Gasser and Peter Oehen for introducing me to psychedelic therapy. Without the experience, confidence, and knowledge they so graciously shared with me, this book never would have come into being. I'd like to thank my colleagues at Fribourg University: Elodie Baumann, Abigail Calder, Adrian Hase, Stefanie Majerus, Max Nietschke, Leonie Keinath, Alexandra Kupferberg, and Polina Ponomarenko. Their ideas, research, and comments were all essential to this book coming together. My thanks to the midwives Caroline Lüscher, Ilse Steininger, and Katharina Tritten for the stimulating conversation about childbirth. I have Ulrich Schnyder to thank for his notes on trauma therapy, and professors Jens Schlieter and Samuel Vollenweider for important contributions to the spiritual aspects of psychedelic therapy.